Cc

Introduction

THE Elan Valley Way runs from Frankley, on the western fringe of Birmingham, to the Elan Valley in mid-Wales. It is loosely based around the course followed by the Elan Valley aqueduct along which Birmingham's water supply has passed for the last 95 years.

In late 1997 I took early retirement from my job of thirty years and decided to devote as much time as possible to my favourite recreational activity – country walking. Within a few months this had developed into a new occupation – the freelance leading of walking holidays. The idea of designing a new long-distance walk then seemed to follow quite naturally, the only question being 'Where?'

Several ideas immediately presented themselves including linear walks along the Heart of Wales Railway Line, the River Teme or the River Lugg but in the event these were all rejected for one reason or another. Then in April 1998 while walking in the Lake District the idea which became the Elan Valley Way happened. I was walking along the lower slopes of Helvellyn, above Thirlmere, with Dave Walker, (a long time friend and fellow walker), when we got to talking about the effect on the Lakes of Manchester's water demands and in particular the pipeline taking the water from Thirlmere to that city. Dave said that he had seen a guide book to a long distance walk along the route and I remarked that if Manchester had such a walk on offer then Birmingham certainly deserved the same. The die was cast!

The walk which developed then is in part a way of saying something of a small 'thank you' to the city which has had me as an adopted son for some thirty years now.

I started work on the route planning in early August 1998. Contact was made with Severn-Trent Water and a visit made to Birmingham's Central Library to establish the course of the Elan Valley aqueduct and then a route, avoiding sections along 'A' and 'B' roads as far as possible, was 'highlighted' onto Ordnance Survey Maps. Remarkably this initial route survived the subsequent walking and mapping phase largely unaltered.

The route was walked, and re-walked as necessary, between late August and the end of October 1998 – sometimes alone and sometimes with Alan Jones, a long-suffering walking companion of over twenty years now. A tape recorder was used to record the route – for maximum detail and coverage. The weather was not at its kindest. I walked the last 2½ stages over the wettest few days Wales had seen for twenty years! The dams in the Elan Valley were like miniature Niagara's, the Wye at Rhayader rose some 12 feet overnight, and the suspension footbridge crossing of the River Ithon was decidedly hair raising. To cap it all I arrived at Llandrindod Wells station to be told that the Heart of Wales Railway line had been closed for over a day due to flooding!

Many new friends were made as the route was walked, including the two brave souls who volunteered to test-walk the route based on my instructions and were covering some of the stages with the word processor ink hardly dry. They got lost only twice over the whole ten stages – both times on Stage 4. Hopefully amendments made as a result of this will prevent others doing the same.

The route of the Elan Valley Way does not aim to slavishly follow the course of the aqueduct but instead visits many of the more obvious signs and sights of the pipelines on the ground. What is seen on each stage of the walk is included in the 'Stage Summary' at the head of each chapter. The walk is never more than about three miles from the line of the aqueduct – but takes 128½ miles to do the journey the aqueduct does in 73½!

Given that the walk is loosely based around the aqueduct which carries water from Wales to Birmingham, ie. west to east, it may seem odd that I have chosen to describe a route running east to west. This was done for two main reasons. First, by walking east to west the sun is usually behind the walker and therefore not in the eyes. Second, I felt that the scenery of the Elan Valley was perhaps a better goal, at the end of ten days' walking, than the high-rise suburbs of the Second City. Having experienced the route on the ground I must also add that it does 'walk better' from east to west.

The walk has been split into stages based on the availability of accommodation and public transport. Within each stage description are included 'Escape Points' also served by public transport. Where no such points exist on a stage then this is stated at the start of the walking instructions for that stage. The walk can therefore be completed as a whole ten-day affair, stage by stage, or even in part stages. No section of it should cause any great problems for the experienced, fairly fit walker. The longest stage is 16 miles and there are no prolonged steep ascents throughout the ten stages.

The walk is suitable for undertaking at any time of the year except that after periods of very heavy rainfall, when rivers and streams are in flood, the latter miles of Stage 2 and the first mile of Stage 3, (along the River Severn), and two fords on Stage 10 may be impassable.

All paths along the route as described were open in June 1999, when I completed a second walking of the entire route, with the exceptions specifically mentioned in the main text. The main problems over the entire route at the time of going to press were three blocked footpaths – one on Stage 6 and two on Stage 9 – where I have indicated ways around the blockage and have reported same to the relevant County Councils.

Mention of any specific accommodation or refreshment stops herein is in no way to be interpreted as a recommendation. As regards the availability of public transport I have given the situation as it existed at June 1999 but bus times in particular, and entire services for that matter, are liable to change at relatively short notice in rural areas. It is always best to check the information beforehand and to that end I have included the relevant telephone numbers of operators or County Councils involved in providing the services.

As far as I can ascertain, all of the route is over either Public Rights of Way or areas of Open Access.

In a public tion of this nature the odd mistake is bound to occur and I hope that any the reader might encounter will not spoil the enjoyment of the walking. My apologies, in advance, for such mistakes – they are down to me or else to 'Father Time'. Nothing remains constant, even in the most 'unspoilt' countryside, and when re-walking sections after the passage of only a couple of weeks I have found stiles replaced, footpaths cleared and others diverted.

I hope the reader enjoys walking the Elan Valley Way as much as I did. As with most things in life there will be 'ups' and 'downs' along the way but the reward at the end of the day is worth the effort put in. Follow the Country Code and respect the land and its people encountered along the way and you may be pleasantly surprised the pleasures you get in return, and the memories you take away with you.

David Milton
Sheldon, Birmingham.
July 1999.

Mileages

Mileage	Total	
0	0	FRANKLEY Church
9	9	Blakedown (+ ½ mile to Blakedown Station)
5	14	COOKLEY (end of Stage 1)
2.5	16.5	Wolverley
4.5	21	Arley
4.5	25.5	BEWDLEY (end of Stage 2) (Alternative route is 4 miles)
3.5	29	Buttonoak
3.5	32.5	Lem Hill / Horse & Jockey
6.5	39	CLEOBURY MORTIMER (end of Stage 3)
4	43	Hopton Wafers (+ ¼ mile to bus stop at Crown P.H.)
5	48	Knowle (+ ¾ mile to bus stop at Cleehill)
7	55	LUDLOW (end of Stage 4)
11.5	66.5	LEINTWARDINE (end of Stage 5)
2	68.5	Parson's Pole Bridge, River Teme (+ 1 mile to Bucknell Station)
10	78.5	KNIGHTON (end of Stage 6)
12.5	91	BLEDDFA (end of Stage 7)
6.25	97.25	Dolau Station
5.25	102.5	CROSSGATES (end of Stage 8)
2	104.5	Gwystre
2.75	107.25	Nantmel
7.25	114.5	RHAYADER (end of Stage 9)
6.5	121	Craig Goch dam
2	123	Pen-y-garreg dam
4	127	Garreg Ddu viaduct and submerged dam
1	128	Caban Coch dam
0.5	128.5	ELAN VALLEY VISITOR CENTRE (end of Stage 10)

Ordnance Survey Maps covering the walk

1:50,000 (Landranger)

138 Kidderminster & Wyre Forest
139 Birmingham
147 Elan Valley & Builth Wells
148 Presteigne & Hay-on-Wye

1:25,000 (Pathfinder)

932 Highley
933 Stourbridge & Kinver
950 Knighton & Brampton Bryan
951 Ludlow
952 Wyre Forest & Cleobury Mortimer
953 Kidderminster & Bromsgrove
969 Rhayader
970 Llandrindod Wells
971 Presteigne

1:25,000 (Explorer)

200 Llandrindod Wells & Elan Valley
201 Knighton & Presteigne
203 Ludlow
218 Kidderminster & Wyre Forest
219 Wolverhampton & Dudley

A Brief History

IT was in the second half of the nineteenth century that Birmingham Corporation's Water Committee, concerned that the population explosion taking place around them would render the existing local water supplies inadequate, first began to look elsewhere for alternative water sources.

In the late 1880s the Corporation, under the leadership of Joseph Chamberlain, approached the engineer James Mansergh for advice on the problem. Mansergh had spent some years with the railways surveying much of central Wales and came up with the suggestion that the Corporation consider purchasing land in the Elan and Claerwen valleys there. His plan was for the construction of dams in these valleys, to create reservoirs there, and of an aqueduct link to Birmingham.

Several features made Mansergh's suggestion very attractive to the Corporation. First, the area suggested received a very reliable high rainfall – up to 70 inches per annum. Second, the valleys earmarked were narrow and so very suitable for the building of dams. Third, the bedrock in the area was impermeable, giving maximum retention of stored water. Finally, the two valleys were high enough above Birmingham to allow water in the proposed aqueduct to reach the city by gravity, rather than having to be pumped.

  syphon.

An act of Parliament was required before the scheme could proceed and, after some weeks of debate, this was obtained in July 1892 – the Birmingham Corporation Water Act. Birmingham Corporation were empowered to purchase the upper portion of the valley of the Elan, (a tributary of the Wye), and the valley of its tributary, the river Claerwen – in all a total of 71 square miles. Three reservoirs were to be built in the Elan valley and a further three on the Claerwen. These were to be linked to a storage reservoir at Frankley, to the west of Birmingham, by a 73 mile aqueduct.

Work on the undertaking began in 1893, the intervening period being taken up with matters concerning compensation to landowners and the like. The first task was the construction of a railway between the sites of the dams and the existing line at Rhayader, some 33 miles of this being built. The second was the construction of accommodation and facilities for over 1500 workmen, the self-contained Elan Village.

While civil engineering had come a long way from the days of the canal and early railway builders – explosives and steam-powered cranes, drills and crushers were available to the work force by this time – much of the work involved was still of the pick-and-shovel kind, with navvies averaging 4 pence per hour for a 60 hour week. The labour force exceeded 5000 at certain times.

James Mansergh was the engineer in overall charge of the project, with George Yourdi the resident engineer in the Elan Valley.

Eighteen cottages, a church, a chapel, a school and two residences – Nantgwyllt and Cwm Elan – were to be destroyed by the Elan valley reservoir works. All but the two residences were replaced. Coincidentally both of the latter had connections with the poet Percy Bysshe Shelley, who lived at both for short periods, in 1811 and 1812, and was greatly influenced by the wild scenery of the valley and whose attempts to purchase Nantgwyllt for himself and his new bride, (Harriet Westbrook), failed due lack of funds. Both houses now lie under water although it is said that the garden walls of Nantgwyllt become visible when the water level of Caban Coch reservoir is low.

The effects of such a massive civil engineering project were not limited to the Elan Valley but were felt all along the line of the aqueduct to Birmingham. The presence of a large itinerant work force could easily disrupt the stability of the mainly rural areas through which they passed. Consider the small village of Bucknell, for example, situated just to the north of the aqueduct, between Knighton and Leintwardine. Here, for three years, 3000 navvies and their dependants were housed in huts in the station yard, outnumbering the villagers by ten to one!

By 1904 the three Elan Valley dams and reservoirs, a submerged dam – (Garreg Ddu, necessary to enable conditions in the 1892 Act regarding the release of compensatory water into the Elan and so to the River Wye to be met without disrupting the Birmingham supply), the Foel Tower – (housing the machinery which controls the water supply to the aqueduct), Frankley reservoir and a 73½ mile long, two pipe aqueduct had been completed. The foundations for one of the proposed Claerwen Valley dams had also been built. It was decided that these works would meet immediately foreseeable water needs and so construction was halted at this point. On 21st July 1904 the opening ceremony took place in the Elan Valley, with King Edward VII, Queen Alexandra and 750 guests in attendance. The first Welsh water reached Birmingham one week later.

Over the next couple of years the construction sites in the Elan Valley were tidied up and later the railway line from Rhayader was closed. In order to house the permanent maintenance force needed for the works Elan Village was rebuilt in 1909.

Before and during the First World War the area was used as an artillery training ground while shipments of the locally abundant sphagnum moss were sent to field hospitals in France to treat the war wounded.

By 1939 three-quarters of the available water supply was being consumed by Birmingham and it was becoming obvious that the balance of the original scheme would soon need to be constructed. A second storage reservoir had been built at the Birmingham end of the aqueduct in 1930 – Bartley reservoir – and in 1939 the addition of a third pipeline to the original two increased the daily capacity from 25 million gallons to 55½ million gallons. It was decided to apply to Parliament for permission to build a single large dam in the Claerwen valley instead of the three authorised in the 1892 act and this was granted in 1940. The Second World War delayed the commencement of work on this dam until 1946.

During hostilities the area once again contributed to the war effort in that a small coffer dam at Nant y Gro, off Caban Coch reservoir, was initially used by Barnes Wallis in preparation for the 1943 'Dambusters' raid, particularly in calculating the size of bomb needed for the mission.

The dams and aqueduct were also seen as obvious targets for both the Luftwaffe and enemy agents and were guarded, the aqueduct throughout its length, by employees and Home Guard units.

After the war work began on the single Claerwen dam, built of concrete unlike its masonry stone Elan Valley counterparts but faced with masonry to harmonise with them. Materials were delivered to the dam site by road from the railway at Rhayader, by way of the viaduct at Garreg Ddu. The dam took six years to complete and was opened by the young Queen Elizabeth II and the Duke of Edinburgh on 23rd October 1952.

In 1949 work had also started on a fourth pipeline for the aqueduct, the demand for water continuing to rise. This was completed in 1961 and increased the aqueduct's capacity to 75 million gallons per day.

Today the Elan Valley continues to meet the increasing water demands of Birmingham but also serves as an important tourist destination, the attractions including walking, angling and bird watching. In 1989 the land was placed under the control of Dwr Cymru Welsh Water with most of the Elan Valley Estate, excluding the waterworks themselves, vested in the Welsh Water Elan Trust on a 999 year lease to protect it for future generations.

Farming, mainly the rearing of sheep, also remains important in the area. Some 100 people make their living from farming on the Elan Valley Estate and there are an estimated 40000 sheep.

A few facts and figures...

Caban Coch is the lowest of the Elan Valley dams and is 122 feet high and 610 feet long. The surface area of the reservoir so created is 500 acres and its capacity is 7815 million gallons. It is bisected by the Garreg Ddu viaduct which carries the access road to the Claerwen dam and reservoir and which is built on piers rising from the submerged Garreg Ddu dam. The submerged dam effectively splits the reservoir of Caban Coch into two and the area above the dam is known as Garreg Ddu reservoir. Alongside the viaduct, in the Garreg Ddu reservoir, stands the Foel Tower which houses the gear controlling the water flow to the aqueduct, the tunnel to which leaves the reservoir at this point.

Pen-y-Garreg is the next dam and reservoir up the Elan Valley. The dam is 123 feet high and 528 feet long. The surface area of the reservoir, which contains a small wooded island, is 124 acres and its capacity 1332 million gallons.

The last of the Elan Valley dams and reservoirs is Craig Goch. Unlike the other two visible Elan dams this is curved in design and is 120 feet high and 513 feet long. The reservoir area is 217 acres and its capacity 2028 million gallons.

The Claerwen dam, (not seen on the walk), is by far the largest at 184 feet high and 1166 feet in length. The surface area of its reservoir is 650 acres with a capacity of 10625 million gallons. It lies to the west of the Elan Valley dams and their reservoirs. Water from it passes through the Dol y Mynach Tunnel to reach Garreg Ddu, entering it just opposite the Foel Tower.

Total capacity of all the Elan Valley and Claerwen Reservoirs is 21800 million gallons.

Water is transported to Birmingham via the aqueduct which is 73½ miles in length, has four pipes, and an average gradient to Birmingham of 1 in 2300, a fall of 169 feet in total. The water travels throughout its journey by

The Garreg Ddu viaduct under construction.
The replacement Nant Gwylt Chapel can be seen top left.

gravity alone and takes about 20 hours to make the trip from the Elan Valley to Birmingham, under normal operating conditions. Current capacity of the aqueduct is over 75 million gallons per day.

The aqueduct consists of conduits, (tunnels and cut-and-cover), and siphons, (pipelines), in about equal amounts by total length. There are 15 tunnels totalling 12 miles in length, the longest being 4½ miles and 2½ miles. The balance of the conduit mileage is made up of 16 separate sections of cut-and-cover. There are 11 siphons. These are used to cross the wider river valleys, that across the Severn valley being 17½ miles in length while the two Teme valley crossings are 9 and 4½ miles long. The aqueduct is at its most impressive where it crosses the rivers themselves such as at the Severn Crossing upstream of Bewdley, Steventon Bridge over the Teme near Ludlow, and Graham's Cottage Bridge over the Teme near Leintwardine.

A crossing of the Staffordshire & Worcestershire Canal, between Cookley and Wolverley, formerly via an arched bridge was replaced in 1988 by underground pipelines.

The original two pipelines were cast iron and each 42 inches in diameter. It was found that water pressure and corrosion caused failures in these and they were subsequently reinforced with concrete. The two later pipelines are of concrete and each of 60 inch diameter.

At the Birmingham end of the aqueduct are the two storage reservoirs – Frankley and Bartley.

Frankley reservoir, built during the first phase of construction, (1893 to 1904), and the original terminus of the aqueduct, has a surface area of 25 acres and a capacity of 200 million gallons.

Bartley reservoir was opened on 19th July 1930 to meet increasing demands. Its dam is 65 feet in height and it has a surface area of 117 acres, a capacity of 500 million gallons.

Finally, in addition to the potential maximum of 75 million gallons of water daily for Birmingham another 29 million gallons per day is provided, by the scheme, as compensation water to keep the Elan River flowing to the Wye.

About the Author

A RESIDENT of Birmingham for over 30 years now, David Milton was born in Worcester in 1949 and spent the first eighteen years of his life there before joining Customs & Excise, for whom he worked for almost thirty years, taking early retirement in 1997 to concentrate on his main interest – walking.

His interest in walking began young – sometime between 5 and 10 years of age – with the Worcester & Birmingham Canal and Worcestershire's Abberley Hills providing early challenges. During the 1970s he walked almost the entire canal system of England and Wales and has since walked widely in Cornwall, the Derbyshire Peak District, the Lake District, Yorkshire, and the Cotswolds in the U.K., and abroad in the Greek Islands, Malta, France, Madeira and India. His declared 'favourite' walking area however is that region around Ludlow where the counties of Herefordshire, Worcestershire, Radnorshire (Powys) and Shropshire mingle.

His other interests include fossils, wildlife, canals, railways, steam locomotives, local history, maps and prints, travel, poetry, and music – especially American folk/blues. He is a dedicated 'non-driver'.

Since his retirement David has divided his time between walking for pleasure, leading walking groups – mainly in the Welsh Marches – and writing. The designer of many 'day walks', the Elan Valley Way is his first long distance venture and also his first time in print.

The Stage Maps

Each of the ten stages of the walk is covered by two stage maps. The numbers on these indicate references within the main text.

The maps are not strictly drawn to scale but are generally at a scale of about 1½ inches to 1 mile. I have expanded this scale where the amount of detailed information to be shown requires this.

These are in no way intended to be a substitute for the Ordnance Survey maps which should always be carried when undertaking the walk.

Public Transport

Brief details of public transport available at the 'escape' points are given in the text. The following is an overview of the position as regards the main stage start/finish points.

Stages 1 to 4

The start of the walk at Frankley church is served by Travel West Midlands bus service 21 – Birmingham City Centre to Merritt's Brook – which stops in Merritt's Hill. From here it is about one mile's walk – along Merritt's Hill, Frankley Lane and Church Hill – past Bartley Reservoir to the church.

Bus route 192/292, operated by Midland Red (Mondays to Saturdays) and Go Whittle (Sundays), serves Birmingham, Kidderminster, Bewdley, Cleobury Mortimer and Ludlow.

Both Kidderminster and Ludlow are also served by rail.

Cookley is linked to Kidderminster via bus service 9, (Hollands Coaches) – or 6A, (Midland Red) in the evenings. No Sunday service.

Stage 5.

Bus route 738-740, operated by Shropshire Link, links Leintwardine to Ludlow and Knighton. Operates Mondays to Saturdays only.

Stages 6 and 8 to 10

The Heart of Wales Railway Line serves Llandrindod Wells (for Rhayader and Crossgates), Knighton, Craven Arms (change for Ludlow) and Shrewsbury (for onward connections to Birmingham). Services are operated by Wales & West Passenger Trains. There is no Sunday service during the period of the Winter Timetable.

A bus service, operated by Cross Gates Coaches, links Rhayader, Crossgates and Llandrindod Wells Railway Station. This operates Mondays to Saturdays only.

A Royal Mail Post Bus service links the Elan Valley with Rhayader and Llandrindod Wells. This operates Mondays to Fridays only.

Stage 7

There is no public transport at Bleddfa. The nearest is the Heart of Wales Railway Line at Dolau Station – see under Stages 6 and 8 to 10 above.

Useful Telephone Numbers

Centro 0121 200 2700

Cross Gates Coaches 01597 851226

Go Whittle 01562 820003

Herefordshire Bus Line 0345 125436

Hollands Coaches 01562 66648

Midland Red 01905 763888

Rail Enquiry Line 0345 484950

Powys County Council 01597 826642

Royal Mail Post Bus 01597 822925

Severn Valley Railway 01299 403816

Shropshire Co. Council 01743 253030

Shropshire Link 01588 673113

Traveline Shropshire 0345 056785

Worcestershire Bus Line 0345 125436

Wales & West Trains 0345 114114

Accommodation

Stage 1: Birmingham – Contact Birmingham Tourist Information (0121 780 4321).

Cookley – None. Use Kidderminster. Contact Kidderminster Tourist Information (01562 829400).

Stage 2: Bewdley – Contact Bewdley Tourist Information (01299 404740).

Stage 3: Cleobury Mortimer – Contact Bewdley (01299 404740) or Ludlow Tourist Information (01584 875053).

Stage 4: Ludlow – Contact Ludlow Tourist Information (01584 875053).

Stage 5: Leintwardine – Very limited. Contact Ludlow Tourist Information (01584 875053). Alternatively use Ludlow. (Note: As another alternative, for those prepared to book in advance to stay at the Riverside Inn, Aymestrey, collection from Leintwardine and return there the following day can be arranged. Contact Steve or Val Bowen on 01568 708440.)

Stage 6: Knighton – Contact Knighton Tourist Information/Offa's Dyke Centre (01547 528753).

Stage 7: Bleddfa – Hundred House Inn (01547 550333) is the only accommodation in Bleddfa. (Note: If fully booked they can usually advise regarding any local farms offering accommodation.)

Stage 8: Crossgates – Contact Llandrindod Wells Tourist Information (01597 822600).

Stage 9: Rhayader – Contact Rhayader Tourist Information (01597 810591).

Stage 10: Elan Valley – Very limited. Use Rhayader. Contact Rhayader Tourist Information (01597 810591).

Publishers' Note

Every care has been taken in the preparation of this book. All sections of the walk have been independently checked and are believed to be correct at the time of publication. However, no guarantee can be given that they contain no errors or omissions and neither the author nor the publishers can accept any responsibility for loss, damage or inconvenience resulting from the use of this book.

Please remember that the countryside is continually changing: hedges and fences may be remove or re-sited; footbridges and river banks may suffer flood damage; footpaths may be re-routed or ploughed over and not reinstated (as the law requires); concessionary paths may be closed. If you do encounter any such problems please let the publishers know, and please report any obstructions to rights of way to the appropriate local authority.

The Route of the Elan Valley Way

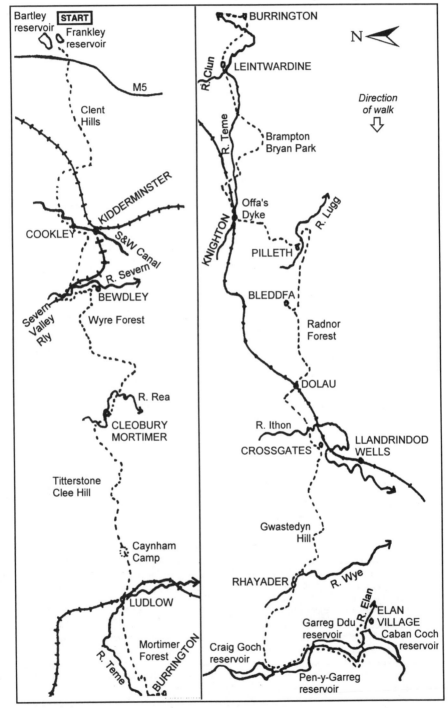

Frankley to Cookley

Distance: 14 miles (Blakedown 9 miles)
Public transport to the start: See page 12
Maps: Landranger 139; Pathfinder 933, 953; Explorer 219

The route commences at Frankley Church, on the western edge of Birmingham, and immediately climbs to the viewpoint of Frankley Beeches. The M5 Motorway is quickly crossed and left behind as is the Birmingham-Black Country conurbation. Thereafter the route is mainly via fieldpaths to Caunsall, with small pockets of woodland. The exception to this is the crossing of the Clent Hills – open hill country with glorious panoramic views. After Caunsall the route uses the towpath of the Staffordshire and Worcestershire Canal to reach Cookley.

The line of the Elan Valley aqueduct is somewhat to the north of the walk at this stage and is crossed only once – evidenced on the ground by a valve chamber (valve chambers contain control valves for the main pipe-line).

THE walk begins at Frankley Church (SO999804), a delightful and unexpected scene of tranquillity and beauty given the encroaching suburbs of Birmingham beyond the reservoirs.

Before setting out, the two reservoirs at this Birmingham end of the Elan Valley aqueduct might be visited. Those using the 21 bus service to get to Frankley – see Public Transport section – will have already walked past the larger Bartley reservoir, but if not it lies alongside the same road on which the church is situated. Turn right outside the church to reach it. Frankley reservoir may be reached by a footpath which leaves the far right-hand corner of the churchyard. Good views of both reservoirs are obtained as the route climbs to Frankley Beeches.

Frankley reservoir was constructed during the original period of the undertaking, 1892 to 1904. It has a surface area of 25 acres and holds some 200 million gallons of water when full. The main pipelines enter here.

Bartley reservoir was opened in 1930 to meet increasing demands and has a dam which is 65 feet in height, a surface area of 117 acres and a capacity of 500 million gallons.

Starting at the gate to the church, facing the road, turn sharp left to walk along a broad dirt track which runs alongside the churchyard wall for some yards before bearing right. Passing a house, on the right, the track continues straight ahead, becoming grassy and starting to climb. On reaching a gate leading into the bottom corner of a field do not enter this but instead take a footpath alongside and to the right of it, to continue climbing. Shortly after passing under some power lines the path enters a field via a metal gate. Continue climbing straight ahead, keeping to the right-hand edge of this field, and on reaching the top cross a three-bar stile onto a road. Cross this and go straight ahead along a path which runs to the right of Frankley Beeches.

There are good views of both reservoirs, but especially Frankley, to be had as the climb from the church to the Beeches is made. Of all the footpaths encountered when this stage of the walk was first walked in August 1998 this narrow climb up to Frankley Beeches was the most overgrown by far. Don't be put off by it.

A height of 256 metres/840 feet is attained at Frankley Beeches, well above that of the surrounding area, with good views over

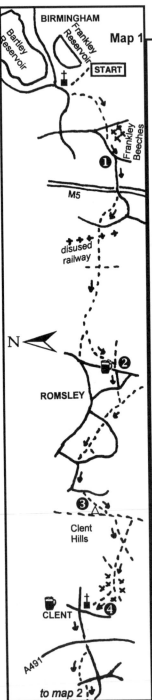

Frankley

The name Frankley – Domesday Book (1086) has it as Franchelie – would seem to indicate the free grant of land here to tenants by a Saxon overlord called Franca, i.e. Franca's Ley.

The church, dedicated to Saint Leonard, dates from the twelfth or early thirteenth century. It was certainly in existence by 1252 for in that year the chaplain of Frankley was in trouble with the abbot of Saint Mary, Hales (Halesowen) – the mother church – for burying a corpse in Saint Leonard's chapel rather than at Hales.

There was a manor house adjacent to the church which was destroyed in 1645, during the Civil War, by troops under Prince Rupert to prevent it being used as a Parliamentary stronghold. The manor was in existence at the time of Domesday Book and during the reign of Henry III came into the possession of the Lyttleton family. Sir Thomas Lyttleton, a local Royalist commander, was captured by the Parliamentarians in a night raid on his Bewdley headquarters and was imprisoned in the Tower of London. It was while he was languishing there that his fellow commander, Prince Rupert, took the decision to destroy Frankley manor to prevent it falling into enemy hands. It was never rebuilt, the Lyttletons moving to their estate at Arley – passed on Stage 2 of the Elan Valley Way – and later at Hagley, below the Clent Hills.

In 1751 the previously wooden church tower was rebuilt using stone from the demolished building. Whether this was a good idea is open to conjecture as the church has had bad luck with its tower since, it being gutted by fire in both 1931 and 1947. The fire of the night of 9 March 1931 was particularly destructive and was fought in freezing conditions. The fire brigade were hampered by both their main source of water – nearby Westminster Pool – and their equipment continually re-freezing and it is recorded that one fireman actually froze to the spot he was standing on!

Birmingham, the Black Country and of the Lickey Hills. The site is a well known landmark on the skyline to the west of Birmingham and is in the care of the National Trust.

Follow the footpath along the edge of the trees and into a field. Here follow to the left hand boundary and descend to a road – the M5 Motorway, below to the right, beginning to make its presence felt both audibly and visibly. Turn left along the road and then almost immediately right, (Yew Tree Lane), at a road junction. **❶**

There are good views of the Clent Hills (right) and Longbridge (left) on first reaching the road.

Follow Yew Tree Lane down to its crossing over the M5 Motorway. Immediately at the end of the overbridge, on the right hand side, take a footpath which goes straight ahead into a field. Initially follow the right hand edge of the field but then gradually bear half left to a stile, next to a water trough, about 20 yards in from the left hand boundary. Cross the stile into the next field and head down this, the footpath making for the left hand boundary and then following this.

Halesowen can be seen directly ahead. To the left are the Clent Hills with part of the village of Romsley visible in the foreground.

Continue straight ahead along the left field boundary. Enter the next field via a gate and walk past a redundant stile to reach another stile in the bottom left hand corner of the field, beside a gate. Over this stile into the next field, bear half left to reach a stile in the far boundary hedge giving access to a road. Cross this road, (Oxwood Lane), and enter the field opposite via a stile. Head directly across and down to another stile leading up onto the embankment of a disused railway line, (SO977797).

This was the line of the Halesowen (Junction) Railway which ran from Halesowen to join the Midland Railway's Birmingham to Bristol line at Northfield, Birmingham – there already being a branch line from Old Hill to Halesowen, (Great Western Railway). The line opened in 1883. When Frankley reservoir was being constructed the line was used to convey some of the the building materials, via sidings at Rubery. Passenger traffic on the line ceased in 1919, with the exception of workers' trains for Longbridge. The line was closed in 1965 and the track lifted, although a section does remain within the Longbridge works.

Cross the old trackbed and proceed down some steps to a stile giving access to a field. Head straight across to a point opposite in the field where the far boundary fence turns away – aiming to the left of a post carrying overhead lines. Follow the boundary fence around, down a slope, to a stile in a wooden fence. Climb over this stile, ignoring the track crossing here, (used by the route of The Monarch's Way), and go straight ahead down a small dip to cross a stream and pass over a stile into another field. Continue straight ahead along the left boundary of this field. After 30 yards or so cross the field boundary via a stile and proceed onwards, now keeping the hedge on the immediate right.

The noise of the M5 Motorway has already been left behind and this section gives an overriding impression of complete rural tranquillity.

At the bottom right hand corner of the field cross a stile to enter a wooded area, bearing slightly right and crossing a stream. Emerging from the trees enter another field. Turn right here to reach the right hand field boundary and then follow this up the field. After a while the boundary becomes little more than a ditch and bank. Continue to follow this, passing into the next field. Again keep the boundary on the right.

Glance behind here to see Frankley Beeches and the M5 Motorway in the distance. Ahead, the houses of Romsley now begin to come into view.

Continue to follow the field boundary until reaching the top right hand corner of the field, where a track is met. Do not leave the field by this but instead turn left to follow the top field boundary – a mast on a hill should be directly ahead. Continue into the next field, keeping the field boundary on the immediate right and ignoring a footpath which passes through it. This field merges into Romsley cricket pitch – pavilion ahead left. ❷

Follow the path until it emerges onto a track behind the Fighting Cocks public house. Turn right, and then left onto a road and immediately right into Poplar Lane, which leads into Dark Lane. Here, opposite bungalow number 24, take a footpath on the left, passing through a gate and up the hill beyond. Cross a stile at the top of the hill and turn immediately right. Descending slightly, bear right to enter trees, emerging after a few yards, via a stile, to run along the back gardens of Romsley. Keep their boundary fences on the immediate right.

Clent Hills are now directly ahead.

Follow the path straight ahead, gradually losing height. Where the garden boundary fences finish a field boundary continues. Keep it on the immediate right and continue ahead into another field, with farm buildings on the left. Proceed through this to reach a lane, via a stile. Turn left and then, by a bungalow, immediately right onto another path in a field. Follow the left hand edge of this, (SO955797).

Halesowen is now clearly visible to the right. Frankley Beeches still dominate the skyline behind.

Follow the path, crossing a stile into the next field. Ignore a footpath turning left but continue on into another field ahead. At the top left hand corner of this field cross a stile to emerge onto a road in a small settlement. Turn left and then immediately right. Proceed along this gently rising road until it swings to the right and reaches a T-junction. Take the lane to the left here. Almost immediately take a path which rises half right from the lane – not signed but with wooden bollards preventing vehicular access, (SO945802). Follow this path as it climbs Walton Hill, (Clent Hills). It emerges very near, but to the left of, the Triangulation Point at the top – 315 metres/1033 feet. ❸

The route is now in the Clent Hills Country Park. In the summer the climb is through tall bracken but usage as a bridleway keeps the path clear.

While climbing look to the left for another view of Frankley Beeches. From the top the views are superb with Birmingham, Halesowen and the Black Country, Bredon Hill, the Cotswolds, the Malvern Hills, and the hills around Abberley all visible.

The National Trust owns 443 acres of the Clent Hills of which 367 are open to the public as a country park. There are two hills – Adams Hill and Walton Hill – the latter being the higher, (315 metres/1033 feet) and the one crossed by the Elan

Valley Way. Walton Hill also bears, near the summit, the indistinct remains of a hill fort where, it is said, a band of Ancient Britons fought off attacks by a Roman force who were camped on nearby Wychbury Hill.

Turn left, (ie. away from the triangulation point), to follow the path signposted 'North Worcestershire Path'. After a few yards, at a junction just before a seat, take the right hand path which bends to the right, gradually descending between scattered gorse bushes. On reaching a footpath 'crossroads', (SO939795), take the right hand path ahead, soon joined by the corner of a field boundary on the left; the path now gradually descending with this boundary alongside it.

Passing the footpath crossroads the Clee Hills appear to the distant right. We will be on more intimate terms with Titterstone Clee Hill on Stage 4. As the path descends more steeply there are good views to the right across the Clent Hills themselves, (Adams Hill).

Continue on the path which levels out and meanders – the field boundary still to the left; the drop on the right of the path getting steeper. After a while the path starts to descend again. Ignore a footpath going sharply off down to the right.

As a National Trust Clent Hills sign is passed there is a parting of ways. Here take the right-hand path which descends through woodland to pass through a kissing gate and emerge from the trees onto open hillside. Proceed half right, (i.e. away from a boundary hedge on the left), over a grassy mound and down the hill ahead, and through a gap in a boundary of mainly hawthorn trees. Continue down the hill ahead in the same general direction, aiming towards the left-hand corner of a iron railing fence. On reaching this bear slightly left along it, (the railings on the right), for about 40 yards to reach a kissing gate. This leads onto a very narrow path, confined on the left by tall garden hedges and on the right by the churchyard wall of Clent church. ❹

Descending the hill the Vine public house can be seen below to the right – the white building. Depending on the time of year the tower of Clent church becomes visible through the trees.

Clent church is another dedicated to Saint Leonard – a sixth century French saint and patron of prisoners and the sick. This is a twelfth century church possibly on an earlier site, with fifteenth century rebuilding and much nineteenth century restoration. A guided tour leaflet is available inside.

There is an Indian restaurant opposite the church gate, although evening openings and a dress code render it of little value to walkers.

Follow the narrow footpath to emerge onto a lane by the church. Turn right, and at the crossroads by the church gate turn left – signposted Belbroughton. Pass underneath the bridge carrying the busy A491 Stourbridge Road. Not quite 100 yards after this bridge leave the road via a short flight of steps to a stile and public footpath on the right – signposted Oldnall. Proceed straight ahead, garden fences on the immediate left. At the end of these gardens bear half left and head for a group of mature willow trees which mark the course of a stream.

Cross the stream by a wooden footbridge, situated under these trees, and bear left to walk alongside it. Go over a stile into the next field, still by the stream. At the end of this field, in the left hand corner, cross another stile into a rough meadow area. Continue straight ahead to emerge onto a road, where the latter crosses the stream. Turn left along the road. After about 100 yards take the public footpath on the right hand side – signposted to Broome. Follow this narrow path as it passes along the right hand side of a cottage, between Prospect Cottage and a parking area, and passes under trees. Go straight on, crossing a stile into a field and following the left hand boundary of this.

To the rear here can be seen Wychbury Hill with its obelisk and the wooded Wychbury Camp hill fort to the left.

The Iron Age hillfort on Wychbury is one of the most complex in Worcestershire and was used in its time by both Ancient Britons and Roman forces – see also the note on the Clent Hills, (above). A legend has it that King Arthur is buried within the hill. The obelisk on the hill was erected in the mid eighteenth century in memory of George, the first Lord Lyttleton, the main estate of the Lyttleton family being, by then, the nearby Hagley Hall – see also the note on Frankley, (above), and that on Arley, (in Stage 2). The obelisk has been leaning and in an unsafe state for many years.

After about 100 yards cross the field boundary to the left by a stile and continue in the same direction, the hedge now on the right. The footpath now becomes a broad green path in a strangely 'artificial' landscape of formal planting. Keep straight on and when a low wire fence, across the path, is reached step over it. Nearing a building the obvious path swings left, away from the field boundary. The public right of way remains along the hedge however, is passable and should be used.

At the far corner of the 'field' turn sharp right through the boundary hedge to descend to a lane, via a flight of steps beneath an Ash tree, (SO917788). Turn right along the lane. After a little over 100 yards turn left onto a footpath, over a stile. Follow the right hand boundary of the field now entered. Continue straight ahead into another field and, via a stile, into a third, the hedge still on the right. The path now gradually widens, a stile or metal gate leading onto an enclosed track.

Proceed along this, ignoring a footpath going off it to the right as you pass a house with a large cedar tree alongside, the track bending first right and then sharply left and becoming metalled. On reaching a junction, (SO906785), turn right to walk down a quiet lane into Broome. This reaches the village by the entrance to Broome House, on the left. Immediately opposite is a gate into the churchyard. Enter, and walk to the left of the church to emerge back onto the road. ❺

Having regained the road follow it to a junction and turn left, signposted Churchill. Leaving Broome the road bends slightly to the right and soon meets the busy A450 Stourbridge to Worcester road at a crossroads. Turn left along the A450 – there is a pavement. When the Hackman's Gate sign is reached, in about 250 yards, cross the road and take the footpath signposted to Harborough Hill – on the right. Proceed along the right edge of the field, the path soon passing to the right of a stand of trees and becoming more of a track as it enters another field.

At the point where the stand of trees is met we found a large clump of wild raspberry bushes which were still in fruit in August and which were sampled along with blackberries, also prolific here.

Look right here, through gaps in the field boundary, for good views of Wychbury Hill and obelisk and the Clent Hills.

Follow the track as it narrows and enters a wood, (SO892785), meandering slightly among the trees. On reaching an area of mainly coniferous trees head downhill on a wider section of path and, at the bottom, go straight across another path, (used by the route of The Monarch's Way – the second crossing of it on this stage of the Elan Valley Way), to exit the wood into a field. Go straight across this, aiming for a white house with red roof tiles opposite.

On reaching the far boundary turn right and, after 20 yards or so, left into trees and alongside the right boundary fence of the aforementioned house. As the end of the house boundary is reached a pool appears to the left of the path, which is here in a small wooded area. Go straight on to emerge from the trees into a large field.

Cross this, bearing almost half left towards a single tree on the skyline, and with a small hill covered in conifers and with a mast and large white house on it to the right, (Harborough Hill). The busy A456 Birmingham to Kidderminster road makes its presence known ahead and is reached via a stile. Cross over – very carefully; it is a well known 'racetrack' – and turn left. ❻

Bus service 192/292 passes along here – turn left for bus stops and for Blakedown station which is half a mile down the A456.

After a few strides cross a stile on the right to enter a field. Follow the path straight ahead along the somewhat incomplete right-hand field boundary to reach a stile in the far right-hand corner. Cross this onto a track and turn left along this for about 30 yards before leaving it over a stile on the right to enter another field. Go straight across this field to

Broome village

The village is thought to have taken its name from the large amounts of broom which grew on the expanses of common land, 145 acres of which survived before the Broome Enclosure Act of 1779.

After the architectural delights of the previous two churches the redbrick of Broome church, (Saint Peter), is initially a disappointment but there is plenty of interest here. Notice the re-hung bell with its dedication to Thomas Monahan, rector here from 1929 to 1939. This was re-hung here after its removal from the belfry in 1940 – apparently it is cracked. Inside the porch is a listing of rectors of Broome back to Alexander de Brimsfield, rector from 1190 to 1203 – revealing the true age of the site. It is likely that the original church here was founded by Maurice de Ombersley sometime after 1154 when land hereabouts was gifted to him by Henry II. The bowl of the font certainly dates from this time and is probably a survivor from that original building. By the late eighteenth century the building had been allowed to fall into a very poor state – possibly as a result of a series of absentee rectors, not an unusual state of affairs in eighteenth century England. The present building dates from 1780, with 1861 additions.

its far boundary where a stile gives access to railway lines, (Birmingham – Kidderminster – Worcester). Cross the rails – *with care* – to a stile leading into another field. Go straight ahead across this field, aiming just to the left of a single oak tree – (the O.S. map shows a field boundary alongside and to the left of the path but this appears to have been removed and a 'temporary' fence was in place as of the time of writing). As the far boundary is neared head towards the left corner, dropping down to a metal gate. Exit the field via this gate, a large pond now visible ahead right.

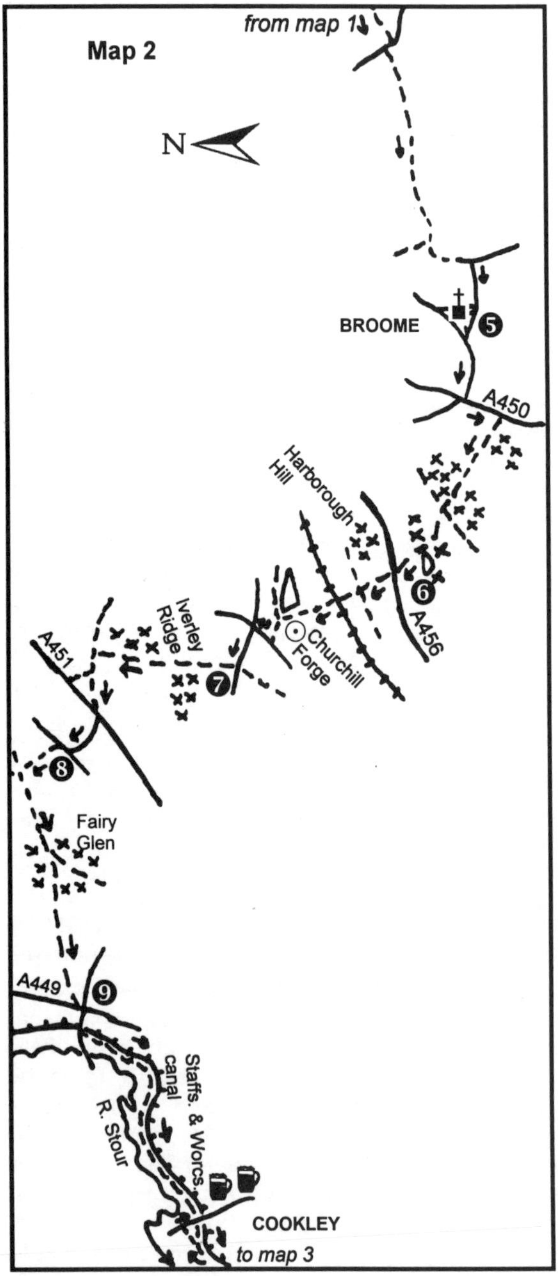

While crossing the field the tower of Churchill church comes into view over to the left – redbrick as at Broome.

Having passed through the gate proceed along a gravelled track straight ahead, with the pond on the right and Churchill Forge on the left. Cross a stream via a brick bridge and then bear left – ignoring a footpath going right. Almost immediately the track reaches a road.

Churchill Forge, (SO883796), was built around 1800 on the site of a thirteenth century water mill. The forge was a spade and shovel works and was run by successive generations of the Bache family. The two waterwheels can be seen from the footpath. The forge is occasionally open to the public – contact Mrs P. Hayward on Kidderminster 700746 for details.

Turn right along the road – (the church and the main village

Map 2

from map 1

N

BROOME

A450

Harborough Hill

Iverley Ridge

A451

Churchill Forge

A456

Fairy Glen

A449

Staffs. & Worcs. canal

R. Stour

COOKLEY

to map 3

of Churchill lie to the left) – to reach a crossroads by a war memorial. Go left here, the road passing through a cutting in the red sandstone rock which is typical of this area. Ahead the road climbs slightly and bends to the left and just before this bend is reached a footpath crosses it. Turn right here – signed Public Bridleway – and enter a field. **❼**

Keeping to the left boundary of this climb up the hill straight ahead. Still climbing, leave the field to walk up a track which is bounded by a plantation on the left and a field boundary on the right. As the end of the plantation is reached, and the track finally levels out, continue straight ahead along a path which runs almost along the top of the ridge, with woodland to the right and a large field to the left as it undulates along.

On eventually reaching a T-junction with another path turn left – onto a much narrower path bounded by raised banks and waymarked 'North Worcestershire Path'. Ignore a footpath going off to the right but descend to reach the A451 Stourbridge to Kidderminster road.

The ridge, Iverley Ridge, attains a maximum height of around 125 metres/410 feet. All the way along the ridge there are good views. In particular soon after the plantation is left behind the obelisk on Wychbury Hill and the Clent Hills are visible due right. To the south, on a good day, the Abberley and Malvern Hills may be visible.

Here we saw overhead the first buzzard of the walk. Formerly restricted to Wales and the Marches these magnificent birds have, through being protected, now re-colonised almost up to the borders of Birmingham itself.

As the A451 is reached the Elan Valley Way leaves Worcestershire for the first time on its journey to briefly enter Staffordshire.

Leaving the A451 along the metalled track, (see below), as the first house on the left is reached a glance into its garden will reveal a grey brick and metal structure which is a valve chamber for the Elan Valley aqueduct, the line of which is crossed here for the first time on the walk. These structures will become very familiar!

Cross the A451 and turn left. After 50 yards or so turn right onto a metalled track, initially crossing a field before passing through a small settlement and bending right to meet a metalled lane, (Sugar Loaf Lane). Turn right into this lane and then immediately left off it and up another metalled lane signed as a bridleway, (SO875810). **❽**

Continue past a farm on the left, and through a metal gate – after which the road surfacing disappears and the lane reverts to a track. Continue straight ahead through another metal gate to walk between two wire paddock fences and then through another gate. Where another track crosses the route turn left along it, through trees – waymarked 'North Worcestershire Path'.

Follow the track which narrows, after a while, and then bends to the left to enter denser woodland, (Fairy Glen), descending slightly. A 'North Worcestershire Path' post marks an otherwise insignificant parting of ways, (SO868811). Take the narrower right hand path, ('North Worcestershire Path'), which descends more rapidly now to leave the wood and enter a field by a stile.

The small woodland interlude of Fairy Glen is well named – it is an enchanting place, and the turning at SO868811 could easily be missed if it were not for the 'North Worcestershire Path' marker post.

Worcestershire is re-entered at the point where the turning is made.

While crossing the fields after the wood the church of Saint Peter, Kinver can be seen in the distance sitting on top of its sandstone hill. Look to the half right.

The Staffordshire and Worcestershire Canal

The Staffordshire and Worcestershire Canal was engineered by James Brindley and was part of his plan for a 'Grand Cross' of canals linking the Rivers Mersey, Trent, Thames and Severn, the Staffordshire and Worcestershire being the south-western arm of the cross. Commenced in 1766, it was fully open by 1772 at a cost of around £100,000 and runs for 46 miles between Great Haywood on the Trent and Mersey Canal and the town of Stourport on the River Severn. The story goes that it was Brindley's original intention to link the canal to the River Severn at Bewdley but opposition from vested interests there – it is said that he was told to take his 'Stinking Ditch' elsewhere – caused him to change his plans. This is unlikely however. The original Act for the canal, (dated 14 May 1766), stated that the southern terminus of the canal was to be 'at some place between Bewdley and Titton Brook' – the town only being mentioned in this respect in a bid to lessen expected opposition from those involved in the lucrative transhipment trade based there. It is very doubtful that Brindley ever intended to end the canal there for no other reason than the route as built was less difficult and expensive to construct. Whatever the true story may be, the net result was that a brand new 'canal' town grew up at Stourport while the trading fortunes of Bewdley stagnated. The silver lining to this particular cloud is however that Bewdley remains to this day an unspoilt and most attractive little town – as will be seen on Stage 2 of the walk.

The oval nameplates on the bridges passed are a feature of this canal.

At Clay House Bridge (No.25) note the towrope wear on both the brickwork and protective ironwork of the bridge, the result of years of horsedrawn traffic.

At Austcliffe Bridge (No.24) note the delightful cast-iron footbridge over the accompanying River Stour. The red sandstone rocks overhanging the canal at Austcliffe are a well-known landmark. A few years ago they overhung a lot more than they do now, it looking like the whole lot might suddenly come crashing down on top of some unsuspecting boatman. Surveys revealed that there was a serious risk of this in fact happening so unstable had the rock become and so it was in part removed. What remains, though a shadow of its former self, is still impressive – especially looking back as the canal swings left.

Cookley Tunnel (No.23) is cut through the sandstone ridge on which the village stands, the River Stour in comparison making a large horseshoe bend around the obstacle. The tunnel is partly lined with brick and has a towpath. It is 59 metres/194 feet in length. Emerging from the tunnel the noise of Cookley Works – a successor to the many small forges that once lined the Stour valley – comes as something of a shock after the tranquillity just left.

Footbridge over the River Stour at Austcliffe

Follow the path ahead, aiming initially midway between the woodland to the left and the hedge to the right then following the latter round slightly right towards a 'North Worcestershire Path' post. At the bottom right hand corner of the field exit into the adjoining field via a stile. Turn half left, diagonally across the field – again a 'North Worcestershire Path' marker post in the middle of the field showing the way.

Exit the field by a double stile about 25 yards in from the left corner. There is a steep drop from the second part of the stile. Follow the same general direction through the next field, the path losing height before reaching the left hand boundary where it enters yet another field via a stile. Head diagonally across this field to its far corner where a stile gives access onto the very busy A449(T) road, here between Wolverhampton and Kidderminster. **❾**

Cross the A449(T), with care, and proceed straight ahead along the road opposite, signposted Caunsall. In about 100 yards Caunsall Bridge over the Staffordshire and Worcestershire Canal is reached. Cross the bridge and turn left to join the canal towpath which is now followed all the way to Cookley – the canal should be on the left throughout. Clay House Bridge and Austcliffe Bridge follow. After Austcliffe Bridge and its sandstone rock overhang an idyllic section ensues with the canal on the left and the River Stour on the right, the towpath all there is between them. The canal then makes a determined left turn and soon Cookley can be seen ahead, the houses on its main street towering above the short tunnel. Follow the towpath through the tunnel. Just before reaching Cookley Works, on the right, turn sharp right off the towpath, through almost 180 degrees, to climb back up over the tunnel to Cookley's main street. On reaching the road turn right, into the village. The Bull's Head public house, from outside which buses run to Kidderminster, is on the left.

Cookley

Cookley is mentioned as early as AD964 when a charter of Edgar, King of Albion, granted two hides of land here to Earl Beorhtnoth. By the time of Domesday Book (1086) there was a corn mill on the River Stour and it seems likely that the original settlement grew up near the river, only later spreading up the neighbouring sandstone ridge.

The village owes much of its later growth to the establishment of an early ironworks on the River Stour, and later alongside the Staffordshire and Worcestershire Canal. By keeping abreast of the rapid changes in technology and demand this survived on the same site until 1884 when it relocated to Brockmoor, near Brierley Hill. Between 1887 and 1904 the site lay derelict but in the latter year it reopened with the new company specialising in the manufacture of steel wheels, as is still the case today.

Formerly part of Wolverley ecclesiastical parish, the village became a parish in its own right in 1849 and the church, St. Peter's, was built in that year.

Modern Cookley has a small supermarket, butcher, fish & chip shop, newsagent, general store/post office, florist, two pubs – with another half a mile up the road – but no accommodation.

Stage 2

Cookley to Bewdley

Distance: 11½ miles (Wolverley 2½ miles, Arley 7 miles).
O.S.Maps: Landranger 138; Pathfinder 933, 953, 952, 932; Explorer 218

This stage begins and ends with waterside walks. It commences where Stage 1 left off, on the towpath of the Staffordshire and Worcestershire Canal. This is followed all the way to Wolverley. A combination of road, track and fieldpath walking then take the route towards the Severn Valley which is reached via a short climb at Trimpley. The way then descends through Eymore Wood to reach the river itself, crossed by footbridge at Arley.

Across the river the route climbs, via minor road and track, into woodland overlooking the Severn Valley – with superb views of the river, Severn Valley Railway and Trimpley reservoir below. After descending to the river, via a short stretch of aqueduct in the woods, the final section of the day is a two mile riverside walk into Bewdley.

An alternative route from Arley to Bewdley uses the riverside path throughout.

In season the sights and sounds of the Severn Valley Railway steam trains add a nostalgic interest to these final miles of the day.

The Elan Valley aqueduct crosses both the canal and river sections of the walk. The canal crossing was formerly overhead by bridge but is now underground – but is still easily recognisable. Just after the section of road leading down to Eymore Wood is reached a valve chamber may be seen in a field. To the west of the River Severn a short length of aqueduct, in the woods above the river, is walked.

The River Severn crossing is by means of a spectacular pipeline bridge.

! Sections of this stage between Arley and Bewdley may become impassable if the River Severn is in flood. If planning to walk this stage after very wet weather the situation should be ascertained beforehand and appropriate action taken.

STARTING outside the Bull's Head P.H., cross the road and turn right. Just before reaching the office building of Cookley Works – in under 50 yards – take the footpath on the left which descends to reach the canal towpath. The mouth of Cookley Tunnel is just to the left. Turn right along the canal towpath which is now followed all the way to Wolverley. The canal should be on the left all the way. It immediately swings to the left as it passes Cookley Works and the towpath crosses a bridge over what was a canal arm into the factory.

Until about 60 years ago Cookley Works received supplies of coal and iron 'pigs' by canal boat into a basin within the works. This has now been filled in but the entrance remains, its bridge bearing the date 1871.

The canal next bears to the right. Debdale Lock is soon reached with the canal continuing to bear slightly right but then making a sharp left turn around a red sandstone spur. A right turn resumes the generally southerly course of the canal and the crossing point of the Elan Valley aqueduct is

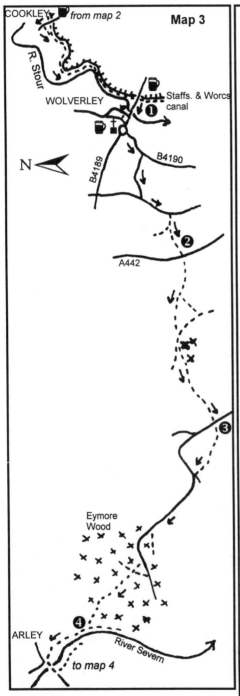

Map 3

The Cookley Works

Cookley Works is the sole successor to several early iron forges which harnessed the water power of the Stour and were established hereabouts by the latter years of the seventeenth century.

In 1665 the river between Stourbridge and Kidderminster was made navigable by Andrew Yarrenton and this made possible the cheaper transport of coal to the area. The coming of the canal in 1770, (it was open throughout its length by 1772), further facilitated transport and the site of Cookley ironworks then expanded alongside it.

The works were owned by the Knight family, of Wolverley and later Lea Castle, and survived successfully by keeping pace with rapidly developing technology. Iron rolling, as opposed to hammering and drawing, was swiftly adopted and in 1815 the manufacture of tinplates began at the works. The work of many smaller local sites owned by the Knights was consolidated at the Cookley site after this date.

In 1884 the business relocated to Brockmoor, near Brierley Hill, and by 1887 the site was derelict. In 1904 the works were acquired by a company specialising in the manufacture of steel wheels, an activity which has continued to the present day. It comes as something of a shock to hear the noise of such heavy industry in this otherwise tranquil setting but it represents 350 years of almost unbroken manufacturing activity on essentially the same site.

passed. The canal now meanders for a while and is joined by a road on its far side. A wooded section follows and a small red sandstone cutting is negotiated. At Wolverley Forge Bridge (No. 21) the canal bears left again, soon reaching Wolverley Lock and Bridge (No. 20). ❶

Debdale Lock is the first lock encountered on this walk down the canal. Look over the wall just beyond the lock house to see one of the circular weirs which are a feature of the Staffordshire and Worcestershire Canal and channel excess water around the lock. The lock house itself is a much more grand affair than many of its fellows elsewhere on the canal, with a bay window giving good views along the waterway. Opposite the lock house there is a cave cut into the red sandstone which is said to have been excavated by the canal navvies as a temporary home while this stretch of the canal was being built. The footbridge below the lock is numbered No. 22.

The Elan Valley aqueduct originally crossed the canal by an arched bridge between Debdale and Wolverley Forge Bridges. In 1988 this was removed and the crossing is now underground, although it can still be recognised as such. It lies soon after the canal has made the very sharp left turn around a red sandstone spur. Look for steel piling on the far side of the canal and a break in the hedgerow vegetation on the towpath side.

This entire section of canal is a very beautiful one and peaceful – once the noise of Cookley Works has been quickly left behind. In particular the stretch around Wolverley Lea, between Debdale and Wolverley Forge, is idyllic.

Leave the canal towpath at Wolverley Bridge, (SO831791), and turn right along the road, (B4189), with the car park of the Lock P.H. on the right – the pub is on the other side of the canal. The road crosses the River Stour over a bridge. Take the first right turning onto a minor road and then left onto a footpath which climbs up a small field towards Wolverley church to emerge onto the road by it, the entrance to the churchyard immediately opposite up steps. Turn left along the road to continue the walk, right to visit old Wolverley, or go up the steps to visit the church. (*See p.30*.)

Walking along the road towards the B4189 an area surrounded by railings, on the left of the road, is passed. This is Wolverley Pound where any animal found straying was impounded until its owner paid a sum of money for its release. Such pounds were quite common in English villages after the Enclosure Acts of the eighteenth century did away with most common pastures. The Enclosure Act for Wolverley dates from 1775 and the pound here is unusual in that it is not merely an enclosure but also incorporates shelters for the animals, cut out of the soft red sandstone rock. For good views of it either enter the enclosure and walk around the edge of the excavated area or else continue to the B4189 and walk a few yards to the left. The iron gate to the pound is early nineteenth century in origin and was made at Cookley.

Bus service 5 to Kidderminster runs along the B4190 (Franche Road). The bus stop is situated en route, just a few yards along Franche Road on the right.

Walk along the road to its junction with the B4189. Here turn right, to reach a roundabout, and then immediately left – signposted B4190 Bewdley and Franche, (Franche Road). Walk down the right hand side of this road – there is a pavement all the way. In a couple of hundred yards, just past a petrol station on the left, take a road going right – signposted Fairfield,

Wolverley Church and Village

The red brick church of St. John the Baptist, Wolverley, stands high up on its sandstone hill overlooking the village, to the north, and the canal, to the east. The present building is the third on the site, the earliest dating back to Saxon times. The second church here was dismantled in 1769, being in disrepair by that date – a similar tale to that encountered at Broome on Stage 1 of the Elan Valley Way. The base of the tower of that church was retained and forms part of the current building.

The rebuilding was mainly down to Edward Knight of Lea Castle and is late eighteenth century and in the Italianate style – Knight having recently visited Italy. The building was opened in 1772 – coincidentally the same year as the neighbouring canal was opened throughout. In the nave of the church is a monument to Sir John Attwood of Wolverley Court which was formerly at the court but was moved to the church in 1916. The Wolverley Legend tells how Sir John escaped from captivity during the Spanish Wars with the help of a swan and the monument has his head resting on his helmet which is part of a swan's neck. Unfortunately the head has been broken.

Immediately inside the gates of the churchyard, on the left, note the very old gravestones built into the path wall, almost indecipherable but one bearing the date 1650 or 1660. There are many old gravestones still standing in this area of the churchyard. Headstones dating from the eighteenth century are commonplace although many have been rendered illegible by the effects of weather and the passage of time on the soft stone. The oldest one I could make out, after a very quick search, commemorates a John Wood Junior of Caunsall who

died on the 16th March 1684, aged about 30.

Walk right around the outside of the church. To its rear, (north), the village of Wolverley can be seen below. To visit it complete the circuit of the church and exit via the steps turning left down the road, (the 'Hollow Way'). On the way down note, on the left, the red sandstone cliff on which the church is perched, a stable cut into the rock, the little plaque depicting St. John, the rear steps and path to the church cut through the red sandstone, and the round plaque on the cottage adjacent to the latter, which depicts the head of a fierce looking man. Crossing the stream, (Horse Brook), proceed along the village street noting in particular the group of buildings on the right around the Court House – bearing a clock, coat of arms, a collection of heads, and the date 1620.

The name 'Court House' is a misnomer and the date misleading. These are actually the old buildings of the Sebright School which was established on this site as provided for in the will of William Sebright in 1620. William Sebright was a member of a successful local farming family who became a lawyer and eventually found fame as Town Clerk of London. He had a school and master's house built on this site sometime before his death – the small house second from the left is thought to be the original master's house – while the building on the very left of the group was a new grammar school built in 1787.

The building which now bears the date 1620 was erected in 1829 as a new school with its design allowing for an existing Right of Way, to the river meadows beyond, to pass underneath it. In the same year the school building on the right of the group was built to match the 1787 building opposite. The date of 1620 on the main building therefore refers to that of William Sebright's bequest and not the date of its construction. There were three schools on the site eventually, all funded by the Sebright charity, although the group of buildings are now private residences.

Wolverley is a very much older settlement than all of these goings on however. It is mentioned by name in a charter of King Ethelbert of Mercia dated 866 and is likely somewhat older than that. It takes its name from its Saxon founder, possibly one Wulfeard. There was a manor court held here for ten townships under the control of the prior of Worcester Cathedral and in the twelfth century, during the civil war between Stephen and Matilda (Maud), the prior, a supporter of Stephen, was granted a licence to rebuild the fortifications of the settlement.

Like Cookley to the north, Wolverley became an early centre for iron forging, using local charcoal and the power of the waters of the River Stour. The coming of the Staffordshire & Worcestershire Canal to the village in 1770, and its opening throughout in 1772, brought much prosperity to it, with coal replacing charcoal in the ironmaking process and cheaper transport for the finished products. Unlike the surviving works at Cookley the forge at Wolverley long ago ceased production.

Today's village has two pubs – The Queen's Head, in the centre of the village, and The Live and Let Live, on the right-hand side further along the road – and a general store cum post office/newsagent.

To return to the church, and the route of the Elan Valley Way, either retrace the route up the road or, if the gate at the bottom is unlocked, climb up the steps and narrow path in its deep sandstone cutting to enter the churchyard on the north side of the building itself, ie. the point from where the village was originally viewed.

(Fairfield Lane). Follow this road which commences by passing through suburban type housing, (as did Franche Road), but then narrows, loses its pavement, bears left, and takes on the characteristics of a country lane, passing between fields and eventually reaching a T-junction. Turn left here, signposted Kidderminster, and remain on this road until, at a fairly sharp bend to the left, (SO817787), Lowe Farm, The Lowe, is reached. Here turn right along a track, indicated by a bridleway sign.

After just under 100 yards, when the track narrows to footpath width and bears right, continue straight ahead over a stile, to the left of a metal farm gate, into a field and along a footpath which follows its left hand boundary to reach a tiny stile in the far left hand corner. Cross this and continue in the same direction through the next field. Cross a stile at the far side onto a stretch of path bounded between two wooden field/paddock fences. Walk along this, the busy A442 Bridgnorth Road visible ahead. Follow the path as it descends to reach this. ❷

Go straight across the road and up a track directly opposite. Cross a stile, (very much the worse for wear at the time of writing), and proceed along the obvious track ahead, which bends to the right to run through a shallow valley, a small stream alongside it to the left, (Honeybrook). Remain on the track as the valley becomes deeper, the cliffs on the right being particularly high. Just before it bends left cross the stream, via a wooden footbridge on the left, and turn right to walk alongside it for a few yards to a stile, situated to the left of a metal gate. Cross this stile. Almost immediately there is a junction of paths, with two stiles ahead – one straight on and one to the left. Take the former, following the stream which is immediately below and to the right. This path can be very overgrown indeed in late summer and care is needed to avoid slipping down into the stream.

Emerging from this very narrow section of path drop down to the right to rejoin the original track, (which has been taking a parallel course to the narrow path but on the other side of the stream), just after the latter has crossed the stream. Follow the track, the stream in trees about 50 yards to the right, until it bears slightly right and rises to reach a metal gate, a stile to its left. Cross the stile to emerge onto another track. Turn right along this. There is a golf course to the left of it.

After a little over 100 yards, with the track becoming stony and rising slightly, cross a stile in the fence on the left to walk along a footpath which immediately drops down to join the stream, now on the left. This path can be quite muddy after wet weather. It follows the stream for a while and then starts to climb, bearing to the right, away from the stream. Here, (SO801787), look for a stile leading into a field on the left. Cross the stile, (crossing a tributary of the main stream at the same time), and enter the field, the left hand boundary of which is formed by the stream. Head half right diagonally across and up the field – quite a steep climb – towards the top right hand corner. At the top pass through a metal gate into another field and again head diagonally across this towards its highest point. On reaching this a stile will be seen straight ahead. Cross this into the next field.

While climbing these fields look behind for views of the Clent Hills – immediately behind – and of Kidderminster – to the right foreground of the hills.

When walking this stage it started to rain and taking shelter under some oak trees, on the right, I discovered the largest mushrooms I have ever seen – well over a foot across.

Go straight across the field, bearing slightly to the left of a large oak tree. Passing this bear very slightly left to exit the field, where a corner paddock fence on the left forms a corner with the far boundary of the field, via a stile next to a metal gate. On entering the next field follow its left hand boundary – a garden boundary of mainly beech hedge – to a stile in the far corner. Cross the stile to reach a path which passes through trees to emerge onto a road, opposite the entrance drive to Bite Farm, (SO792785). ❸

Cross the road and head down this drive but after only about 20 yards – long before the drive swings sharp right to the farm house – cross a stile on the right into a paddock and head diagonally across this, (i.e. half left under the trees), to cross into another paddock via another stile which is almost immediately in front of the farm house. (*Note: Take care when crossing these two paddocks. The fences which surround them are electrified and the protective rubber coverings at the stiles were not that extensive or substantial when we were last here.*) Heading in the same general direction across this paddock cross a stile in the far corner – just in front of and to the right of the farm house – to enter a field. Continue across this field in the same general direction.

Crossing the field, Titterstone Clee Hill can be seen directly ahead in the distance while to the left are the Malvern Hills and on the half left the wide expanses of Wyre Forest. Wyre Forest is crossed on Stage 3 of the Elan Valley Way and the lower slopes of Titterstone Clee Hill on Stage 4 – see these stages for notes. In between Wyre Forest and the Malverns can be seen the Abberley Hills – see note in Stage 4 – Abberley Clock Tower showing at the right end of the body of Abberley Hill itself.

On reaching the far side of the field cross into the next field via a stile. Continue in the same direction across this field until the left hand wire boundary fence – not shown on O.S. Explorer Map 218 but where that map does indicate a bend in the path, (SO787785) – is reached and then turn right to follow this to the corner of the field where a lane is reached over a stile, (or through the gap in the hedge here). Turn right along the lane but then almost immediately left, along a road. The road is initially in gradual descent and bending to the right. Follow it as it straightens and then bends right again with the descent becoming steeper.

After about 100 yards on the road a glance over the hedge to the left, just past some metal gates, will reveal one of the Elan Valley aqueduct's valve chambers in the field just beyond.

Depending on the time of year the sound of steam trains on the Severn Valley Railway should be heard for the first time as the road is walked – a sound of a bygone age which will accompany the walk for the remainder of the day.

Continue on the road, another straight section of which ends with a fairly long bend to the right – the trees of Eymore Wood visible ahead. Ignore a footpath going off steeply down to the left – although there are further good views of Titterstone Clee Hill to be had here. Instead remain on the road which now enters Eymore Wood, passing a car parking area, (to the right), and making a sweeping left turn before straightening in preparation for a steeper section of descent. Before reaching this – and about 50 yards before a Severn Trent sign announcing Trimpley reservoir, on the left – take a track which leaves the road on the right, (SO776793), waymarked 'Worcestershire Way'.

Follow the track as it descends through the trees of Eymore Wood. After about 100 yards go straight on at a 'crossroads' of tracks – following the 'Worcestershire Way' markers. Follow the track onwards, ignoring another track going off to the right through a gate into a field, but instead bordering the field which is on the right. The 'Worcestershire Way' markers continue to indicate the route, and in fact do so all the way to Arley, (or to Bewdley if the alternative route beyond the river crossing is used). When the gates to Huntsfield Farm and Cottage, marked 'Private', are met take a path which leaves the track on the right by means of a stile to cross into an open field area. Bear round to the left, skirting the boundary of the farm and cottage, to reach a gate giving access to a field. Go half left diagonally across and down this field.

The village of Arley is first seen as this field is crossed, both the church tower and Arley Tower are clearly visible.

Crossing the field the descent becomes much steeper and the path passes through a gap in a hedge to continue through a scrubby but still open area – hawthorn bushes and bracken. At the bottom left hand corner of this area re-enter the woodland via a stile. Continue to descend, first bending to the

The Severn

At almost 220 miles in length the River Severn is the longest river in Britain. Known to the Romans as Sabrina, it rises on the Plynlimon plateau in mid-Wales to plunge through the Hafren Forest. In Wales it is known as Afon Hafren. It flows through Newtown and Welshpool to enter England and then passes through Shrewsbury, Ironbridge, Bridgnorth, Bewdley, Worcester, Tewkesbury and Gloucester on its way to the Bristol Channel and the sea. It is now accompanied on much of its journey by a long distance footpath, the 'Severn Way', running 210 miles from the source to Severn Beach.

Although there is now virtually no commercial traffic remaining on the river, in its heyday the fortunes of many riverside settlements – notably Bewdley – depended on river trade.

At the close of the seventeenth century the Severn was the second busiest river in Europe, after the Meuse, while the latter eighteenth century saw it linked with the heavily industrialised Midlands via the growing canal system – such as the Staffordshire & Worcestershire Canal at Stourport, (1772), and the Worcester & Birmingham Canal at Worcester, (1815).

left then the right – the path can be quite muddy and slippery in wet weather. Ignore various minor paths joining and leaving the main path but follow the waymarked route. The River Severn is soon visible through the trees ahead and as the path drops down to it the 'Worcestershire Way' markers are joined by those for the 'Severn Way'. On reaching a T-junction of paths, turn right to pick up the riverside path at the bottom of the slope. ❹

Follow this path alongside the river into Arley, the river on the left hand side. Almost immediately cross a footbridge over a small stream, just below an isolated cottage. Ignore various small paths going left to the very edge of the river but remain on the main riverside path which runs about 20 yards from the water and about 10 yards above it and is easily recognised here by having a metal handrail on its left. As this handrail ends cross a stile to continue along the path, which eventually becomes metalled. Cross another stile and descend a short flight of steps to a footbridge over a water channel. Through the trees half left Arley footbridge will be seen. This is soon reached.

> *On the east of the river bus service 297 runs to Kidderminster, while over the river there is the train service on the Severn Valley Railway, from Arley station to Bewdley and Kidderminster.*
> *The bus stop is situated at a road junction about 400 yards up the road which runs to the right, away from the river, as the settlement is entered on the walk. The railway station is on the main route after crossing the river.*

Cross the footbridge over the River Severn. This replaced the former ferry in 1972.

> *There is now a choice of routes to Bewdley – an alternative, all the way along the river or the main higher, and slightly longer, route which goes through the Wyre Forest, with some fine views, before descending to continue along the river into Bewdley. For the main route now continue reading from ✪ on page 37.*

River Route (Alternative): After crossing the footbridge over the river turn left to follow the riverside path, (waymarked 'Worcestershire Way'). This avoids the climb just starting on the main route and shortens the distance to Bewdley by half a mile. There are several stiles along the riverside path. The main route is rejoined just before the Elan Valley aqueduct's Severn Crossing is reached. The route passes under Victoria Bridge which carries the Severn Valley Railway across the River Severn. Just after passing under this a Great Western Railway cast iron boundary post, dated 1897, will be seen, against a wall. A little further on a high bank on the far side of the river conceals Severn Trent's Trimpley Reservoir. The route runs in part through riverside woodland and in late summer can seem almost like being in a jungle, with Indian Balsam, Bracken and Japanese Knotweed each staking its own claim for superiority waterside. It is as the wooded section is left that the main route rejoins from the right. *Now continue reading from ★ on page 42.*

Arley

Arley is a pretty riverside village which used to be home to at least six public houses of which only the one – The Harbour – now remains open. It was originally the site of a ferry across the River Severn but this has now been replaced by the footbridge. Most of the village is on the east of the river but the pub and railway station, (Severn Valley Railway), are over the footbridge on the west side.

Arley is mentioned in Domesday Book (1086) and even earlier – a documentary reference exists for 996 when ownership of the manor was transferred to the college of canons at Wolverhampton. The ferry is mentioned as long ago as 1331. The Saxon name for the settlement was Ernley – 'the clearing where eagles live'.

In the twelfth century the lord of the manor was Henry de Port and it was he who probably was responsible for building the oldest remaining parts of the church of St. Peter here. In due course of time the manor passed under control of the Mortimer family – powerful Marcher Earls whose claim to the throne of England passed to the Yorkist cause during the Wars of the Roses. In 1270 the manor was given to Isolda, daughter of Ralph de Mortimer as her marriage settlement when she wed Sir Walter de Balun, a very short-lived marriage – see below.

In 1425, after the direct male Mortimer line had died out and the family estates had passed to the House of York via marriage to the female line, the manor was in the possession of Richard, Duke of York and was sold to a Sir Thomas Burley. His daughter married into the Lyttleton family and Arley then passed to them. The Lyttletons already held the manors of Frankley and Hagley – see the notes on Frankley and on Wychbury/Hagley in Stage 1. After the destruction of their manor house at Frankley in 1645, during the Civil War, the family moved to Arley as their main residence until again moving to Hagley Hall in the mid eighteenth century. In 1767 Lucy Lyttleton married Arthur Annesley, Viscount Valentia, and the Valentias came to live at the manor, willed to Lucy and so into the Annesley family control in 1779. Arthur Annesley's son – generally known as Lord

Valentia – inherited Arley on his father's death in 1816. A bit of an eccentric, he decided to beautify the house by remodelling it as a modern castle – or, some would say, 'folly'. Village roads were diverted and any buildings blocking the view of the river were demolished. An arboretum, which still exists, was laid out. Arley Tower, on the left alongside the road up to the church, was built – supposedly to hide the Valentia Arms pub from the castle. Lord Valentia died in 1844 before all the work had been completed and the manor was then bought by the Woodward family who held it until 1959. In 1962 new owners had the castle largely demolished.

Arley has a post office cum general store which is passed on joining the road through the village just after the footbridge. Further along this road, on the left beyond what was the Valentia Arms pub are public toilets. Continuing up the village street Arley Tower is passed. The church soon comes into view on the left.

The oldest part of St. Peter's Church, Arley, is the nave which dates from the twelfth century and was probably built by Henry de Port,
then lord of the manor. There are some traces of an even older structure however. Some rebuilding took place around 1525 and the only major building work since then was the tower in the late sixteenth century. In 1886 much internal modification was carried out which did little for the church except install more comfortable seating, a heating system and a bigger chancel with room for a choir and organ. A lot of the past was swept away, including the medieval floor tiles – although a few of these can still be seen between the chancel and chapel near the 'Crusader' monument.

The 'Crusader' monument relates to the tomb of Sir Walter de Balun who married Isolda de Mortimer in 1270. Sir Walter had been summoned by Henry III to Southampton to join the Eighth Crusade, which was led by Prince Edward. While there he married Isolda, daughter of Ralph Courthope Mortimer who gave her the manor of Arley as her marriage settlement. A tournament was held to celebrate the wedding during which Sir Walter met with an accident which caused his death. Isolda brought his body to Arley and buried him in the nave of St. Peter's.

The Severn Crossing under construction in 1901

⚙ **High Level Route (Main Route):** Walk up the road ahead, past the Harbour Inn – on the left – to reach a bridge over the Severn Valley Railway. Arley Station is situated on the right here.

The Harbour Inn, the sole survivor of Arley's pubs has old photographs of the village, ferry and castle on the walls of its bar. The inn also has a picture of the Arley Ferry as its sign.

Arley Station, on the Severn Valley Railway, has been a favourite location of film and TV. crews over the years, most recently for the B.B.C. television comedy series Oh, Doctor Beeching.

Over the railway, continue on the road which climbs and bends to the left. As it levels out ignore a track and a footpath going off to the right. The road drops slightly and bends first right and then left again. A more substantial bend to the right begins. At the start of this ignore a track going off down to the left - a private road to Meadow Farm - but within 50 yards turn left onto a track which is indicated by a Public Footpath sign. The turning onto this is by a pond - on the left of the road and to the right of the track - just as the road starts to climb again.

Almost immediately, while still alongside the pond, at a junction of tracks go right, (or straight ahead). Just past the pond ignore a footpath going off up to the right but remain on the track.

Climbing the track, good views of the River Severn and of Victoria Bridge, which carries the Severn Valley Railway over it, open up down to the left while slightly ahead Trimpley Reservoir also comes into view, alongside the river. A glance behind will reveal a distant view of Arley church, surrounded by trees.

Victoria Bridge was completed in 1861 to the design of Sir John Fowler. The contractors were Brassey & Co. and the span was manufactured by the Coalbrookdale Iron Company. At the time of its construction it was the longest single cast-iron clear span in the world at 200 foot.

Continue the gentle climb up the track past an isolated bungalow - down to the left. About 100 yards past the entrance drive to this, just after a gate on the track, take a footpath which leaves the track on the right to climb up into woodland, (Seckley Wood).

Victoria Bridge, carrying the Severn Valley Railway over the River Severn

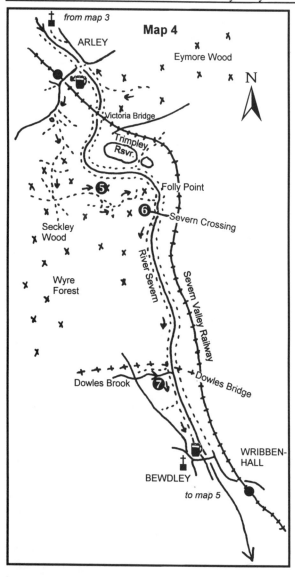

At a path junction, after about another 300 yards, go left. About 10 yards further on, at another junction, ignore a path going steeply downhill to the left. The path now climbs more gradually and meanders through the woods high above the river valley, although generally bearing to the right - away from the river and above the valley of a side stream.

With the side stream in a dip just to its left the path reaches a T-junction with a track. Turn left here. After about 30 yards a five-way junction of tracks/paths is reached. Take the track on the immediate left here - it is waymarked with RED ringed posts and has a wooden seat about 20 yards along it.

Walk along the track through the woods. It is fairly level and heads towards the river, bending gradually to the right. As a significant bend to the right begins a small 'slip' path to the left leads to an obvious viewpoint, with wooden picnic benches/tables, above the river valley. ❺

There are superb views from here over the Severn Valley. Trimpley Reservoir is immediately opposite with Eymore Wood - walked earlier on this stage of the Elan Valley Way - beyond. To the left can be seen Victoria Bridge and Arley church and village. An information board is provided.

Trimpley Reservoir and water treatment works were built in the early 1960's by Birmingham Corporation to supply additional water for the city, over and above that provided by the Elan Valley aqueduct. There is a naturally deep site in the bed of the river hereabouts and water is pumped from this into the reservoir and thence to the treatment works. The works were modified and extended by Severn Trent in 1996 and the reservoir now supplies water to various locations between Birmingham, Worcester, Tenbury Wells and Ludlow.

Return to the main track along the other arm of the 'slip' path. After just over 100 yards on the track ignore a path/track going right. Within about 10 yards of this, by a wooden seat, the track with the RED ringed marker posts swings left downhill. Leave it by continuing straight ahead along a grassy path between conifers.

The grassy path initially runs straight ahead but then bears slightly right to reach a wide break in the woods - the course of the Elan Valley aqueduct.

Turn left and walk down the left hand side of the break. (*Note: This is the only point on the Elan Valley Way where the line of the aqueduct is followed in the direction of its water flow, ie. west to east.*)

Part of the way down the break a track is crossed - (the RED ringed waymarked track recently left) - and after this the path down the left hand side of the break becomes an obvious stony track. Remain on it.

As a brick valve chamber - on the right - is neared the track swings to the left around the corner of the boundary of a residential caravan site. Another track joins it from the right as it does so and the resulting track is much wider.

Follow the now very wide track as it skirts the caravan site, (on the right), gradually bending right and descending. As it makes a steep bend down to the left to enter private woodland leave it by walking down a path on the right, towards the river - the junction is indicated by a footpath marker post.

The Severn Valley Railway

The Severn Valley Line was built between 1858 and 1862 between Hartlebury, north of Droitwich, and Shrewsbury – a total of some 40 miles. The original Severn Valley Railway was absorbed into the Great Western Railway empire in the 1870s and in 1878 a link line was constructed from Bewdley to Kidderminster. There was also a line running off the Severn Valley Line through Wyre Forest to Cleobury Mortimer, Tenbury Wells and Woofferton and thence to the line between Shrewsbury and Hereford.

The line was never a financial success and was closed to through traffic in 1963, the track north of Bridgnorth being lifted. A limited passenger service continued between Bewdley, Kidderminster and Hartlebury until 1969 and freight trains served Alveley Colliery until 1970.

In 1965 the Severn Valley Railway Society, a group of enthusiasts, was formed through whose fund-raising efforts the line was re-opened from Bridgnorth to Hampton Loade by 1970, to Bewdley in 1974 and finally to Kidderminster in 1984, the former Bewdley to Kidderminster link now forming part of the main preserved steam railway line from Bridgnorth to Kidderminster, a total of 16 miles.

Details of services over the line can be obtained from Severn Valley Railway (Holdings) PLC. on a free Talking Pages number – 0800 600 900 – or on 01299 403816.

At a Y-junction, near the river, bear right to walk the last few yards down to a T-junction with the riverbank path. Turn right along this, immediately crossing a stile. Across the field ahead can be seen the structure of the Elan Valley aqueduct's Severn Crossing, the actual bridge over the river initially hidden by trees which line the riverbank.

The riverside path is now followed all the way into Bewdley, a distance of two miles. The route is shared with that of the 'Worcestershire Way', as indicated by the latter's waymark signs - with the logo of a pear.

Bewdley

Bewdley is architecturally a town frozen in time, that time being the late eighteenth century when the opening of the Staffordshire and Worcestershire Canal to the River Severn at Stourport saw its lucrative river transhipment trade decline.

Its name is derived from the French *Beau Lieu*, meaning 'beautiful place', the first reference to the settlement dating from 1304. It appears to have grown from a forest clearing to become a busy river town with a royal palace on the hill behind it. One of the first descriptions of the town was given by John Leland, the official historian to Henry VIII. Writing in 1539 he said :

'The towne of Bewedley is set on the syd of an hill so coningly that a man cannot wish to set a towne bettar. It riseth from Severne banke by est upon hill by west so that a man standing on the hill...by est may descrive almost every house in the towne and at the rysinge of the sonne from este the hole towne gliterithe, being all of new buylding as it wer of gold.'

The oldest part of the town is probably around the streets high above the river now known as Sandy Bank and Wyre Hill. The latter lies close to a prehistoric trackway which ran from central Wales and probably crossed the Severn by a ford near where Lax Lane is now situated. The first bridge over the Severn was built in 1447 and this would have encouraged further development nearer the river, and across it at Wribbenhall.

In 1472 the town was granted its first charter, by Edward IV, in thanks for the area sending a company of soldiers in support of him at the battle of Tewkesbury, (1471). Amongst other things this charter granted the town freedom from tolls, very useful for a community already involved in trade by land and river.

The two biggest factors which contributed to the growth of the town up to the late eighteenth century were the transhipment trade, based on the town's position on the Severn, and the establishment of the royal manor at Tickenhill, above the town.

The town was ideally sited to act as a river transhipment point for raw materials and finished products en route to and from the Black Country, Shropshire and Midlands generally via wagon or packhorse. At Bewdley these goods were transferred to or from flat bottomed Severn trows which could navigate the shallows of the river, still tidal almost to the town as late as 1842. These trows, (a depiction of one is used as the waymark logo for the Severn Way), were towed up river by gangs of men known as bowhauliers and great fortunes were made by the merchants of the town, reflected in the fine 17th and eighteenth century houses which remain. It was traditional for transactions between merchants and boatmen to be agreed over a mug of ale and the Mug House P.H. on Severnside North is a reminder of this.

Tickenhill Manor was held for many years by the Mortimers, the powerful Marcher Lords. Their lands passed to the House of York in 1425 and so to the Crown when the Yorkist Edward IV became king in 1461. Later in the fifteenth century the manor became one of the seats of the Council of the Marches set up to control the border counties and Wales – Ludlow Castle, another former Mortimer stronghold, was the other seat. Henry VII appointed his elder son Prince Arthur to be President of this Council and it was while Arthur was in residence at Tickenhill in 1499 that he married Catherine of Aragon by proxy – see also the note on Ludlow Castle at Stage 4. Henry VIII's elder daughter Mary Tudor, later Queen Mary, also lived at Tickenhill during the years 1525 to 1527 when she was banished from court while her father was trying to divorce her mother, the same Catherine of Aragon. Parts of the fifteenth century hall are incorporated in the present eighteenth century house.

During the Civil War Tickenhill was a Royalist stronghold and it was in bed at Tickenhill, in April 1644, that the local Royalist leader Sir Thomas Lyttleton was surprised and captured by the Parliamentarian Colonel 'Tinker' Fox – see note on Arley (above) and on Frankley (Stage 1). Charles I stayed at the Angel Inn in Bewdley after his defeat at Naseby in June 1645.

The mid to late eighteenth century saw Bewdley at the peak of its prosperity but all that was to change with the opening of Brindley's Staffordshire and Worcestershire Canal, in 1772, to Stourport. This entered the Severn five miles to the south of Bewdley and effectively bypassed it as the port for the increasingly industrial Midlands. Within a few decades most of Bewdley's river trade had gone and the merchants had moved south to Stourport. Since then the town has changed very little.

Bewdley does not possess individually spectacular buildings. Instead it is as a whole eighteenth century Georgian town that it impresses. A Town Trail guide can be obtained from the Tourist Information Office in the Guildhall, Load Street – the street which runs down to the current river bridge, i.e. a right turn from Severnside North where the Elan Valley Way enters the town.

The present bridge was built by Thomas Telford in 1798 at a cost of £11,000. It used to have a toll house on it but this was demolished in 1960. The bridge replaced the earlier medieval structure of 1483, the third bridge on this site, which was largely destroyed by floods in 1795. The site of the old bridge can be made out from its approaches on either riverbank just to the south of the present bridge.

Load Street takes its name from the Saxon word 'lode', meaning a ford, and recalls Bewdley's early importance as a river crossing on the road to Wales.

At the top of Load Street is St. Anne's Church, built between 1745 and 1748 to replace a previous wooden structure of the sixteenth century.

Across the river, Wribbenhall is older than Bewdley – the name is of Saxon origin – and is mentioned in Domesday Book, (1086), unlike its neighbour. Bewdley station on the Severn Valley Railway is on this side of the river.

★ *The alternative route from Arley rejoins the main route as the riverside path is reached.*

There is a small island in the river just above where the riverside path is reached. O.S. Explorer Map 218 names the large bend in the river here as 'Folly Point' but this perpetuates a long standing misnomer. The correct name for this area is 'The Falley', meaning 'the fall near the island' and refers to a former ford across the river at this point.

There were formerly many fords across the river, six in the four miles between Arley and Bewdley alone, and this must have presented great difficulty to navigation, especially at times of low water. Their positions are not difficult to recognise even today – one below Dowles 'Bridge' being evidenced by 'broken water' when I walked this stretch.

The aqueduct's Severn Crossing is at its most impressive when viewed from underneath. As at April 1999 it was undergoing remedial work at an estimated cost of £1 million.

Walking this stretch I disturbed a green woodpecker on the riverbank.

Follow the riverside path to pass underneath the aqueduct's Severn Crossing, through a metal gate underneath the structure itself. ❻

The path along the riverbank continues past a redundant gate, through a still functional wooden gate and through a very long field. At the end of this it crosses a stile to run along the outside of the riverside boundary fence of another very long field. As this ends the piers of Dowles Bridge will be seen in the river ahead. The path passes a redundant stile and becomes a much more substantial track with a firm surface.

The piers seen in the river as Bewdley is neared are all that remain of Dowles Bridge which carried the line of the Great Western Railway's Tenbury & Bewdley Railway – see note at Stage 3. The bridge was dismantled in March 1966.

Passing the piers of Dowles Bridge the track swings right but both the Elan Valley Way and the Worcestershire Way bear left to continue to follow the riverbank, along a path which crosses Dowles Brook by a footbridge, a stile just beyond this. (The wide track will however be used on Stage 3 of the Elan Valley Way when the path from Dowles Brook to Bewdley – itself just coming into view – is walked in reverse.) ❼

After crossing the stile the path runs along the outside of the riverside boundary fence of a large field. Ignore a footpath going off right into the field. At the end of the field another stile is crossed and the path becomes well maintained – with dog waste bins, litter bins and seats – as Bewdley is approached and the town bridge comes into view.

Remain on the riverside path until the bridge is reached, the last 100 yards along a road, (Severnside North, formerly Coles Quay). This stage of the Elan Valley Way finishes at the bridge, at the foot of Load Street.

Stage 3

Bewdley to Cleobury Mortimer

Distance: 13½ miles (Buttonoak 3½ miles, Horse & Jockey 7 miles).
O.S.Maps: Landranger 138; Pathfinder 952; Explorer 218.

A stage of two halves. The first is spent crossing Wyre Forest and is mainly along woodland paths. The second uses fieldpaths, tracks and short sections of quiet road as the route loops south to enter Cleobury Mortimer from that direction, visiting the attractive village of Bayton along the way.

A long section of the Elan Valley aqueduct is walked to the south west of Buttonoak in Wyre Forest.

! If the River Severn is in flood the start of this stage may be impassable as far as, and including, the broad track after the first Dowles Brook crossing. If this is the case then leave Bewdley by walking up Load Street away from the river, passing the church, and then taking a right turn to follow the B4194 road until the abutments of the former railway bridge across it are reached. Here rejoin the main route.

STARTING at the bottom of Load Street by the river bridge, facing the river, turn left to walk along Severnside North and onwards along the riverside path towards Dowles – the river on the right all the way. There is only one stile on this section until the one immediately before the footbridge over Dowles Brook. (This is the last half mile or so of Stage 2 in reverse).

Having crossed Dowles Brook turn immediately left onto a broad track – ie. do not pass the piers of Dowles railway bridge.

Follow the track as it makes a marked turn to the right before resuming its original direction, the brook alongside to the left. On reaching the busy B4194 road, via a metal stile, turn right along it, passing between the abutments of the railway bridge which once spanned it. Here cross the road and make a left turn onto a path which runs alongside and to the right of the old railway embankment. It commences by passing between two round posts, entering Wyre Forest. The path can be very muddy indeed in wet weather. (*See* ✪ *below for an alternative route.*) ➊

Soon it crosses a steep bridge, where Dowles Brook passes under both it and the railway embankment, and continues between the old railway line on the left and the brook on the right. After a little while take a path signed as a bridleway which branches off to the right to drop down to Dowles Brook and hug its bank even more closely. Again this can be very muddy.

Soon the path emerges through a wooden gate onto a partly metalled track. *Now continue from* ➡ *on page 44.*

✪ (Alternative Route: To avoid the initial muddy path in Wyre Forest an easy alternative is when leaving the B4194 road instead of passing between the two round posts onto the forest path turn more sharply left and climb up onto the embankment of the disused railway. Walk along this until reaching the crossing of the partly metalled track where the railway overbridge has again been removed. Here leave the old trackbed by climbing down some steps on the left onto the track. Turn right down the partly metalled track which almost immediately bends to the left. The main route comes in from the right on the bend, through a wooden gate, and is rejoined here.)

➡ Turn right along the track, blue bridleway signs still in evidence. At a junction in the track turn right, again following the bridleway signs. To

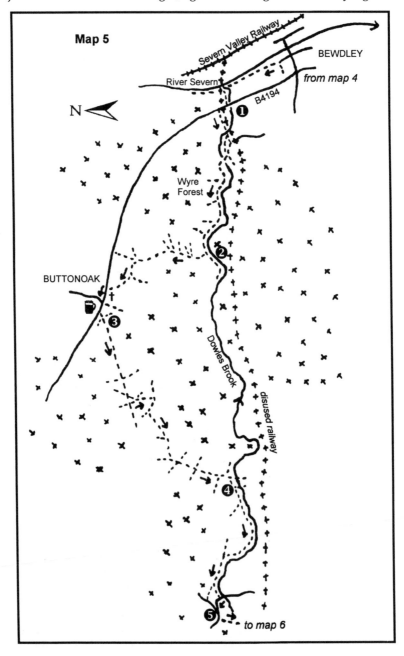

the right a locked wooden gate and some steps lead down to a wooden hut by the brook but continue ahead on the track which has, since the junction, lost its metalled surface. Just after the wooden hut is passed the track swings right to cross Dowles Brook by means of a brick footbridge, (SO771764). There is an isolated house to the right here. Continue along the track which bends to the left to follow the brook, the two meandering along together for a while, the brook on the left.

As Dowles Brook is crossed the route leaves Worcestershire to enter Shropshire.

This section is a lovely peaceful stretch of forest walking, especially atmospheric in the early mornings.

Wyre Forest

This is the remnant of a vast forest which, prior to the Middle Ages, stretched from Bridgnorth down the Severn Valley as far as Worcester. The current woodland still covers an area of 6500 acres. The area was formerly a royal hunting forest where kings and nobles – such as the Mortimers – hunted bear, wild boar, wolves and deer. The deer still remain – a very large herd of Fallow deer which is so successful that it has to be controlled by culling.

The forest supported a vast range of associated 'industries' including timber felling, (especially for shipbuilding), charcoal manufacture, (for industrial use such as iron smelting), bark peeling, (for the leather tanning industry), and birch broom making. The economy of nearby Bewdley and countless other small settlements was very dependent on these trades.

Along Dowles Brook there was industry too with several mills using the power of its waters – mainly corn and felt mills. The remains can be seen today.

In 1955 part of Wyre was designated a site of Special Scientific Interest and became a National Nature Reserve in 1978. The area so covered was enlarged in 1985 and finally, in 1989, the whole of the main area of forest between the A456 and B4194 was designated a Forest Nature Reserve. The forest is run by Forest Enterprise with the 1700 acres of National Nature Reserve managed by English Nature.

A large acreage of woodland to the west of Wyre is still privately owned.

The disused railway running through Wyre Forest was the Great Western Railway's line to Cleobury Mortimer, Tenbury Wells and Woofferton – the Tenbury & Bewdley Railway. Opened in 1864, it left the Severn Valley line to the north of Bewdley, crossed the River Severn at Dowles Bridge and then ran east-to-west through the forest. Passenger traffic ceased in 1962 and the line closed in 1965. It is crossed twice more on this stage of the Elan Valley Way – once in Bell Coppice and again near Norgrovesend.

It is tempting to imagine that this was the railway line the poet A. E. Housman had in mind when he penned the lines:

'...through the wild green hills of Wyre
The train ran, changing sky and shire,
And far behind, a fading crest,
Low in the forsaken west
Sank the high-reared head of Clee,...'

(Alfred Edward Housman: *A Shropshire Lad*, Poem XXXVII.)

Follow the track as it continues to meander, ignoring a footpath going uphill into the wood on the right. Just after this there are a couple of houses on the left of the track. The first, and nearer to the track, is currently the Liepmoor Boxer Kennels – with two sculptured heads of boxer dogs on plinths by its entrance. Continue past a gate to a Worcestershire Nature Conservancy Trust reserve, on the left, which is locked – access being by permit only. Another track departs right, and up into the woods just beyond this but again is not taken. Instead remain on the main track which soon bends to the right and passes a second access point, (a stile), to the WNCT reserve. Knowles Mill is on the left across the brook here, a footbridge leading to it. Continue ahead on the main track.

Both track and brook now begin to bend to the left. The track has a surface of large stones here which aid drainage but can be slippery. Ignore yet another turning on the right, going up into the woods, and on reaching a green metal gate with a 'step-over' to its right cross this to continue along the track. On the right here is an English Nature notice board indicating that the route is now entering the 1989 protected area and almost immediately a footpath departs right up a small side valley into the woods. Again, remain on the track which now narrows considerably to a path of about four foot width. There is a small field/pasture between the track and Dowles Brook, on the left, here. ❷

On reaching a T-junction with a stony/gravel surfaced track, (SO758768), turn sharp right to climb up into what is marked as 'Withybed Wood' on O.S. Explorer Map 218. There is another English Nature notice board at the junction. As it gains height the track swings sharply to the left. Ignore two tracks departing right, the main track winding about as it continues to climb – a good stony surface with drainage channels cut across it keeping it dry underfoot. As the rate of climb eases and the track becomes undulating ignore a further path, right, and then two more also going right, where the main track makes a sharp left bend.

As a guide to navigation here – at the time of writing the main track was waymarked as a forest trail with marker posts bearing RED rings. The overall bearing of the track is NNW.

Another wonderful section of forest walking, much more open than down by Dowles Brook. The trees are still mainly deciduous but as the B4194 at Buttonoak is approached some stands of conifers are encountered.

As the track makes a turn to the right, (SO758774), it reaches a 'crossroads' of tracks/paths. Take the major track going left here. (NB. The RED ringed forest trail markers continue on the original track ahead, which is not taken. If for any reason this turning is missed then the net effect will be an exit onto the B4194 road too far to the east, which can easily be remedied by making a longer journey along the road to the left or retracing the route.)

After about 30 yards the new track bends sharply left to head back into the woods towards Dowles Brook. At the start of this bend turn right along a grassy woodland track which heads off in a generally NW direction. Follow this track, ignoring one or two small footpaths which go off to the right. Eventually the track narrows to footpath width and becomes less distinct. Remain on it until reaching the edge of the woodland where there is a metal gate with a stile over a wooden fence to its right – the latter being very worse for wear when last visited.

Cross the stile into a paddock area and follow the wire boundary fence, on the right, towards a single pine tree, with a redbrick house behind, and a tall green metal fence. Exit the paddock area through the green fence via a matching large green metal gate. Turn right along a rough track which almost immediately emerges onto the B4194 road. Alongside the track as it meets the road, on the left, is the brown-painted wooden chapel of St. Andrew, (SO756778). On the opposite side of the road is a white cottage – Weathertop Cottage.

Turn left along the road. It may be easier to cross the road as there is no pavement here. A road going right to Pound Green and Arley is ignored. Just after this a pavement commences on the right-hand side of the road. At a telephone kiosk the pavement switches sides. Ahead, on the left of the road, is the Buttonoak P.H. Just before this is reached cross a stile on the left to take a footpath which initially follows the right-hand boundary hedge of the field entered.

Limited bus service 125 to Kidderminster along the B4194 through Buttonoak. 🚌

Just before reaching a metal gate in the far right corner of the field bear slightly left to a wooden stile which is situated about 20 yards in from the corner. Cross this and go straight ahead over a path which crosses here. Ahead will be seen a very wide break in the trees. This marks the course of the Elan Valley aqueduct which is now followed for something in excess of half a mile. Walk straight ahead through the break in the forest, keeping to its right-hand boundary. ❸

Wyre Forest is one of the few remaining Midlands strongholds of Britain's only poisonous snake, the adder. 50 to 100 yards along the break in the forest there is a large colony. Probably NOT a good place for a picnic lunch!

The path through the break climbs quite steeply. As the top is reached a valve chamber for the pipelines comes into view and is passed. Descending, after a while a major forest track is crossed. At the start of a steeper section of descent ignore a bridleway sign indicating a path going off left into the trees. As the descent lessens again a second valve chamber will be seen ahead. About 25 yards before this is reached a wide path crosses the break, (SO741777). Walk across the break to turn left down this, into the trees. The path can be quite muddy in wet weather.

After about 100 yards ignore a narrower path going right and almost immediately the wide path makes a T-junction with a track. Turn right here. In a few more yards there is a parting of ways – the left track has a barrier to stop motor vehicle access and carries a wildlife conservation notice board while that on the right bears a blue bridleway sign. Take the latter. The wide track winds among the trees and drops down to a T-junction of tracks. Turn right here – the bridleway goes left but the right turn is signed as a public footpath, (SO741772).

Follow the track which immediately bends back on itself, turning sharp right and heading downhill. Just beyond a left bend is a Y-junction of tracks. Ignore the track going up to the right but keep left here, the track still dropping and now narrowing. Very shortly, through the trees on the left, a stream will be seen below. Follow the path down to a wooden fence/stile which leads to a ford across this stream. Reaching this the path continues around to the right. Do not follow it but instead cross the fence/stile and ford the stream – the area by the ford can be very muddy indeed in wet weather but there are large stones to help with the ford itself. Having crossed the stream the path emerges through trees into the bottom right-hand corner of a field. Head up the field half left, diagonally across to the top left-hand corner. Here a stile/fence gives access to a footpath which runs between two hedge boundaries and initially bends to the right. This is an old established path which is quite 'sunken' in parts.

After a little under 200 yards emerge right from the sunken path into the corner of a field to pass into another field by means of a farm gate. On entering the new field drop left again back onto the sunken path, which runs up the left-hand boundary of it, passing a ruined farm building, on the right. At the top of the field are two farm gates. Pass through the one on the left to follow the now much narrower path which is confined between two hedges. Passing an isolated cottage on the right, (Lower Kingswood), the path widens into a grassy track which meets the access track to the cottage at a T-junction. Turn left here onto the broad access track which immediately bends sharp right. Follow it between the buildings of Kingswood Farm, then through two gates to eventually reach a T-junction with another track, (SO731769). The two gates may be open.

Turn half left to proceed along a forest track. After 50 yards or so pass around a locked barrier, preventing vehicle access into the forest. Follow the track as it bends right and then left. At a 'crossroads' of tracks go straight across, (SO730768), the track soon bending to the left again, starting to lose height and meandering through the forest. This section is marked on O.S. Explorer Map 218 as 'Brand Wood'. At another track 'crossroads', this time with a major forest track crossing, again continue straight ahead.

As a significant bend to the left commences, and with the track still descending, ignore a footpath going off and up to the right but almost immediately – on the same left-hand bend – turn onto a track going off and down to the right. Immediately ahead Dowles Brook will be seen, with a footbridge crossing it. Do not cross this but instead take another path to the right which immediately splits, a path to the left crossing the brook by a ford while that to the right follows the brook along – the brook on its left, (SO729763). Take the path along the brook. ❹

Follow the path as it winds alongside Dowles Brook. Do not attempt to struggle along the very banks of the brook but take the path which rises slightly. Almost immediately there is a junction with a path which rises even more sharply to the right. Keep left, on the lower path. The brook is about 15 to 20 yards away on the left at this point. As the brook is followed there is a veritable maze of paths crossing and re-crossing, many leading to the water's edge. The best rule to follow as regards navigating this stretch is to keep the brook about 10 yards or less away to the left.

On reaching a section where the opposite bank of the brook becomes an open field area the path approaches the brook to hug its bank. As a building, at the top of the field opposite, is passed the path veers away from the bank again to meander alongside, sometimes nearer to, sometimes further from the water. When a T-junction with another path is reached turn left to continue to follow the brook.

This is a beautiful and peaceful section of woodland walking along the banks of Dowles Brook.

The path is now some 40 to 50 yards from the brook and as much as 30 feet above it. Follow it as it continues to meander along, sometimes approaching the bank where its height above the brook can be more readily appreciated. A side water course is crossed. Often dry, this may be in water in wet weather but there are stones there to help ford it. The path bears left and approaches the brook again at a section where care needs to be taken not to slip down the slope into the water. (*For an alternative route from this point see ★ below.*)

After a long period of flirting with the stream the path seems now to have decided to do all but join it. A precipitous section follows with steps cut into the steep banks to aid footing and help with the slopes. Eventually, as the path shies away from becoming as one with the brook it emerges onto a road, just to the right of where the latter crosses the brook, (SO721765).

Turn right to walk along the road, almost immediately passing the entrance to Furnace Mill, on the left. Remain on the road as it climbs to reach a junction. Go left, signposted Kinlet. **❺**

Now continue from IIII➤ *below.*

★ **Alternative Route**: The final section along Dowles Brook can be quite hard going in bad weather or for those less agile/sure of foot! An alternative is as follows.

About 60 yards after crossing the seasonal side water course, with the path alongside the brook, take a path which goes off and up to the right. As a rough navigation guide look for a very large flat topped boulder in the far side of the brook; the turning off the main route is just before this is reached.

Follow the narrow path up to the top of the initial climb from the brook, just before conifers begin, and then bear left to walk along an indistinct path which parallels the brook. Take any one of several paths off to the right to reach a road. Turn left along the road to a junction and then right, signposted for Kinlet. The main route is rejoined at the road junction.

IIII➤ In under 50 yards a drive is reached on the left – marked Furnace Mill Farm and Stud/Fishery. Take the footpath on the left here – it runs along the left side of the drive.

Cross a stream by a footbridge to proceed up the very narrow path, a garden boundary of firs on the left and bushes separating it from the main farm drive on the right. Cross another footbridge. Ignore a stile and gate on the left but continue on the narrow path to emerge onto the main metalled drive. Turn left up it and just before the parking area for the stud/farm is reached turn right off the drive to proceed through a metal gate, which bears a footpath sign, and into a field. Turn left to climb up the field alongside the left boundary fence – not too close, it is electrified! On reaching the top of the initial climb continue to follow the boundary towards the far left-hand corner of the field, woodland beyond it.

On reaching the corner negotiate the electric fence, using the protectors provided, and pass through a wooden gate into the woodland. Head straight ahead along a path. After about 50 yards this crosses the disused railway line, here in a slight cutting. On crossing this the path becomes a track which rises. At the top of the initial rise from the old railway, where the track bears right, take a footpath which goes off to the left. On reaching a footpath 'crossroads' – with the paths straight on and to the left marked as Public Footpaths – go straight on.

This is a wonderful stretch of woodland walking with a good path passing between bracken and brambles, in season, beneath deciduous trees. One of the lesser walked corners of Wyre Forest, it is known as Bell Coppice.

Follow the path as it begins to climb gently and nears the edge of the wood, to the left. At a T-junction with a track, (SO716755), turn right, continuing to climb until the edge of the wood is reached and the track levels out. Remain on the track until it reaches the A4117 road; just after some farm buildings, on the left, and having passed through a gate, which may be open. **❻**

Along the A4117, about 100 yards to the left, is the Horse & Jockey P.H.

Bus service 192/292 runs along the A4117 and can be boarded outside the Horse & Jockey.

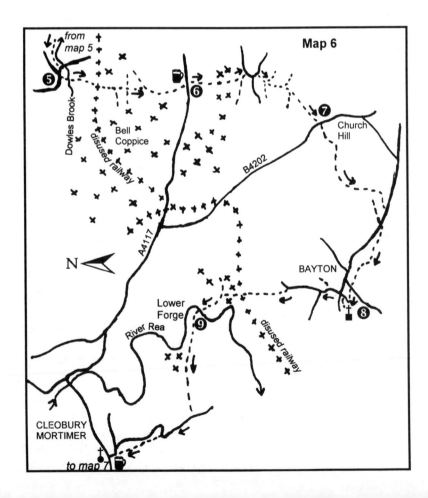

Cross the A4117 and turn left. Almost immediately cross a stile on the right – sited by a small metal gate – to enter a field. Proceed up the field following the left boundary. Cross a stile into the next field – the boundary crossed is an electric fence – and continue to follow the left-hand boundary up the hill which now steepens. On reaching the top left-hand corner of the field cross two stiles in quick succession to enter another field. Head diagonally across this field to its far left-hand corner – passing an isolated house, 'Stone Barn' which is in the next field to the left. On reaching the corner cross a low wooden fence into the next field and head directly across this towards the far boundary which has woodland beyond it. Cross a stile in this boundary to enter the wood and then go straight ahead, dropping down through the trees on a initially meandering path. There are footpath marker posts hereabouts to point the way.

The descent through the woods is quite steep and the bottom is soon neared. On reaching a fence turn a few yards left along it and then cross it via a stile. Then follow the fence down to the left – fence on the left – to reach a track at the bottom of the descent. Turn left along the track to pass over a stile next to a wooden gate, the track then emerging onto a road – opposite a house called 'Tanners Bow'.

Reaching the road the route leaves Shropshire behind to re-enter Worcestershire.

Turn right along the road. Almost immediately turn left at a road junction, signposted Buckridge. 50 or so yards along this road turn right up a track, signposted Public Footpath Church Hill, which is initially the metalled entrance drive to a house, (SO717744). On reaching the house pass to the right of it, the track now becoming grassy and climbing. As the rate of climb lessens ignore first a footpath going off it over a stile to the right and then almost immediately one going off left over a stile. Continue along the track to reach a stile to the left of a gate which may be open. Another footpath goes off to the left over a stile just before this but is again ignored in favour of the track.

Having crossed the stile/passed through the gate proceed along the track which now begins to descend slightly and bends to the right towards the buildings of Teddon Farm.

A group of giant puffballs found growing along here in September were unfortunately all a little too mature for eating.

Do not pass between the farm buildings but instead swing round to the right alongside them to pass into a field, (SO716740), via a wooden farm gate as the end of a barn, on the left, is reached. The gate may be open. (Ignore a track going up to the right here – the access track for Teddon Farm.)

Follow the right-hand boundary of the field, the track still clearly distinguishable as it now begins to descend. At the bottom of the slope ignore a track which passes through a wooden gate on the right but instead swing left to another wooden gate. Go through this and proceed half right over the highest point of the field now entered. As the field is climbed head towards a stile in the far boundary, situated just to the right of two large trees (oaks). Cross this stile with care – there was barbed wire hidden behind it at the time of writing but this has been reported for appropriate action.

Follow the left-hand boundary of the field now entered, the buildings of Carton Farm visible half left ahead. Passing these buildings, which are beyond the boundary hedge and well to the left of the path, proceed through a gap in the field boundary ahead. Just after the farm buildings (left) end cross a stile in the boundary on the left and bear right to emerge onto a concreted farm track. Walk up this to reach a road. ❼

As the fields adjacent to Carton Farm are walked views of the Clee Hills, (Titterstone Clee and Brown Clee), begin to open up to the right, on a clear day, while at the top of the concreted farm track, on reaching the road, a look behind reveals a view back to the two Clent Hills, (Walton Hill, crossed on Stage 1 of the Elan Valley Way, on the right and Adams Hill on the left), with Wychbury Hill to the left of them, its obelisk just visible.

Go straight across the road to proceed up a sunken dirt track opposite, signposted as a bridleway. After 35 yards this narrows to path width with an initial conifer plantation on its right-hand side soon replaced by open fields. At a bend to the left it regains its original width. Follow this obviously very old sunken track as it climbs around Church Hill.

It is while walking the track around Church Hill that the best views on Stage 3 of the Elan Valley Way may be obtained. The modest summit of Church Hill, (230 metres/755 feet), lies well to the left of the course of the track which remains on its lower slopes throughout. Superb views across rolling countryside begin to open up on the right as the track starts to level out at the top of its climb and meanders between its well established tree boundaries. A delightful section of walking ensues.

Visible to the right on a clear day are the Clee Hills with the town of Cleobury Mortimer in the foreground and the large residence of Mawley Hall, (see note below), nearby. Further along the village of Bayton comes into view. On a really clear day there are views over as far as the hills of Radnor Forest with the top of the conical shaped Whimble, (599 metres/1965 feet), just visible on the far horizon, while to the south the northern escarpment of the Black Mountains may be seen.

Continue to follow the track as it levels out. It begins to undulate and wind along between its borders of trees, passing through a metal farm gate. Still following it, pass through another gate, which may be open, to descend slightly towards farm buildings ahead, (Colliershill Farm). Pass through a third metal farm gate and follow the track as it bends around to the left and emerges into the open. It drops to pass between the farm buildings. Proceed straight ahead through a wooden gate and down the farm drive, a bend to the left and then a final straight section leading onto a road, (SO702727). Turn right to walk along it.

As the track emerges into the open above Colliershill Farm look right to see the village of Bayton with its prominent church tower.

As the road is walked Bayton church is ahead while to the distant left the spire of Mamble church may be visible across the fields on a clear day.

After about 150 yards on the road ignore a footpath going off over a stile to the right but instead cross the road to pass through a gate on the left. Turn immediately right to follow the right-hand boundary hedge of the field now entered, with the road on the other side of this. After a while, still following the boundary, a field replaces the road over the hedge and a small stream now appears in a depression to the right, between the path and the boundary. Cross a stile, (with care; there was barbed wire behind the bars of it at the time of writing), into another field where the path continues to follow the boundary, the stream now on the far side of it. Eventually a stile will be seen on the right, crossing the boundary. Cross this and then a wooden footbridge over the stream. Another stile gives access to a field ahead.

Turn half left across this field, passing to the right-hand side of an oak tree and a fenced compound, (Leominster Marches Housing Association wells), to reach a stile mid way up its left-hand boundary. Cross the stile and head directly towards the church tower across the field. As the field is walked the church tower disappears from view but head onwards towards a small willow tree and a lone house beyond the far boundary. Exit the field via a stile alongside a metal gate, just to the right of the aforementioned

Bayton

Bayton is a very pretty village with a large number of 'black and white' houses. Unfortunately its only pub closed in 1997. Walking around the village it is difficult to imagine that the area hereabouts was once a centre for coal mining. Several small pits took advantage of outcrops of coal seams occurring in and around Wyre Forest, south of Dowles Brook. These included mines at Hunthouse, Pensax, Mamble and Bayton itself. In 1913 Bayton pit was linked to railway sidings on the Tenbury & Bewdley Railway at Cleobury Mortimer station by an aerial ropeway in an effort to increase coal sales outside of the immediate locality. The workings were soon exhausted and pit and ropeway closed in 1923.

Bayton Church, St. Bartholomew's, dates from the twelfth century but was heavily restored in 1818 and again in 1905, when the chancel was entirely reconstructed. Some notable features from the original building do remain however of which perhaps the most striking is the beautiful drum-shaped font with its elaborate deep carving. Other survivors are the dog-toothed rounded Norman arch over the south doorway and three massive oak beams in the roof.

Over the door to the vestry and tower, (the west end of the building), is the heraldic lozenge of Edmund Meysey-Wigley, a former M.P. for Worcester, (died 1821). It was he who financed the restoration and building of the tower in 1818, the church previously having just a timbered bell-turret.

Walk through into the vestry and look out of the west window of it for a superb view of distant rolling countryside across the Rea Valley towards Titterstone Clee Hill. A similar view can be obtained outside the church, standing beside the tower. The spire of Cleobury Mortimer church may be seen rising from a fold in the rolling hills on a clear day.

On leaving the church look left to see a curiously carved rectangular gravestone resting against the wall of the building. The inscription is roughly carved and in Latin and is a memorial to or by a 'T.M.' to someone who died on 3rd September 1654, the stone being presumably of a contemporary date. A rough translation of the full inscription would be: 'Be righteous living and dying. If you are always righteous you will be among the righteous when you die. He departed, not died. September 3rd.'

house. Proceed straight ahead along a short track to emerge onto a road in the village of Bayton.

Turn left along the road and almost immediately right onto a metalled narrow lane which runs to the right of Bayton C. of E. Primary School. Before the end of the school buildings are passed the lane loses its metalling to become a stony track. Pass through metal barriers and proceed straight ahead along the track and where it reaches a road bear left to reach the entrance to the churchyard. Enter through the lychgate and proceed along the left of the two paths ahead to visit the church. **8**

If Bayton Church is locked a notice on the door gives details of where the key may be obtained.

On leaving the porch of the church turn right to exit the churchyard by means of small wooden gate. Turn immediately right to follow the boundary wall of first the churchyard and then a cottage beyond. The path soon emerges onto a road, with the garden gate to the cottage on the right.

Turn left along the road to reach a staggered crossroads – the left arm of this being marked as a private road. Go straight on here. (Turn right to look around the village – the pub was along this road but closed in 1997.)

Proceed along the road ahead, ignoring a track which goes off to the right as the road makes a first bend left. The road next swings right before making a pronounced bend to the left. At this bend, (signposted Cleobury, Nineveh), take a narrow road going off to the right which is signposted to Norgrovesend, No Through Road. After about 300 yards this road bends to the right, (SO693738). Here take a public footpath to the left which exits the road over a sturdy stile, (railway sleepers), and is signposted to Lower Forge. Go straight ahead from the stile, following the left-hand boundary of the field so entered – Explorer Map 218 shows the path initially to the left of the boundary but this is not the case. The buildings of Norgrovesend Farm are ahead half right.

Still following the boundary, descend to the bottom left-hand corner of the field where a second sturdy stile is crossed to enter another field. Again follow the left-hand field boundary here. The path initially rises but then drops steeply towards the bottom left-hand corner of the field where there is another sturdy stile alongside a farm gate. Cross this and the trackbed of the disused railway – perhaps the source of materials for the stiles hereabouts.

Cross another stile opposite to leave the old trackbed and enter a wooded area.

Passing through the fields leading down to the disused railway track Mawley Hall may be seen directly ahead, on higher ground. This imposing building was built around 1730 probably by the architect Francis Smith of Warwick, on the site of an earlier hall, as the seat of the Blount family who owned the Mawley estate from 1535 until 1960. The hall was restored in 1962 and is still a private residence.

On crossing the old railway trackbed there are warning signs as regards not straying from the footpath into these private woods but also as to snakes. These are not empty warnings. This is the second adder stronghold passed on today's stage of the walk.

Having crossed the stile, follow the winding path ahead through the trees to descend to a footbridge over a stream. Cross this and climb straight ahead to reach a track; turn left along this, (SO691745). The track makes a sweeping bend around to the right, following the stream just crossed. As it straightens the stream bends away to the left to join the River Rea. Continue on the track, the river now some 60 yards or so to the left. The track bears left to cross a water channel and then right to cross the River Rea via a ford above a weir. Leave it briefly to cross the river by a metal footbridge, situated just below the weir, and having crossed it turn right to regain the track and then left along it. ❾

The area hereabouts is called Lower Forge and was formerly the site of such. The forge here was started in the seventeenth century by Robert Dudley, Earl of Leicester, who was Lord of the Manor at that time. The forge produced wrought iron from pig iron but had ceased production by about 1800.

At the footbridge crossing of the stream which then enters the Rea, (SO691745), the route of the Elan Valley Way finally leaves Worcestershire to re-enter Shropshire.

The River Rea is formed by the amalgamation of several streams, including Rea Brook, to the north-east of Titterstone and Brown Clee Hills. It flows south past Cleobury Mortimer and then south west to join the River Teme near Newnham Bridge, about three miles east of Tenbury Wells.

Remain on the track as it climbs steeply and bends sharply left before beginning to meander along, a substantial stone wall bordering it on the right – the river now hidden in rough woodland over that wall and far below. The track levels out, straightens and passes through a wooden gate, which may be open. After this a fence which has been on the left of the track gives way to an open field while to the right the wall continues. Pass through another wooden gate, again possibly open, and between a farm house and some stabling, (The Rookery, on Explorer Map 218). Continue on the track which climbs and bends to the left to emerge onto a road. Turn right to walk along it.

On reaching the road look directly behind for a distant view of Bayton Church. To the left of it will be seen the long mass of Church Hill. The course of the track around it, walked earlier on this stage, can be recognised by the line of trees along the length of its lower slopes.

Follow the road as it undulates and winds along before making a steep descent to an extremely sharp right-hand bend, (SO679752). At the bend leave the road, left, for a track – as indicated by a public footpath sign. After only about twenty yards on this – and just before it reaches a metal farm gate leading to private land – leave it over a wooden fence/stile on the right. Having crossed the wooden fence/stile climb up the path ahead which soon bends right and steeply up to another stile. There is a small stream in the dip to the left along this section.

On crossing the stile go straight ahead, still climbing, through a very narrow field. Keep the right-hand field boundary about 10 yards distant throughout.

The long narrow field, (or 'slinget'), is known locally as Rowley's Sling and is a rare survivor of the medieval open field strip system hereabouts.

Mawley Hall is visible again, to the right and slightly behind, as the narrow field is climbed.

As the top of the narrow field is approached the spire of Cleobury Mortimer church suddenly looms large ahead half left. Pass through a metal gate in the top boundary of the field, which may be open, to enter another field. Head for the near left-hand corner of some farm buildings ahead, which is also directly towards the church spire. As the corner of the farm buildings is passed maintain direction towards the spire to soon pass through a gap in a field boundary ahead.

Passing through the gap in the field boundary pause for a moment to take in what is possibly the finest view of the town of Cleobury Mortimer immediately ahead and below.

Head straight down the field now entered, towards the church, to reach a stile at the bottom which gives access to a lane, (Lion Lane). Proceed straight up Lion Lane to cross the main street of the town, (A4117), at the top and so reach the church of St. Mary the Virgin where this stage of the Elan Valley Way ends.

Until 1794 when Thomas Telford, as County Surveyor for Shropshire, re-aligned the local road system and built New Bridge over the River Rea, to the east of the town, Lion Lane formed part of the main road from Bewdley to Cleobury Mortimer rather than the quieter back road it now is.

If staying at the Old Cider House it is the first building on the right as Lion Lane is entered.

Cleobury Church with its crooked spire

Cleobury Mortimer

Cleobury Mortimer, (pronounced 'Clibbery'), is an old established settlement, almost certainly Saxon in origin. In Domesday Book (1086) it is shown as 'Claiberie', a name derived from the Old English words 'Cleofu' (= a steep, ball-shaped place) and 'Burg' (= a settlement within a defensive structure, or manor). The name Mortimer comes from the family of powerful Marcher Lords, based at Wigmore Castle and later Ludlow, who were Lords of the Manor here after the Norman Conquest.

Before the Normans came Cleobury had belonged to Queen Edith, the wife of Edward the Confessor and was still nominally under Saxon ownership until 1069, after the rebellion under the Herefordshire nobleman known as Wild Edric had been defeated, when William the Conqueror redistributed land amongst his followers. Ralph de Mortimer alone received the titles to 130 different manors at this time, among them Cleobury. The Mortimers built a castle in the town – on the raised land behind the present church – although no trace of this structure now remains. It is thought that it was destroyed around 1154 by Henry II, in an attempt to curb the increasing power of the dynasty, and the site was cleared in the late eighteenth century for use as the town's bowling green.The Mortimers also held hunting land in Wyre Forest to the east of the town.

It was under the Mortimers that an existing Saxon church was rebuilt in 1160, although the only parts of that rebuilding which survive are the base of the tower and fragments of walls in the nave. The church was much added to up to the early fourteenth century, also under Mortimer patronage.

In 1226 the Mortimers were granted the right to hold a market in Cleobury, by Henry III, and this aided the early growth of the town.

The Lordship of the Manor of Cleobury Mortimer eventually passed to the Childes of Kinlet who still hold it today.

By the eighteenth century the town seems to have been very prosperous and many of the properties which can be seen along the main street today were either rebuilt or rendered in brick at this time. The dominant building of the town remains the church of St. Mary the Virgin. Its most immediately obvious feature is the famous crooked spire, of oak construction and probably built in the early fourteenth century. The essentially fourteenth century building was in urgent need of repair and in danger of collapsing by 1793 when Thomas Telford, then Shropshire County Surveyor, was called in to advise. His solution was to erect brick buttresses to support the structure – later replaced by the extant stone ones to the right of the porch, (in 1874 by Sir George Gilbert Scott).

In 1993 the wooden steeple was found to be unsafe and was restored by securing the bottom of the 34 ton structure to steel girders. The steeple was re-shingled in English oak at the same time. The total cost of the work was in excess of £200,000, the project winning the 1994 John Betjeman award, which can be seen on the wall in the north aisle. Also inside the church, and much cheaper at the time of its installation in 1875, (£235 for the glass), can be seen the Langland Window, (East Window), which commemorates the life of William Langland, author of the fourteenth century poem *The Vision of Piers Plowman*, who was born nearby in Kinlet parish and was educated by the Augustine Friars at Woodhouse

Priory, just off the route of Stage 4 of the Elan Valley Way.

In the road outside the church porch a small stone figure is carved in the boundary wall. It is not known what this represents or what age it might be, although some maintain it may be a god or goddess of water.

Up the road to the west of the church is the much eroded remnant of a cross. This may have been a market or preaching cross or might be the 'weeping cross' where the funeral procession carrying the body of Prince Arthur from Ludlow to Worcester Cathedral for burial rested, in 1502 – see the notes on Ludlow in Stage 4.

Down the road to the east of the church lie the Wells, formerly the source of the town's water supply. In 1895 the graveyard of the church was closed for burials when it was feared that the springs leading from it to the Wells might become contaminated. It might be felt that by then any damage would already have been done although it was not until sometime after the Second World War that the Wells ceased to supply the town. Cleobury now receives its water from Trimpley reservoir – passed on Stage 2 of the Elan Valley Way.

Cleobury Mortimer railway station, on the Great Western Railway's Tenbury & Bewdley Railway, was over two miles to the east of the town. It closed for passenger traffic in 1962. The station was the junction for the Cleobury Mortimer & Ditton Priors Light Railway, built primarily to serve the dhustone quarries on Brown Clee Hill but which also carried passengers during the earlier years of its existence, until 1938 in fact. Cleobury Town station on this line was slightly nearer to the town itself – about one mile distant.

There was a thriving paper making industry at Cleobury Mortimer until the late nineteenth century, with two paper mills alongside the River Rea to the north of the town.

Cleobury Mortimer to Ludlow

Distance: 16 miles (Hopton Wafers 4 miles, Knowle 9 miles).
Maps: Landranger 138; Pathfinder 952, 951; Explorer 203.

The longest stage of the Elan Valley Way begins by visiting the small settlement of Neen Savage, with its church and ford, the walking being mainly over quiet road and track. The route then turns west and heads for Hopton Wafers, using quiet roads and fieldpaths. The next section crosses the lower slopes of Titterstone Clee Hill, initially using fieldpaths but then climbing above the level of the farmland to reach open hillside. There are superb views to be had here.

After descending again the route uses tracks, fieldpaths and roads as it turns towards Ludlow. It visits the hill fort at Caynham before making a final descent to enter Ludlow alongside the River Teme.

The Elan Valley aqueduct is much in evidence on this stage of the walk. It is first seen as it crosses the River Rea between Cleobury Mortimer and Neen Savage. Next, one of the original well houses is encountered in a field near Earls Ditton. (Well houses usually occur at junctions of tunnels and pipeline sections and contain stop gates to halt the flow of water. They also sometimes contain an overflow to a nearby stream or river. Tunnels were built where ground excavation to lay pipes would have been too deep.) Two sections of the aqueduct can be seen while the crossing of Titterstone Clee Hill is made, both of them where the aqueduct crosses the valleys of minor streams. Descending from Caynham Camp, the route actually crosses Ledwyche Brook with the aqueduct immediately below it – over a metal footbridge which has been installed as a permissive path at this crossing. Finally the crossing of the River Teme via Steventon Bridge is seen as the route hugs the river entering Ludlow.

STARTING outside the porch of St. Mary's church, facing the road turn left to walk along it, (A4117). On leaving the 'churchyard' it is advisable to cross the road to gain the pavement on the right-hand side until a pavement is provided on the left of the road as well – which happens as a red telephone box, on that side, is passed. Continue along the road. Shortly after passing the Old Lion P.H. turn left into New Road. After 150 yards or so this road bends left, becoming Furlongs Road. Take the first right turn off this – Furlongs Close – and walk to the top of this cul-de-sac.

Here descend a flight of steps, with metal handrails, to walk along a very narrow path which runs about 80 feet above the River Rea which is to the right – this path is so narrow that on meeting anyone along here retreat may be the only option. Turn right where the path emerges onto a road and descend the steep hill which takes the latter down to river level. Continue along the road by the river until it bears left away from the waterside. Here take the track which goes off to the right, (SO674765), and soon bears right to cross the river via a footbridge – Walford's Bridge, as shown on the adjacent house on the far side. Having crossed the bridge bear left to follow the river. The track can be quite muddy in wet weather. The distance between it and the river increasing, the track begins to climb and passes a farm building, which is on the left.

Walford's Bridge was the site of one of Cleobury's two paper mills. The other was a short distance down river.

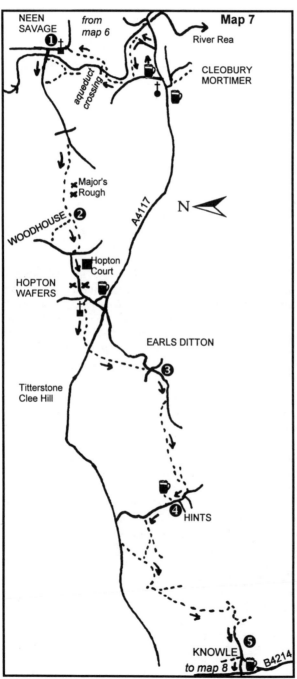

Just after passing the farm building look over a gate on the left to see the Elan Valley aqueduct crossing the River Rea.

Cleobury Mortimer has already disappeared from view behind. As the track continues to climb all that can be seen of the town is the top of the church steeple of St. Mary's.

Continue along the track. As the top of the climb is finally reached and the track begins to descend the church at Neen Savage appears ahead. A farm access track joins from the right and the main track widens and becomes much better surfaced, finally bending right to meet a road. Turn left along this to walk past the church. **❶**

St. Mary's church, Neen Savage, is late Norman in origin. In 1179 it was given to Wigmore Abbey by Hugh de Mortimer – at that time head of the increasingly powerful family based at Wigmore Castle, south of Ludlow, who were later to become Earls of March. On the dissolution of Wigmore Abbey, (1536), the patronage reverted to the Crown. The tower of the church was originally surmounted by a wooden spire but this was struck by lightning and burnt down in 1825 and was never replaced.

Beyond the church the road meanders and passes beneath trees, with the River Rea flowing alongside to the left, to reach a junction, a road to the left crossing the river via a ford. Turn left here to cross the river by a footbridge just upstream of the ford, the path to which leaves the road at the junction. Having crossed the river join the road which immediately starts to climb and bears slightly left. At a break in the climb, on the left, is Bank Top Farm from where a track returning to Cleobury Mortimer departs, (SO671775). Remain on the road which starts to climb again.

Look over the hedgerows to the right here for a view of Brown Clee Hill. To the left just the spire of Cleobury Mortimer church is still visible.

Eventually the road levels out and at a crossroads go straight across, signposted Hopton Wafers 2¼ Miles. About 100 yards after this, at a metal gate on the right, (SO663771), leave the road for a public footpath. Head half left, diagonally down and across a field to reach a footbridge at its bottom boundary. Cross this and climb the short slope on the other side to enter another field. Here follow the right boundary, formed by the stream just crossed, to reach the far right-hand corner. Go through the gap on the right into the next field. The track through this gap crosses the stream as the new field is entered, (SO657771).

Turn half left towards, and then to pass to the right of, a small area of coppice. Keeping the boundary of this immediately to the left head towards a stile directly ahead. Cross this into the next field. Proceed straight across this field, climbing slightly, to reach a metal farm gate opposite. Pass through this and on entering the next field head half left to another metal gate in the far left-hand corner – the grounds of a new farm house immediately alongside on the right as the gate is reached. Pass through the gate and turn right to follow the boundary of these farm grounds – the right-hand boundary of the field entered – to reach a metal farm gate in the far right-hand corner. ❷

The small area of coppice passed is known as Major's Rough after the late Major Woodward, of nearby Hopton Court, who owned much of the land hereabouts.

On reaching the metal farm gate in the field corner look behind, on a clear day, for a distant view of the Clent Hills on the far horizon. Not quite the last time these will be seen on the Elan Valley Way!

About 600 yards along the track beyond the gate lies the moated site of the former Woodhouse Priory founded in 1250 by Augustinian (Austin) Friars and dissolved in 1536. The moat is all that remains of the original structure. Its main claim to fame is that William Langland, author of The Vision of Piers Ploughman *– considered by many to be the greatest English poem of the late Middle Ages – was educated here. He was probably born in neighbouring Kinlet parish. The area around Woodhouse was, until recently, the smallest parish in the British Isles, at 12 acres.*

Passing through the metal farm gate turn immediately left over a stile in the hedge to enter a field – (Note: this stile may be very overgrown and

Hopton Wafers

The settlement is Saxon in origin. The name comes from a Celtic word 'Hope' meaning 'lying between two hills' and the Anglo-Saxon 'Ton' meaning an 'enclosure'. It took the name 'Wafers' from the Norman Le Wafre or Le Waffre family, the name being derived from an old French version of the modern word *gauffre* which meant a honeycomb, bee-hive or sweet cake.

At the time of Edward the Confessor the manor of 'Hopstone' was held by the Priory of Worcester but Sweyn, the eldest son of Earl Godwin, conspired to get the Priory stripped of its lands hereabouts in retaliation for the Bishop of Worcester and the Archbishop of Canterbury compelling him to give up an abbess he had abducted. Just prior to the Norman Conquest the manor was held by Siward, 'a free man'. Hopstone and three other manors held by Siward passed to Roger de Lacy after 1066 and by the time of Domesday Book (1086) Hopstone was held for him by one Widard.

The Le Wafre family originated in the village of the same name near Evreux in Normandy. They appear to have come to the Marches and Wales with the Norman conqueror of mid Wales, De Newmarch, and the first mention of the family is when Robert le Wafre was one of the signatories to a charter regarding Brecknock Priory, in 1201. By 1243 his son, also Robert, is recorded as owning the manor of Tedstone Wafer in Herefordshire and by 1255 he was also Lord of Hopton, the village becoming known as Hopton Wafers from this time.

It was probably this Robert le Wafre who had the first church built on the present site. A church is first mentioned here in 1236 when it paid tithes to Brecknock Priory. The daughter of Robert le Wafre later married the third son of Roger de Mortimer, of the powerful Wigmore based dynasty and himself called Roger, and the manor subsequently passed under his control. By 1279 the church at Hopton Wafers was paying its dues to the Abbot of Wigmore who promoted its first known rector William de Bray, installed on the 26th April of that year.

Hopton Wafers later passed to the Earls of Arundel and on to the Talbots of Shrewsbury, although the Le Wafre family retained ownership of some lands in the area. The manor passed to the Pleyleys and the Hydes until those lines died out. In 1756 it was purchased by Joseph Oldham, who owned paper mills locally, and it was he who had the old hall of the manor pulled down and the present Hopton Court built on a new site above it, in 1779. In 1812 Thomas Botfield, owner of several coal mines, purchased the manor and had the Norman church, by then very dilapidated, pulled down and rebuilt on the same site. This rebuilding – the present church – was completed in 1825. The Botfield line soon died out and the manor then passed to the Woodward family who own it to this day.

The church is dedicated to St. Michael and All Angels. Very little remains of the original Norman building except for the old font beneath the pulpit, (it spent some years exiled to the churchyard), and a fragment of fourteenth century glass depicting the head of St. Michael. The building as now seen is largely the 1825 rebuilding. The new font is of local marble.

Like Cleobury Mortimer and also Neen Savage, Hopton Wafers was a centre for paper making.

concealed; it is situated immediately beyond the gate before the farm track is reached, at SO650768). Go straight across the field to a stile in the fence opposite. Cross this and head half right to the far right-hand corner of the next field to exit by a gate. This leads to an enclosure immediately behind the farm house of Sproseley, a pond to the left. Follow the left boundary and cross a stile therein. Keeping the walls of the farm buildings immediately to the right, pass through a gate which is to the left of and immediately against the last of them. Head straight across the field now entered to a stile opposite and cross this to emerge onto a road. Turn right and then immediately left along a road signposted Hopton Wafers ½ Mile.

As Sproseley Farm is passed there are good views of Titterstone Clee Hill, the route here heading directly towards it.

Passing the walls of the gardens of Hopton Court the road bends right and begins a sharp descent. As the slope eases it bends left and crosses a bridge over Hopton Brook, in a short wooded section, and leaving this behind begins to climb slightly. On reaching a road junction go straight on, Hopton Wafers church now on the right.

A short walk along the road past the church – taking the left option at the road junction soon met – leads to the A4117 road by The Crown P.H. for bus service 192/292.

Enter the churchyard through the green gates and walk to the church porch. On reaching this bear half left towards the left boundary of the churchyard to leave it through kissing gates. Proceed along a garden boundary fence, on the left, for about 10 yards and through a gap in the boundary ahead – which lies immediately to the right of a large tree. Bear slightly right across and up the small field now entered to a stile in the fence opposite – situated just to the right of where the fence opposite makes a right-angled turn away – to enter another field. Follow the left-hand boundary here to exit via a metal gate which leads onto a footbridge over a stream. Just across this is a stile into a field. On entering the field head directly across to a stile in the boundary opposite, a gradual climb.

On climbing the field after the footbridge over the stream, (above), there is a nice view of the church behind.

Cross the stile and turn half left to head towards a fairly obvious gap in the field boundary opposite – a slight rise as the next field is entered. Turn right to follow the right boundary of the field. On reaching the top right-hand corner of the field follow the boundary around and exit the field via a red metal farm gate on the right. Entering the next field pass through a similar gate, in a fence on the left, and bear half left to a stile in the left-hand boundary hedge which leads immediately onto the A4117 road, (SO631765). *Take great care when crossing this often overgrown stile as there is practically no verge on the busy road here.*

As the corner of the penultimate field, (above), is rounded turn around for views of the Abberley Hills and Clock Tower and the Malvern Hills – a taste of views to come.

Go straight across the road and through a gate opposite into a field. Follow the right boundary of this and cross a stile into the next field. Again follow the right hedge to pass through a small metal gate into another field.

Continue along the right boundary here, a rectangular equestrian paddock on the left. Ahead is a metal gate with a stile to the left of it. Cross this into the next field, still following the right-hand boundary, the path now beginning to descend. Enter the next field via a stile (to the left of a farm gate) and descend alongside the right boundary to a stile in the bottom right-hand corner. This gives access to a footbridge over a stream. Cross this and climb up the bank opposite to emerge into the bottom of a field. When we last walked this section the footbridge had certainly seen better days while the bank was a thorny scramble.

While crossing the fields to descend to the footbridge, (above), the views across to the Abberley Hills, on the left, are superb while the Malvern Hills are just visible as they peep over the horizon, half left. The low hills in front of the Malverns are those which border the south side of the Teme Valley between Stanford Bridge and Tenbury Wells. Immediately ahead the settlement of Earls Ditton soon comes into view on the skyline.

On the climb up the field to Earls Ditton, after the footbridge, look right for a sighting of Doddington Church which is sited just above the A4117, some height above Earls Ditton. The right-hand turning at the crossroads just after Earls Ditton is a lane which leads directly to this church.

Climb straight up the field ahead, bearing half left towards the farm buildings as the top is neared. Pass through a metal farm gate onto a road at a point where the latter bends. Turn right along the road to pass through the farm settlement of Earls Ditton. ❸

Go straight across at the crossroads just after the farm. The road begins to descend and bends sharp right. A little way along the road after the bend a wooden stile – marked 'No public right of way' – gives access to field containing one of the old Elan Valley aqueduct well houses – at SO626755. Do not enter the field but continue along the road to the near corner of the

The Abberley Clock Tower

Situated between Abberley and Walsgrove Hills, Abberley Clock Tower was erected on Merritts Hill in 1883 for the then owner of Abberley Hall, Joseph Jones. The tower is a mixture of thirteenth and fourteenth century Gothic in style and used to contain a carillon of bells which played a selection of forty-two tunes as well as chiming the hours and quarters. It is 161 feet high and, because of its siting on the hill, dominates the view for many miles around.

Several stories exist as to the reason for Jones having it built. One is that it was a memorial to his late cousin from whom he inherited the Hall while another is that it was intended as a tribute to his wife who used a room near the top of the tower as a sewing room. More colourful but equally likely was that it was built in order that none of his employees might have an excuse for arriving late for work. Finally it has been suggested that it was built where it was so that he was able to look down on his near neighbour the wealthy Earl of Dudley, whose residence was at Witley Court. If this last seems far fetched then it should be remembered that this same Joseph Jones was the man who had a flagpole erected on the top of neighbouring Abberley Hill from which a flag was flown whenever he was in residence.

next field on the right where a public footpath, (unmarked at the time of writing), leaves the road on the right to enter the field through a metal gate, (may be open).

The well house is first visible just before the sharp right bend as the road descends from the crossroads at Earls Ditton. Look right here, over two metal gates, to see it. For a closer view climb off the road to the wooden stile with the 'No public right of way' sign and look half left into the field. Hardly a thing of beauty the building is of some interest as an original aqueduct structure. It bears the Birmingham coat of arms and legend, 'Forward'. Another good distant view of the building is to be had by looking back as the farm buildings at Marsh Down are reached. Good views over to the Abberley Hills and the hills of the Teme Valley are also to be had at this point.

Walk up the right-hand boundary hedge of the field. On reaching a gate in that boundary, (and where a glance left reveals the road just vacated bending sharply off to the left), bear half left diagonally towards the far left-hand corner of the field, passing well to the right of a large tree. About 20 yards to the right of the corner a stile, (beware barbed wire), gives access into the next field. Again head half left across this field towards buildings – Marsh Down, (SO620755), almost at once crossing a small watercourse. On reaching the farm buildings of Marsh Down keep their boundary fence on the right to reach a stile onto a track, with a makeshift footpath sign alongside. Turn right along the track but immediately before reaching a concrete bridge over a culvert, (on a bend to the right, at the entrance to the farm), turn left off the track to cross a stile into a field. Follow the left boundary of this field.

The upper slopes of Titterstone Clee Hill suddenly become visible on the right here. The views across to the Abberley Hills and the Teme Valley continue to improve to the left.

On reaching the end of the field cross a stile into the next. Again follow the left boundary but only for a few yards, continuing straight ahead as the boundary bends away 90 degrees to the left. Cross a stile in the far boundary – in wet weather it may cross a small stream as well as the field boundary but there is a large flat boulder to aim for if this is the case. Go straight across the field so entered. As the far side is neared bear half right to a stile in its right-hand boundary, about 20 yards in from the corner.

Cross the stile and bear left to follow the left boundary of the field now entered to a stile beside a gate. Once over this go straight across the next field, crossing a footbridge over a small stream and then a stile into another field. Initially bear straight across this field but then go half left to a metal gate in the far left-hand corner. Go through the gate and turn right onto a track which leads, almost at once, out onto a quiet lane. Turn right here, (SO613751). The lane drops down to a T-junction. Turn right, signposted Hints ¼ mile, Clee Hill 1¾ miles. The road immediately climbs, bending left, to reach another T-junction at the small settlement of Hints. Again turn right to walk up the road past a telephone box and then over a cattle grid to reach open hillside. **❹**

The Collier's Arms P.H. is visible here up its access track to the right (open evenings only on weekdays; lunchtimes and evenings at weekends).

The route is now at about 270 metres/885 feet in height on the open slopes of Titterstone Clee Hill which rises to 533 metres/1748 feet at its highest point. This stage of the Elan Valley Way soon reaches its maximum height of 325 metres/1066 feet but even at this relatively low height the views are phenomenal on a clear day.

Continue the steep climb up the road. About 300 yards after the cattle grid, just as the road makes a very sharp right bend, turn left onto a fairly level gravelled track, (SO609756). A short distance along this on the left is a white house, (Pond House), with a pond immediately to the left of the track. Just before reaching this take a track up to the right. As it climbs this track becomes somewhat 'sunken' and may be overgrown in late summer or boggy after wet weather – in which case climb out of it and walk alongside. It passes above a cottage, along a stone wall. Remain on it as it becomes less distinct and narrows to footpath width. As it levels out leave it, bearing half right up an indistinct track to pass above a house. Keep the garden wall of this house to the immediate left and as the far corner of its garden is passed, and a T-junction with a broad gravelled track is reached, turn left, (SO606756). Walk down the gravelled track.

Look left along this section for the best view yet of the Malvern Hills. The entire chain is visible from North Hill, (398 metres/1305 feet), and Worcestershire

The Clees

The summits of both Titterstone Clee Hill and its neighbour, Brown Clee Hill, were formerly extensively quarried for dhustone – a form of basalt especially good for paving streets and roads. To facilitate transport of the quarried stone down from the hill a branch railway was built from the main Shrewsbury & Hereford Railway line near Ludlow to the foot of steep inclines climbing the hill. There was also an aerial ropeway link to the Cleobury Mortimer & Ditton Priors Light Railway. This latter line left the Great Western Railway's Tenbury & Bewdley Railway at Cleobury Mortimer and primarily served the quarries on Brown Clee Hill, via another incline. Quarrying of dhustone has now ceased although much evidence of the former activity remains at the top of both hills.

Coal and ironstone were also mined up here, both being beneath the dhustone capping of the hill. This in turned spawned other industries such as brick and glass making and ironworks.

It was the hard dhustone capping of Titterstone and Brown Clee Hills which protected their summits through millions of years of erosion and left them as the highest hills in Shropshire.

Also covering the summit of the hill are the remains of an Iron Age hill fort, its ruined stone ramparts enclosing an area of 68 acres, making it the largest hill fort in central Marches, three times the size of any other.

None of the above is visible from the route of the Elan Valley Way but the views on a clear day more than compensate. As the cattle grid is crossed and the road climbed the views behind already encompass, left to right, the Clent Hills, Abberley Hills, Malvern Hills and over into South Wales.

Beacon, (425 metres/1394 feet), on the left along past Herefordshire Beacon to Midsummer, Hollybush and Chase End Hills on the right.

On a clear day the Cotswold Hills are visible behind and to the left of the Malverns, between them and the nearer Abberley Hills.

As the garden wall of the house, (above), is first reached look down the hill to catch a first glimpse of the Elan Valley aqueduct crossing below.

Remain on the gravel track as it descends, passing a bungalow – aptly named 'Panorama' – en route. Bearing right the track descends to negotiate the crossing of a side valley, turning sharply left as it crosses the stream therein.

Look to the left down the hill to see the Elan Valley aqueduct crossing the same stream, (Corn Brook).

Look up to the right as the track turns sharp left for a good view to the top of the wild side valley.

On reaching a junction, almost immediately after crossing the stream, take the right track which climbs sharply. (The left track continues to descend.) At a second, and almost immediate, parting of tracks again go right. (The left option here only runs to the house ahead.) Follow the track as it climbs past the aforementioned house, which is on the left, and then levels out, becoming grassy and undulating between high bracken in season.

Just after passing the isolated house stop for awhile to take in the view – here about as good as it gets on a clear day, (SO603754).

To the left down the hill the course of the Elan Valley aqueduct can be clearly seen.

Owain Glyn Dwr

Woodbury and Abberley Hills had their moment in history in the early fifteenth century during the Wars of Welsh Independence of Owain Glyn Dwr. In 1405 Glyn Dwr marched east at the head of a combined Welsh and French force. He reached the city of Worcester, the part of which to the west of the River Severn he sacked, before being confronted by an English force under Henry IV and retreating to the old hill fort on Woodbury, the English following and setting up their own camp on Abberley Hill. Thereupon a stalemate of some eight days ensued, with the two opposing armies facing each other each morning but only light skirmishing and jousting taking place – about 200 killed – before the English retreated to Worcester, 12 miles distant, and Glyn Dwr's force marched back into Wales. In truth both armies were probably too exhausted to enter into a full scale battle and the French had lost most of their horses at sea and so would have been at a grave disadvantage in the exchanges that did take place. The moral victory, if any, was with Henry and this invasion by Glyn Dwr marked the pinnacle of his success.

The distant views of the various hills are sensational. In addition to the Clent Hills, Abberley Hills, Cotswolds, the entire Malvern Hills chain, and the Teme Valley the northern escarpment of the Black Mountains may now also be visible beyond.

The nearer Abberley Hills dominate the left foreground as they have done since the views first opened up along this stage. Three hills and the clock tower are clearly visible. The hill on the left is Abberley Hill itself, (283 metres/928 feet in height) while next to it is the smaller Walsgrove Hill. Finally, on the right is Woodbury Hill, (276 metres/905 feet), which bears an Iron Age hill fort on its summit.

Remain on the grassy track which soon begins to descend and narrows to footpath width. Passing through bracken, in season, it continues its steady descent and eventually bends very sharply left and then just as sharply right to join a similar green track at a T-junction. Turn right here to continue the descent. The new track makes a sharp right turn to reach a stream at the bottom. Walk to the right alongside this for a few paces and then cross it at an obvious ford. Once over the stream bear left up the bank on the other side on a rough footpath, with a boundary on its immediate right. On reaching a track turn right. Within a few yards the track takes on a metalled surface to become a quiet road, (SO600744), immediately starting to climb. ❺

Walk up the road. After about mile it crosses a cattle grid and reaches a junction. Turn right here. Almost immediately the Golden Lion P.H., on the left of the road, is passed and the road then emerges onto the B4214 road as the latter climbs to the village of Cleehill. There is a telephone box just down the B4214 to the left. Cross straight over the B road and take the track opposite.

The Golden Lion P.H. opens evenings only on weekdays and both lunchtime and evening at weekends.

Cleehill village lies about three quarters of a mile up the B4214 to the right. Bus service 192/292.

Almost immediately as the track over the B road is entered the hills behind Ludlow and beyond into Wales come into view. As the junction in the track is reached these views really open up. On a clear day should be visible, on the left: the hills of the Mortimer Forest behind Ludlow, Bircher Common and Croft Ambrey, the hills of the Radnor Forest – the conical shaped one in the distance is the Whimble, (599 metres/1965 feet), – and the hills around Knighton and Clun.

After about 100 yards, on reaching a junction in the track, (SO595743), turn right to walk past Heath Farm, which is on the right. Ignore a footpath going off left but pass to the right of a house. As the track descends slightly as if to enter the grounds of a bungalow, 'Heathfields', turn half right through two gates in quick succession (the second off its hinges at the time of writing) to pass along its boundary fence (immediately to the left) the track now narrowing to footpath width. Having passed the bungalow continue along the boundary fence, ignoring a footpath which climbs up the slope to the right.

To the left along here the Malvern Hills now make a reappearance while, between them and the hills behind Ludlow, the northern escarpment of the Black Mountains may also be visible in the far distance.

Continue along the path following the contour. Pass into the next field through a gap in the boundary. The path immediately becomes indistinct but continues to follow the contour. When an area of woodland, (Gorstley Rough), comes into view half right aim half left towards the bottom corner of

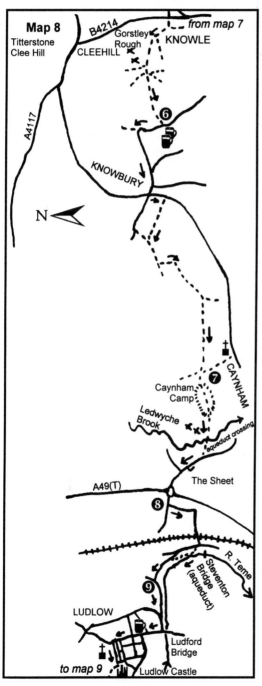

the field to pass into the next field through a large gap in the boundary hedge, between trees. Climb half left up the new field – quite steep – towards its top left-hand corner. Cross a stile here into the next field where a choice of footpaths is indicated.

Go straight ahead to walk alongside the left boundary of the field. Almost immediately a stile in that boundary is reached. This bears little finger posts indicating three destinations – Hope Bagot, Whitton, and Bennettsend. Ignore all these options but remain on the same side of the field boundary, continuing to follow it.

Rounding a corner of the field a depression in the ground starts to develop alongside the left boundary. Drop down into this as soon as is practicable, continuing to walk alongside the boundary, now among trees. On reaching a stile over the boundary fence, just before the next field corner, cross this and turn half right along a path which, after a few yards, emerges from the trees into an open field. Continue in the same direction down this field towards a large white building below. Pass

The old pump in Cumberley Lane

through a gap in the hedgerow onto a road immediately opposite the white building which should by now have been identified as the Bennettsend Inn. Turn right along the road. **❻**

Descending to the Bennettsend Inn look to the left to see another section of the Elan Valley aqueduct as it crosses a stream, Colly Brook, via Bennettsend Bridge.

There are two pubs here side by side – the Bennettsend Inn, bearing the date 1640, and the Penny Black Inn. There is a bowling green behind the former.

Walk up the road past the large tarmac car park of the Bennettsend Inn, the bowling green and the car park and entrance to the Penny Black – all on the left. Colly Brook now flows alongside on the left and the road crosses it via a bridge, now bending left. A very sharp left bend follows.

After just over a quarter of a mile of further gentle ascent along the road ignore a turning to the left – Cumberley Lane.

Passing the Cumberley Lane turning, (SO578746), look on the grass verge to the right where a black painted tap/pump is sited. Made by Glenfield & Kennedy of Kilmarnock, this wonderful contraption is a long way from home but is still in perfect working order. Unfortunately there is nothing to indicate whether the water so obtained is drinkable, but then again there is nothing to say that it is not!

A lot of new building was taking place along here in 1998/99 with a great many housing plots for sale.

Continue along the road, passing through housing now, to reach a T-junction with the Caynham Road, (SO575746). Turn left here, (signposted Caynham 2 miles, Ludlow 5 miles), down the hill. As the road begins to swing to the right take a footpath going off to the right, which is accessed over a high step stile. Follow the left-hand boundary across the field so entered to cross another step stile into the next field. Again follow the left boundary across this field to another step stile – the highest of the three yet encountered – which is crossed into an orchard area. Go across this, still hugging the left boundary, to a step stile in the very far left corner. Cross this and immediately another to enter a field.

Follow the left-hand boundary across the bottom of this but then, as the far boundary is approached, ignore a small gate in the bottom corner of the field and bear half right up the hill to pass through a full size farm gate into the next field, (this gate may be open). Go straight across the field to a gate opposite and pass through this onto a stony track, (SO569747). Turn left down the track – not however the immediate left which is the entrance to Myrtle Cottage. Almost immediately the track loses its stony surface and becomes a dirt/grass track. Remain on it as it passes a house, which is on the right, and descends through a metal gate into a field where it follows the left-hand boundary, bearing to the left and continuing to descend.

As the track bears to the left Ludlow makes an appearance straight ahead – not its first, as it is initially visible half left as the fields after the Caynham Road are walked. Caynham Camp is also visible in the foreground.

Follow the track to the bottom of the field where there are two farm gates – a wooden one on the right and a metal one on the left. Pass through the metal gate on the left and follow the left-hand boundary ahead across the field now entered. On reaching the far left corner of the field pass through a wooden gate into the next field and turn right. Follow the boundary – on the right – across this field passing through another wooden gate into the next field. Continue to follow the right-hand boundary as this field is walked. At the far corner pass into the next field through a metal gate. Follow the left-hand boundary of the field now entered to reach a metal gate at the far side, the gatepost of which bears a yellow arrow to indicate the right of way, (SO563742).

Pass through the gate to follow the left-hand boundary of the field now entered.

The hill fort of Caynham Camp is now clearly visible just slightly to the right ahead.

Follow the left-hand boundary as it bends to the left to reach the far left-hand corner of the field where a gap leads through to the next field. Initially turn as if to pass through this but instead cross a stile in the hedge on the right of the gap to enter another field. (*Care needs to be taken not to miss this stile.*) On entering the field one of the pipeline valve chambers will be seen ahead. Bear to the right of and past this – half right from the stile – to a wooden gate about half way along the right-hand field boundary. Go through this gate into the field beyond and turn left to follow the initial direction of its left-hand boundary hedge.

When this boundary bends slightly away to the left continue to hold its original course and head towards a group of trees and bushes at the far boundary of the field. On reaching this head down a slope into the trees and bushes to find some wooden steps leading down to a footbridge over a stream – the steps lie about 100 yards in from the left-hand corner of the field just crossed. Cross the footbridge – a single but sturdy plank of wood at the time of writing – and climb the wooden steps on the far side to emerge over a stile into a field, (SO557739). (The steps down to the footbridge and up from it, the footbridge itself, but especially the stile can all be very slippery in wet weather.) On entering the field turn half right to walk up it towards its far boundary, crossing a track after 25 yards or so. Maintain direction up the field to reach a stile which is sited about 25 yards to the left of two trees in the boundary. A steep climb up to and over this stile leads into the next field.

Climbing the field from the stream, ahead and to the right another pipeline valve chamber can be seen in an adjacent field. When climbing over the stile look behind to see where the pipeline crosses the stream.

Turn right to follow the boundary of the new field to the corner and then along its right-hand side. In the far right-hand corner cross a stile into the next field. Go straight across and up this field to the far boundary to locate a stile which is situated about 10 yards to the right of a small tree in the boundary. Cross this and continue straight ahead to another stile in the field boundary opposite, (SO549738). Cross this stile into another field and head half right across this towards the far right-hand corner behind which Caynham Camp hill fort looms large. Cross the stile in the very top right-hand corner and go straight ahead, either over a stile or through the gap in the ramparts, to enter Caynham Camp. ❼

As the final field before Caynham Camp is crossed there are wonderful views to be had all around on a clear day. The Clee Hills are directly behind. The Malvern Hills and Abberley Hills may also be visible.

Caynham Camp hill fort – at a height of 173 metres/567 feet – is thought to date from the Late Bronze Age which makes it probably the oldest inhabited of the hill forts passed on the Elan Valley Way. Fragments of pottery found there suggest it was already occupied by about 870BC. It was abandoned sometime after the coming of the Romans. Late in the evening, as the sun sets, Caynham Camp can seem a very atmospheric place indeed and it is easy to imagine those early residents here looking out across the wild country below them.

Follow the obvious path straight through the middle of the hill fort – the ramparts on the left-hand side being particularly prominent. Passing

Approaching the ramparts of Caynham Camp

through a gap in an internal ridge turn half right to walk along the very top of the right-hand rampart. This leads to a well defined gap in the rampart of the fort furthest from where the path originally entered. Exit the hill fort here.

While walking along the top of the right rampart there are superb views of Ludlow, half right.

Leaving the hill fort there are good views ahead – to the mass of radio aerials at Woofferton on the left and to the Mortimer Forest above Ludlow, directly ahead.

Leaving the hill fort through the ramparts turn sharp right to take a grassy track which curves back around the hill fort, losing height, a fence alongside to the left. On reaching a wooden gate through that fence pass through it to head downhill on an obvious grassy track, above bushes. At the bottom right-hand corner of this field cross a stile alongside a metal gate and head half right across the field so entered to a stile half way along its right boundary, just to the left of two trees in that boundary. Cross this and head diagonally across the next field towards the left edge of a wooded area below where a metal structure can be seen. As the path descends this reveals itself to be the Ledwyche Brook Crossing of the Elan Valley aqueduct, (SO538738). Descend to it and take the permissive path over the footbridge.

A serious case of sheep worrying hereabouts in September 1998 – with me being worried by two sheep! As I was searching for the stile to the left of the two trees in the field boundary, (above), the guilty parties ran up to me and proceeded to harass me as I attempted to consult my map. Presumably these two were bottle raised as lambs and were just on the lookout for a free meal but it was certainly a novel experience and one which did not stop until I had managed to locate the stile and beat a hasty retreat.

A good specimen of a giant puffball was found in one of the fields during the descent from Caynham Camp to the Ledwyche Crossing.

Alone among all of the Elan Valley aqueduct crossings that over Ledwyche Brook carries a permissive path. The footbridge crosses immediately above one of the pipes and some 30 or so feet above the brook. Quite an exciting crossing with both pipeline and brook visible through the metal bridge underfoot.

On reaching the road to The Sheet (below) there are good views of Titterstone and Brown Clee Hills to the right, the hills of the Mortimer Forest to the left, and Caynham Camp behind.

Having crossed Ledwyche Brook by the aqueduct footbridge, go half right across and up the field entered to a stile leading onto a road – (the stile is situated about 90 yards to the right of a prominent metal farm gate which leads onto the same road). Turn right along the road which soon reaches the oddly named settlement of The Sheet. When a pavement commences on the left-hand side of the road cross to it. The road bends left and eventually reaches a road island on the A49(T) Ludlow Ring Road.

'The Sheet' appears a strange name for a settlement at first sight. It is apparently a quite common name in Shropshire around older settlements and often refers to the area wherein are the streams into which the sewage of the settlement was discharged. Given the distance from both Ludlow and Ludford and the drainage system hereabouts this derivation seems unlikely in this particular instance however. A more likely origin of the name is the early English 'sceat' which means a 'corner projection'.

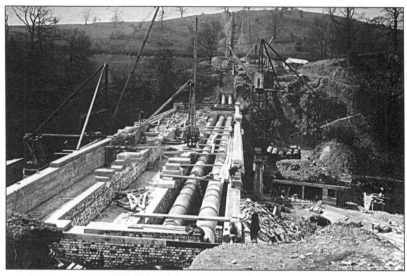

The Teme Crossing under construction

In 1339 the owner of the land here, Richard Goldsmith, was murdered during a property feud by another local landowner, John Ace, such feuds and associated killings being common at this time. In 1494 there was a corn mill here which later became a fulling mill.

Go straight across the ring road and along the road opposite but then take the first road on the left. ❽

Walking this road look through the hedgerow to the right for views over Ludlow – in particular the castle and the church of St. Laurence – and beyond to Mortimer Forest.

Walk along the road which, after a short distance, bends sharply to the right and shortly afterwards crosses a bridge over a railway, (the line from Shrewsbury to Hereford), and then descends to a T-junction. Here turn right, signposted Ludlow 1 Mile. About 50 yards down the road from the junction turn left down a flight of stone steps – indicated by a footpath sign – which lead to the River Teme. These may be very slippery in wet weather. On reaching the river turn right along its bank.

Look left downstream here to see the Elan Valley aqueduct crossing the River Teme over Steventon Bridge.

Follow the riverside path until it emerges onto a road. Cross this and turn left along it. Follow the road to reach a T-junction, an old toll house on its right corner. Turn left here, crossing the road, (Temeside), to gain the pavement. ❾

Shortly before reaching the T-junction with the toll house a large cream-painted building will be seen on the left. This is Temeside Mill, built in the nineteenth century in a mixture of stone and brick and with cast iron window frames. Known as the New Mill until the 1880's, corn milling ceased here at the turn of the century but in 1921 the premises reopened as the Temeside Case Mill where cases for cutlery and jewellery were made. This enterprise only lasted a decade and since then the building has variously turned out false teeth and wood-burning stoves. It is still commercially active.

The toll house itself is an early nineteenth century building. The blank window above the door probably contained the toll board.

As Ludford Bridge is approached look over the wall to the river to see the sites of the old mills.

Proceed along Temeside to another T-junction. Again turn left, to walk along the road beside the river. Ludford Bridge soon appears half left ahead. On reaching it turn right to go up Lower Broad Street and through Broad Gate into Broad Street. Proceed up Broad Street until the Butter Cross is reached, at the top, and then turn left into High Street to reach the Market Square and castle. This stage of the Elan Valley Way finishes at the castle gates.

Ludlow

Whilst neighbouring Ludford, across the Teme, is mentioned in Domesday Book (1086) Ludlow is not and it is not until 1138 that it is first recorded as a place name. The name itself is derived from Ludelaue meaning a hill or mound beside loud waters, ie. rapids.

Ludlow is very much a medieval planned town, begun under the de Lacy family – supporters of William the Conqueror who were given land hereabouts and began building the castle in about 1086. The town's obvious grid plan incorporates an earlier through route along the present Corve Street and Old Street. The only other distortion of this grid is where the existing castle was enlarged into it, at its north west corner. It is likely that the original crossing of the River Teme was at the bottom of Old Street, where it forms a junction with Temeside – passed on the walk. Between 1233 and 1304 the town was walled. The walls were one mile around with 7 gateways through them. Only one of these, Broad Gate, still stands although many sections of the wall remain, such as that in St. John's Road which runs off Lower Broad Street

by Broad Gate. By 1377 the population of the town was 1700, making it the 33rd largest settlement in England.

In the fourteenth century one third of the properties in the town were owned by the Palmers' Guild, a quasi-religious organisation formed in the thirteenth century and claiming links with the crusaders. The Guild invested in property and used its profits to help its less fortunate members and the town in general through the provision of almshouses and schools. It was dissolved in 1551, a late casualty of the Dissolution of the monasteries and religious orders started under Henry VIII.

Also in the early fourteenth century Ludlow Castle passed to the powerful family of Marcher Earls, the Mortimers, and thence to the House of York on the cessation of the direct Mortimer male line in 1425. In 1459, during the War of the Roses, the town was sacked after the rout of the Yorkists by Henry VI at the battle of Ludford Bridge.

The town was at the zenith of its power and influence between 1534 and 1689 when it was the main seat of the Council of the Marches. Much building and rebuilding took place during these years – the Feathers Hotel is an example.

During the Civil War the town was besieged by Parliamentarian forces, in 1646, and many buildings outside of the town walls sustained damage. The Council of the Marches was suspended during the Civil War and was finally dissolved in 1689. Thereafter history has largely bypassed the town as did the major effects of the Industrial Revolution. A railway from Shrewsbury reached the town in 1852 – the Shrewsbury & Hereford Railway.

For such a small town Ludlow is rich with interesting buildings, in fact almost 500 of the town buildings are listed as being of historical interest. A walking guide such as this could not hope to do full justice to all the town has to offer but to briefly cover the highlights, there are:

(A) On the route of the Elan Valley Way:

(1) Ludford Bridge – a fifteenth century structure crossing the River Teme, but the foundations may be older. There was formerly a chapel on it. An older crossing of the Teme existed on the through route which pre-dated the town, probably at the bottom of what is now Old Street.

(2) Broad Gate – the only remaining gate through the town walls. The original medieval gate is now hidden by 16th, 17th and eighteenth century domestic architecture but is visible from beneath it.

(3) The Butter Cross – built 1742 to 1744 to replace the medieval High Cross. The architect was William Baker. The ground floor serves as a covered market; the upper has been a school and a museum in its time.

(4) Ludlow Castle – the original castle here pre-dates the town and was built between 1086 and 1094 by Roger de Lacy, a supporter of William the Conqueror. The castle was constructed of stone from the start – quite unusual as most were wooden initially – and it is likely that the earliest part of the town grew up between it and the river around the area now called Dinham. The castle has been much extended over the years, especially after it passed into the hands of the powerful Mortimer family, through marriage, in the early fourteenth century. When the direct male Mortimer line died out in 1425 the castle passed, via the female line and marriage, to the House of York and thence to the Crown after the Yorkist Edward IV's victory at Mortimer's Cross (1461), about 8 miles to the south-west of Ludlow, effectively ended the Wars of the Roses. It then became a royal palace. The two sons of Edward IV – better known as 'the Princes in the Tower' stayed here for a time and it was at Ludlow Castle that Arthur, the elder son of Henry VII honeymooned with his bride Catherine of Aragon in 1501. Tragically Arthur was dead within five months and his wife went on to marry his brother, later Henry VIII. Arthur's heart is buried in St. Laurence's Church while his body was taken for burial in Worcester Cathedral. Mary Tudor, Henry VIII's daughter by Catherine of Aragon, who spent several winters at the castle, was its last royal resident. After 1534 the castle became the main seat of the Council of the Marches – the town effectively becoming the administrative and legislative centre for Wales and the English border counties. It was a Royalist stronghold during the Civil War and was besieged by a Parliamentarian force under Colonel Birch in 1646, surrendering after a few weeks. The Council of the Marches was dissolved in 1689 and

after that the castle became disused and soon fell into disrepair. In 1811 it was purchased by the Earl of Powis whose descendants own it to this day.

(B) Off Route:

(1) The Chapel of St. Thomas – the oldest building in Ludlow outside of the castle walls, built about 1190 and dedicated to St. Thomas a Becket. The chapel is now incorporated into a later building. It is situated just off Dinham, the road leading from the castle down to Dinham Bridge.

(2) The Feathers Hotel – situated at the top of Corve Street, this was a 1619 rebuild of an existing structure for one of the members of the Council of the Marches whose initials can still be seen on the surviving original door lock frame. It became a pub in 1670. The balcony on the front of it was added in the nineteenth century for electioneering use.

(3) The Bull Hotel – is the oldest pub in Ludlow, having been carrying out that function for 500 years. Its frontage in Corve Street gives no clue as to the true age of the building as this was rebuilt after a fire in 1795. However, pass through to its inner yard to see its true character. The earliest record of it is as Peter the Proctor's House, in 1343, but it is thought to date back to 1199 in part. A priest hole and indoor well have been discovered within.

(4) The Tolsey – situated in the Bull Ring and probably of fifteenth century origin, the Tolsey was where the market courts were held. These dispensed instant justice and were known as the Court of Pie Powder – after the French 'Pieds Poudre' literally meaning the 'Dust off the Feet', ie. justice was dished out before one had time to shake the dust off one's feet.

(5) The Reader's House – after 1551 Ludlow corporation appointed a reader to carry out some of the duties of the Church. In the eighteenth century the reader lived in this house, situated behind the church. The main building dates from the sixteenth century with a splendid Jacobean porch added in 1616.

(6) St. Laurence's Church – dominates the whole town and is the largest parish church in Shropshire at 132 feet in height and 203 feet long. It dates from 1199 with much fifteenth century rebuilding. Full of interest inside the undoubted highlights are the fifteenth century carved wooden misericords. Dating from around 1440 these are amongst the finest of their kind in the country. Also contains St. John's Chapel, the chapel of the Palmers' Guild, with its Golden Window containing a representation of St. Catherine and her wheel and Palmers' Window telling the legend of how that organisation got its charter from Edward the Confessor. Across the church is the Lady Chapel which contains a restored fourteenth century Jesse Window. This chapel was formerly used to house the town fire engine and the wooden pegs for the fire buckets and a blocked access doorway remain. The West window of the church depicts the Lords of Ludlow Castle ending – at bottom right – with Prince Arthur whose heart is buried somewhere in the building. He died in Ludlow Castle in 1502 while staying there with his bride of five months, Catherine of Aragon. The entrance porch to the church is hexagonal in shape – one of only three such constructions in the country, the others being at Chipping Norton and at St. Mary's, Redcliffe, in Bristol. It is of mid-fourteenth century origin.

Stage 5

Ludlow to Leintwardine

Distance: 11½ miles. *No public transport 'escape routes' on this section.*
Maps: Landranger 138, 148; Pathfinder 951; Explorer 203.

Leaving Ludlow by rounding the castle and dropping down to cross the River Teme, the first half of this stage consists of a long crossing of Mortimer Forest, using clearly defined tracks throughout. The first mile or so of the route is shared with the waymarked Mortimer Trail and, once that is left behind, the markers of one of the forest trails then take over for most of the way.

Leaving Mortimer Forest along an 'interesting' farm track, the second half of the stage begins by dropping down to visit the small settlement of Burrington with its fascinating church. A section of road walking takes the route across the River Teme for the second time on the stage and leads to the settlement of Downton on the Rock after which a mix of footpaths and tracks climb over the hill behind to descend into Leintwardine via Church Hill.

A long stretch of the Elan Valley aqueduct is walked in Deep Wood, within Mortimer Forest. This includes two significant bridges crossing side valleys and two of the small well houses, seen previously on the walk. Later in the day the line is clearly recognisable in several places by its valve chambers, while the crossing of the River Teme via Downton Bridge is also seen from a distance.

FACING the entrance to Ludlow Castle turn right to walk along an obvious path beneath the castle walls, past a notice board marking the start of the waymarked Mortimer Trail. The first mile of this stage of the Elan Valley Way shares its route.

The cannon and drinking water fountain outside the castle gates are worth looking at. The water fountain was manufactured by Glenfield & Kennedy of Kilmarnock, one of their 'Hygienic Fountains' – the same manufacturers who produced the much simpler tap/pump seen on Stage 4 of the Elan Valley Way, at Knowbury. Like the Knowbury pump this model features lions heads but this time surmounted by a trident and dolphins and mounted on a much more ornate plinth. Unfortunately, for all its splendour, unlike its Knowbury counterpart it does not work. The cannon is Russian in origin and was captured by British forces during the Crimean War, at Sebastopol, in 1855.

As the path bends to the left beneath the high walls look up to see the North Range of the castle. This was the part of the castle much developed and improved by the Mortimers when they came into possession of it, via marriage, in the early fourteenth century. The most impressive structure of the castle, as seen here from the outside, is the early fourteenth century Garderobe Tower which was actually built onto the outside of the Norman walls. It provided extra accommodation for the Mortimers who entertained lavishly. The tower had a number of bedrooms each with its own garderobe, (toilet), a very unusual luxury in those days. Exactly how medieval castle toilets functioned can be imagined by looking up at the apertures in the outside walls which indicate their positions!

The path bends to the left around the castle walls and, passing below the buildings of the North Range and Garderobe Tower, begins to descend. Ignore a narrow path coming in sharply from the right but at a Y-junction of paths go right – as indicated by the Mortimer Trail sign. The descent becomes steeper, the path becoming metalled and dropping to the road which is reached through metal barriers.

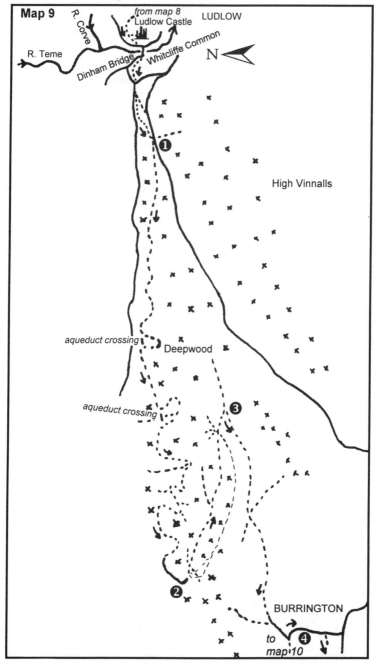

Map 9

R. Corve

R. Teme

from map 8
Ludlow Castle

LUDLOW

Dinham Bridge

Whitcliffe Common

N

❶

High Vinnalls

aqueduct crossing

Deepwood

aqueduct crossing

❸

❷

BURRINGTON

to
map 10

❹

Turn left along the road to reach a T-junction. Go right here to cross the River Teme via Dinham Bridge.

Dinham Bridge was built in 1823 and replaced an eighteenth century structure which itself had replaced a timber bridge built on stone piers, the latter probably being used by the eighteenth century builders. The old piers can still be seen just downstream of the current bridge when the river is low.

Dinham takes its name from Joce de Dinan who was granted land here in 1130, after the de Lacy family - the founders of the castle and settlement at Ludlow - fell out of favour with the Crown.

The high land across the River Teme from Ludlow is Whitcliffe Common, used for common grazing of animals and collection of firewood since it was granted `common' status in 1221. Good views to be had of Ludlow Castle across the river as this section is walked.

Having crossed Dinham Bridge leave the road via a gap in the continuation of the left parapet wall of the bridge to climb the flight of steps ahead. Bear right at the top to follow the edge of the cliff along an obvious path which rises slightly. Take note of the warning notices hereabouts regarding collapsing cliff edges and the like. The path soon bears gradually left to climb more steps. Ignore a path going off it to the left by a seat but continue straight on. At a 'crossroads' of paths go straight on, still following the signs for the Mortimer Trail. On reaching a road turn right and walk as far as a sharp right-hand bend on it, (SO503745), and then go left along a minor road – Lower Wood Road.

After about 50 yards take a footpath going off on the left and heading up through the woods. Almost immediately this splits into two paths. Take the right-hand option, again following the Mortimer Trail signs. Lower Wood Road is still running parallel to the path but some distance below it on the right. The path undulates and winds along for a while, gradually gaining height above the road, but then drops again before once more climbing and turning away from it. The climb becomes steeper and the main road through Mortimer Forest – that to Wigmore – is soon approached.

At the top of a longer, straighter climb ignore a narrow path going off left, (almost straight ahead), and up to the road but stay on the main path which levels out and parallels the road for a short spell. Mortimer Trail signs point the way. On reaching a T-junction with a path/track turn left

---

River Teme

The River Teme rises in the Kerry Hills of Powys and flows generally east or south to join the River Severn just below Worcester, a total length of over 75 miles. On the way it accepts the waters of several important tributaries – the Clun, (at Leintwardine), the Onney, the Corve, (at Ludlow), and the Rea, (at Newnham Bridge). The confluence of the Teme and Corve is just north of Ludlow, about half a mile up-stream of Dinham bridge. It is thought that the Teme may have originally flowed northwards beyond where Leintwardine is now situated but that it became trapped by ice at the end of the last Ice Age and, after flooding what is now the Vale of Wigmore, cut a new channel eastwards – now Downton Gorge.

along it to reach the road, within a few yards. The entrance to the Forestry Commission's Mortimer Forest Office and Centre will be seen opposite. The Elan Valley Way leaves the route of the Mortimer Trail here. Do not cross the road but instead turn immediately right down a forest track, (SO494742). ❶

Proceed along the track, almost immediately passing a wooden barrier. (A white ringed forest trail marker was nearby in September 1998 but was missing by May 1999. It is, however, the route of this waymarked trail which is followed for most of the remaining time in the forest.) The track runs fairly straight and level for a while but then a gradual descent begins and it bears slightly to the right. The walk here is along the edge of the forest with open fields to the right. Ignore a path crossing the track – going steeply up into the woods to the left and through a gate into the field on the right.

Mortimer Forest

This is a name which does not appear on O.S. maps, the reason being that it is purely a term used by the Forestry Commission to describe all the forest areas it manages in the central Marches. It is however particularly used to describe the main forest near Ludlow which covers some 2500 acres on two main ridges to the south-west of the town and includes Whitcliffe Wood, Deep Wood, Bringewood, Haye Park Wood, High Vinnalls, Climbing Jack Common, Sunny Dingle Wood, Mary Knoll, and Upper and Lower Evens. The wooded ridges rise to a maximum height of 370 metres/1200 feet, at High Vinnalls. There are several well waymarked forest walks in the area, including the 'Mortimer Walk' which is a complete circuit of the two main ridges waymarked with white ringed marker posts – followed in part by the Elan Valley Way.

Continue to follow the good, obvious track as it begins to wind more and plunges into thicker woodland – marked as Deep Wood on Explorer Map 203. Eventually, on rounding a sharp bend to

Laying a section of pipeline

the left, high above a side valley to the right, a bridge carrying the Elan Valley aqueduct over the valley will be seen ahead and below, (SO470740).

This is the first of two of these structures to be seen in quick succession. Such is the style and scale of these two bridges that on first seeing them one could be forgiven for thinking they were part of a disused railway line. Between the two pipeline bridges the walk is along a wonderfully springy section of grassy track which follows the line of the aqueduct. Good walking!

Remain on the track as it bends left and then right to round the side valley and, on reaching the other end of the bridge carrying the pipelines, swings left to follow the line of the aqueduct along a straight grassy section.

As the far end of the pipeline bridge is reached look half right for a first view of Downton Castle which stands downstream of Downton gorge on a bank above the River Teme.

A deer was seen nearby. Mortimer Forest contains herds of fallow deer including a long-haired variety unique to this location. We also found, at the start of the grassy track section, a large patch of autumn crocus, (or meadow saffron).

The track passes a pipeline valve chamber and at the end of the grassy section another sharp left bend heralds a second aqueduct bridge, an old lime kiln on the left here. The track again bends left then right around the head of the side valley crossed by the bridge but this time there is also a junction at the head of the valley with a wide forest track going off right to drop down the side valley under the aqueduct. Take the left track here to maintain height and reach the far end of the bridge where it bends to the left to follow the course of the aqueduct, now some height above the land to the right. A well house will be seen ahead.

A good view of the second pipeline bridge can be had by proceeding some way down the forest track on the right at the track junction. The well house is similar to the one seen near Earls Ditton on Stage 4 of the Elan Valley Way. It bears the date 1902 and the legend 'Elan Supply. Birmingham Corporation Water', together with the Birmingham coat of arms and motto, 'Forward'.

On reaching the corner of the building look beyond it to see a line of pipeline inspection covers marking the course of the aqueduct. Also look half right here for a good view of Downton Castle.

On reaching the redbrick well house the track swings to the left of it. After about 200 yards, at a junction of tracks, (SO461736), turn left onto a partly metalled track which immediately makes a sharp bend to the right and soon loses its metalled surface.

Shropshire is left behind here, the route entering Herefordshire.

Downton Castle

This was built between 1772 and 1778 by Richard Payne Knight, a member of the Knight family of Madeley, Shropshire, whose fortunes were made in ironfounding. The estate was landscaped at the same time, again under his instructions. See also the note under Burrington, on page 86. Richard Payne Knight was something of a scholar, anthropologist and archaeologist and a leader of the Picturesque movement in landscaping which rejected the more formal parkland layouts of the likes of Capability Brown in favour of wilder and more natural features. Downton Estate reflects these ideas.

Follow the track as it winds along through the woods, ignoring a grassy track going off down into the trees on the right. On rounding a bend to the left more pipeline valve chambers will be seen on the right-hand side. Ignore a track going off left up into the woods at this point and also a very steep and winding narrow path going off left soon after but remain on the obvious main track, still with the white ringed marker posts.

On reaching a second well house, on the right, the track becomes metalled again and starts to climb, bearing left. As the climb steepens a sharp left bend is followed by one to the right and then an even sharper left bend by one just as sharp right. At a further sharp left bend the track reaches the edge of the forest, (SO452736). ❷

Look right here for the best view yet of Downton Castle. The River Teme runs below and in front of the building, its course marked by the trees seen in the foreground. The woodland below to the left marks the course of Downton gorge.

Well to the left of the castle may be seen the spire of St. Giles church, Downton-on-the-Rock. The old church at Downton was abandoned in 1861 and this replacement building is sited in a field on the Downton Castle estate, at the end of a long vista from the castle. The architect was Samuel Pountney Smith.

Rounding the sharp left bend the track loses its metalled surface. Here ignore a path/track going sharp right up into the woods – the white ringed waymarked forest trail's route – but remain on the main track which straightens, the climb lessening. Ignore another track going off sharply to the right and up and also a path going off down to the left. At a major track Y-junction, (SO456735), take the right-hand track, continuing to climb.

On reaching a group of eight mature pine trees, on the right of the track, ignore a path going off sharp right, (the white ringed route returning), and three paths going off on the left-hand side but remain on the obvious main track which now bends to the right, continuing its steady gradual climb. Eventually it levels out and passes a wooden barrier, designed to prevent vehicular access. ❸

Just before reaching the barrier there are good views to the right. Ahead half right the fire hut on the summit of High Vinnalls – the highest point in Mortimer Forest – can be seen. Continuing to follow the hills along to the right the sails of Leinthall Starkes windmill may be seen across the valley while further along the hills known as the Wigmore Rolls may also be visible on a good day. Wigmore Castle – original stronghold of the powerful Mortimer dynasty – is unlikely to be seen in the summer months, due to its ruinous state and surrounding tree cover, but may be visible in winter. It is situated below and in front of the hills, at the edge of the woodland. The wooded hill behind the windmill at Leinthall Starkes is Gatley Long Coppice.

Immediately after passing the barrier turn sharp right off the forest track and onto another track, (SO465733). Wide and stony, it immediately passes through a farm gate, (may be open), and begins to descend. The forest which has dominated this stage of the walk so far is left behind.

Walking down the track look left to get the same views which were on the right a short time ago when the barrier on the forest track was passed. The windmill at Leinthall Starkes now seems much nearer while to the south the views now extend to include the wooded hills above Aymestrey and the Lugg gorge.

On a clear day Wigmore village, below the castle and the Wigmore Rolls, can be seen. Beyond, to the left of the Wigmore Rolls, is the long wooded Shobdon Hill, while the northern escarpment of the Black Mountains may also be visible. Beyond and to the right of the Wigmore Rolls it may be possible to pick out individual hills in Radnor Forest, such as the conical Whimble, (599 metres/1965 feet), or, to the right of this, a long hill bearing a mast which is Black Mixen, (650 metres/2133 ft). Looking straight ahead the higher hills towards Knighton may be seen. The Elan Valley Way will be among these on Stage 6.

While sampling the views do not ignore the track underfoot. Its stony surface is most interesting as it contains a wide variety of fossils, including corals and primitive squid-like creatures among others – especially on the section just below New House Farm. Unfortunately many of these have been damaged slightly by vehicles using the track so perfect specimens are the exception.

Persistent tapping from trees on the left along here revealed a green woodpecker at work.

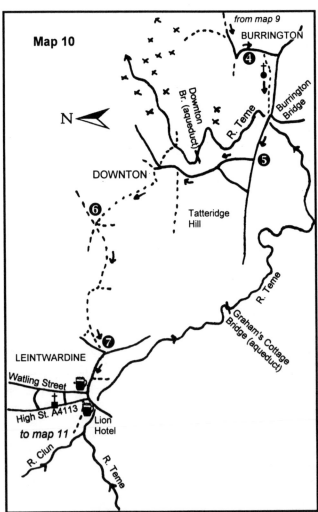

Remain on the track as it descends, passing through another gate. Soon the isolated New House Farm appears ahead, to the left of the track. Just before reaching this there is another farm gate, with a stile to its left. Cross this to continue down the track past the farm.

Passing the farm house, ignore a track going off and up to the right, ('Private'), but continue straight ahead. The track makes a large curve around a depression in the land on the right, that contains a pond, and reaches another farm gate, this time with a small footpath gate alongside on the left. Having passed through this, a metal farm gate soon follows and just afterwards a bungalow and then a house, both on the right-hand of the track, are passed.

The track now begins to climb and at the top of the rise gains a concrete surface. Ignore a footpath that goes off to the right just after this but remain on the track as it descends and bends sharply to the left. The descent steepens and the village of Burrington is soon reached. The half-timbered Burrington Farm, on the right, is the first building passed. **❹**

While walking the road through Burrington look right to see Tatteridge Hill, shaped like an upturned boat and with a line of trees across its top.

On reaching the settlement proceed straight ahead down the road. After a little less than 400 yards on the road take a footpath which goes off right, alongside a house called Church Bank and opposite the School House, and leads – initially up a short track – to the gate of Burrington churchyard. Enter the churchyard and follow the gravelled path around to the left-hand side of the church, through a short avenue of yew trees.

Continue down the road through Burrington beyond the footpath turning to the church to reach a telephone box.

The gravelled path finishes at the church porch. Here go straight on to a stile in the churchyard boundary ahead. Cross this and proceed along a narrow path between a fence on the right and bushes on the left. The path opens out into a rough paddock area, the boundary fence remaining on the right. Follow the fence to reach another stile giving access to a field. Head straight across this to cross another stile into the next field. Again go straight across this field, a pond on the left, to another stile. Cross this to enter a field which has a watery depression along its left boundary. Walk along the edge of this and then bear left to the far left-hand corner of the field to cross a stile by a metal farm gate. This leads onto a road at a junction, another road joining opposite, (SO436721).

While walking these fields look ahead right to see Tatteridge Hill and behind for a good distant view of Burrington church.

Turn right along the road, which immediately crosses the River Teme via Burrington Bridge, and remain on it as it starts to climb. At the first road junction turn right, signposted Downton. **❺**

The road junction is by a large oak tree. Opposite the junction is a farm gate. Look over this, slightly left, to see the windmill at Leinthall Starkes and, half-right, the village of Wigmore with the hills of the Wigmore Rolls behind. It may be possible to pick out Wigmore Castle, former stronghold of the Mortimers, above the village. Standing at the junction itself look right for a final view of Burrington church, already well in the distance.

After the turn Tatteridge Hill becomes very prominent on the left while to the right, on a clear day, the wooded hills of Mortimer Forest can be seen, the fire hut on High Vinnalls still visible. Look high on the slope of Tatteridge Hill to see one of the aqueduct's pipeline valve chambers.

Proceed along what is a very quiet road, as evidenced by the growth of grass and moss along its centre. It climbs gently and bends towards Tatteridge Hill. At a junction, where another road comes in from the left, go

Cast iron grave slabs at Burrington Church

Burrington

The settlement of Burrington dates back beyond Domesday Book (1086), when it was known as Boritune, to Saxon times. Its name means 'farmstead by a fortified place'. At the time of the Norman Conquest the manor was held by the Herefordshire nobleman known as Edric the Wild, the source of many legends and an opponent of William the Conqueror during the English uprising of 1069.

Burrington Church – St. George's – was largely rebuilt in 1864 and has a timber spire. Little is known of the earlier building on the site but a rough drawing of 1842 suggests it was a much lower structure than its replacement. The current building is the work of two architects – Samuel Pountney Smith and G. F. Bodley. Pountney Smith worked on the nave, Bodley the chancel. This unusual job-sharing arrangement was the result of a disagreement between the local landowner, Mr. A. Broughton-Knight of Downton

Castle, who was meeting the cost of the nave and the Vicar (Philip Hale) who was responsible for the chancel. Fortunately that difference of opinion has not affected the finished product, the church being very simple in style and decoration – more typical of a thirteenth century building than the Victorian construction it actually is.

Burrington church is famous for something other than the actual building however. Outside, at the east end of the church lie a series of cast-iron grave slabs (covers) dating from the early seventeenth century. These would have originally been inside the old church – the chancel of which was longer than the present building – and if not unique are certainly the finest collection in the country. There are eight slabs, all cast at Bringewood forge, and they commemorate members of the local ironfounding families, such as the Walkers and the Knights.

Bringewood, on the River Teme near Downton gorge, became an ironfounding centre in about 1600,

Kinnenley, too !

using locally produced charcoal and iron ore and limestone from the Clee Hills, (brought in by packhorse). Job Walker purchased the lease of the works in 1690, having previously worked it for the earls of Essex and Craven. The Walkers sold out in 1727 to Thomas Knight, who also owned furnaces at Wolverley, (see note on Wolverley at Stage 2), and Madeley, Shropshire – where the Knight family originated. The Knights built up a large holdings of land in the area, various members of the family buying the manors of Lucton (in 1707), Leintwardine (in 1720), Burrington (in 1721), Leinthall Starkes (in 1721), and Downton (in 1727; the Walkers had bought it in 1716).

Ironfounding ceased at Bringewood in the late eighteenth century, the area being overtaken by developing Coalbrookdale, and the Downton Castle estate was then landscaped by Richard Payne Knight.

straight on. The road now begins to descend gently and starts a long bend to the right.

At SO427728 a small Severn Trent building, on the left-hand side of the road, is passed – with access gates to a path leading up to the valve chamber on Tatteridge Hill. Opposite, on the right of the road, is a wooden stile. Look over this for a view of the pipeline crossing the River Teme via Downton Bridge. The river cannot be seen but the line of the aqueduct over the hills beyond it is unmistakable.

Finishing its long bend to the right, the road bears left and begins to climb. Passing through a short cutting the first houses of Downton on the Rock are met. Ignore a footpath going off to the left here.

When walking this section, as we passed the name-sign for Downton a small vole ran along the road ahead of us for some considerable distance before finally diving for cover.

As Old Downton Farm with its high walls, on the left, is reached there is a road junction of sorts, (SO427734) – to the right a track leads down to Bow Bridge over the River Teme, the 'main' road bears right, and another metalled road goes left, (or almost straight on). Take the latter of these options, following the high walls of the farm to pass through a gate (probably open) with a stile alongside it. Almost immediately, at a parting of ways marked by a footpath sign, turn left onto a partially metalled track which climbs, the metalling ceasing as it bends to the right.

At the bend, and about 40 yards past the farm buildings on the left, head left off the track towards two metal farm gates. Do not pass through either but instead take a sunken track which goes off to the right through another metal gate. (This sunken track initially runs to the left of and parallel to the track just vacated.)

Proceed up the sunken track – which can be very overgrown in late summer – to reach, after about 40 yards, the bottom left-hand corner of a field. Climb up into this and head half right across it to a stile in its right-hand boundary, an avenue of trees beyond. Cross the stile and turn left to proceed up a slightly sunken grassy track between the trees.

While climbing the field to the stile look right to see the spire of Downton church, (St. Giles), rising above trees.

Climbing the track, glorious views open up. Behind, on a good day, the hills of Mortimer Forest can be seen – with the high points of both the main ridges in view and the fire hut on High Vinnalls still recognisable. Again behind, and to the left, Clee Hills may be visible with the eastern and northern parts of Ludlow peeping out from behind the Mortimer Forest in front of them.

A brown hare was disturbed near the top of the avenue of trees while a second was seen during the descent to Leintwardine.

Continue to climb the grassy track between the trees. Towards the top the trees thin out – no longer a complete avenue although replanting is taking place. On reaching the top of the avenue the track begins to descend, very slightly, towards a 'double' wooden gate ahead. Pass through this to reach a three-way junction of stony tracks, (SO420739).

Take the middle track option – straight ahead from the gate. It immediately bears left. ❻

Before starting to descend on this track look straight ahead to see the village of Leintwardine nestling in the valley below. The wide valley of the River Teme stretches out beyond the village. The hills beyond this are Bucknell Hill and its neighbours, leading towards Knighton and Wales, with the lower Coxall Knoll in the foreground. The route is at a height of 230 metres/755 feet here.

Walk down the stony track and through a gate, which may be open. A ramshackle farm building, on the right, is passed as the track continues to descend and bears to the right, becoming more grassy.

The Wigmore Rolls are now visible on the left while ahead Coxall Knoll becomes more distinct from the higher hills behind it. It has a hill fort at its summit.

Follow the now grassy track as it descends, heading directly towards Coxall Knoll. It swings suddenly right and then left to enter a field and follow its left-hand boundary, public footpath signs pointing the way.

Below, half left, the River Teme can be seen making some large loops in its valley. This section of it is often called Leintwardine Fishery.

Follow the left-hand boundary down the field. On reaching a stile at the bottom cross it into another field and bear half right across this. The grassy track/path drops down through a obvious gully – heading directly towards Leintwardine church below – curving round to the left of a large ash tree as it descends. Becoming slightly wider and sunken it bears sharp right to head down the steepest part of the hill, (Church Hill). Where the track starts to bend diagonally down towards the bottom right-hand corner of the field leave it and follow the left-hand boundary of the field down to cross a stile in the bottom left-hand corner and emerge onto a road. ❼

Turn left and then immediately right – signposted Leintwardine – and walk along the road into the village. Ignore a footpath going off left just after the Recycling Centre but continue past the Sun Inn and a fish and chip shop, (the Fiddler's Elbow), which are both on the right of the road, (Rosemary Lane). Ignore a road on the right, (Watling Street), and on reaching a T-junction cross over the road to the Lion Hotel, where this stage of the Elan Valley Way ends.

Leintwardine

Leintwardine represents that most unusual of settlements, a Saxon village built on the exact site of a Roman garrison town. The Saxons were a superstitious people and generally regarded it as unlucky to build over previous remains. In this instance however the importance of the site, on high ground above the confluence of the Teme and Clun, appears to have outweighed their fears.

The Roman fort and settlement here – known as Bravonium – was established around AD160 at the point where the Roman road of Watling Street crossed the Teme. The settlement was rectangular in layout and surrounded by a wall and ditch. Watling Street ran to the immediate east of the wall. There were baths on a site by the Teme, passed early on Stage 6 of the Elan Valley Way. The present main street, High Street, runs north-south through the middle of the site.

The Saxon king Edward the Confessor owned the 'Hundred' of Leintwardine which extended into more modern Shropshire, Herefordshire and Radnorshire and contained forty-nine manors at that time.

By the time of Domesday Book (1086) the manor of Leintwardine was under the control of the powerful Mortimers of Wigmore Castle, one of some 130 manors given to Ranulph (Ralph) de Mortimer by William the Conqueror in return for his support.

The village is dominated by the church of St. Mary Magdalene which stands just inside the original eastern Roman wall. Built on Saxon and Norman foundations the current building is of mainly thirteenth and fourteenth century origin with 1865 rebuilding. The oldest visible part is a blocked doorway in the west wall of the nave which is twelfth century. The church is mentioned in Domesday Book.

The tower of the church is thirteenth century and was built as much for defence as any other reason – with walls up to six feet thick. It is 76 feet in height and there is a spiral staircase of 103 steps to the top.

Inside the entrance porch is a peculiar iron grille which looks as if it might have been used as some form of punishment but in fact is to prevent anyone from standing under the weights of the church clock and meeting with an accident.

The old clock of the church may be seen preserved inside – made of wrought iron and brass and with two crude stone weights it worked only one hand on a slate dial which is now hidden under the stucco and later dial on the tower outside. It is one of the oldest of such mechanisms in the country, dating back to at least the early sixteenth century.

Also in the church is an octagonal fourteenth century font on a more modern base.

Standing at the steps leading from the nave to the chancel look at the base of the arches left and right to see carved heads of King Edward III and a lady, possibly his wife Philippa. In 1328 Roger de Mortimer set aside the income from some of his lands to pay for nine chaplains to say mass daily, in the church, for the souls of himself, his wife Countess Joan, his mistress Isabella, (known as the She Wolf of France because of her numerous political intrigues – such as with Roger against her own husband Edward II), Isabella's son Edward III, and his wife Philippa.

In 1181 Hugh de Mortimer had given the church to the abbey he had founded at Wigmore. At the time of the Dissolution (1536) the carved wooden misericords, choir stalls and benches of the Abbey, dating from the fifteenth century, were brought to the church where they can still be seen. The misericords are very similar to those in St. Laurence's Church in Ludlow but the Leintwardine examples have suffered far more damage.

The unusually great difference in floor levels between the nave and chancel is down to the church being built upon the old Roman embankment. Roman bricks and tiles have been discovered below the floor of the building.

The name 'Leintwardine' means the 'enclosure on the River Lent'. The Lent was the old name for the River Clun.

The modern village of Leintwardine has a fish & chip shop, (The Fiddler's Elbow – passed in Rosemary Lane on the way into the village), a post office cum store, a petrol station with shop, a general store, (on Watling Street), a butcher, and a very small HSBC bank branch with limited opening hours.

There are three public houses. There is the Lion Hotel by the bridge over the Teme and at the far north of the village, (well off the route of the Elan Valley Way), is the Cottager's Comfort – still known as 'the Poker' or 'the Poker and Hole'

by some of the village's older residents. Then, on Rosemary Lane, there is the Sun Inn!

When we were last here the Sun Inn might well have been claimed as being the most unspoilt and traditional pub in the country. With no 'bar' but just a brick tiled room with a few benches and tables, no bar meals, music, games or machines, and with 'real ale' straight from the barrel this establishment is a real throwback to a mellower bygone age. The obvious question has to be asked as to how long it will be until someone thinks of 'improving' it or, even worse, it closes, but for the time being it remains a gem.

We spent a wonderful few hours talking to the landlady and a few of the elder statesmen of Leintwardine. One old gentleman could remember the laying of the third pipeline of the Elan Valley aqueduct in the 1930s and recalled a fatal accident when a worker fell into the pipeline trench. He had also been in the local Home Guard during the Second World War and had been detailed to guard the aqueduct's two local crossings of the Teme – Downton Bridge and Graham's Cottage Bridge – against enemy action.

We left the Sun Inn a lot wiser and happier than when we entered and found that the cloudy night we had left outside earlier had now cleared to reveal literally millions of stars above, with the familiar 'plough' group right over our accommodation. A magic moment in an evening of the same.

Stage 6

Leintwardine to Knighton

Distance: 12 miles (Bucknell station 3 miles)
Maps: Landranger 148; Pathfinder 951, 950; Explorer 203, 201.

Leaving Leintwardine the route crosses the River Clun and makes its way, via fieldpaths and tracks, towards Coxall Knoll. It then turns south, on quiet roads, to cross the River Teme and enter the village of Brampton Bryan. A climb up through Brampton Bryan Park to Pedwardine Wood follows, using paths and forest tracks. Next a sunken track is climbed to Stanage Park where the route turns north to cross the estate and regain the Teme Valley.

The River Teme is crossed for a second time on the stage as a section of road walking climbs to Stowe Church. Finally fieldpaths and forest tracks are used to descend to Knighton, the Teme being crossed for a third time as the town is entered.

The Elan Valley aqueduct is not much in evidence on this stage of the walk. It has made its own final crossing of the Teme at Graham's Cottage Bridge, to the south-east of Leintwardine, and so is well to the south of the walk in the early miles. It is crossed at Brampton Bryan but no evidence is seen on the ground. The walk then loops well to the south of it until, having crossed Stanage Park and reached the A4113 road, one of the familiar valve chambers is spotted. As the A4113 is crossed before the climb to Stowe Church a small stream crossing is seen – in someone's garden – but this is its final appearance of the day and it is not crossed again.

STARTING outside the Lion Hotel, facing the road, turn left up High Street. After a few yards turn left into Mill Lane – between the Post Office and the Petrol Station. Follow the lane and where it swings right, into the grounds of Seedley House, go straight ahead and onto an unmetalled track.

Just after entering Mill Lane the premises of Teme Valley Travel will be seen to the left. Underneath here was the site of the Roman Baths, (see note on Leintwardine at Stage 5).

The river alongside to the left as the track is walked is the Clun. The confluence of Teme and Clun may be seen by looking across and beyond the garden of the house called 'Troutbeck', on the left-hand side of Mill Lane.

Following the track, pass through a metal gate, the River Clun now much closer on the left. On reaching another metal gate, leading into a field, do not pass through it but instead turn left to a footbridge over the Clun, (SO400741).

Having crossed the river pass through the small wooden gate, on the right, and immediately turn left, (that is away from the riverbank), to cross a stile into a field. Head straight across this field to cross a stream via a footbridge, and so enter another field. Here turn right to cross a depression – possibly containing water – and to walk alongside another depression, (on the left of the footpath), which again may contain water after wet weather. Follow this across the field – half right from the point where the field was entered over the footbridge – to a stile in the far boundary. Cross the stile and two others which follow immediately.

Head straight across the field now entered to a stile in the far boundary. This is situated just to the right of a group of wooden buildings which can

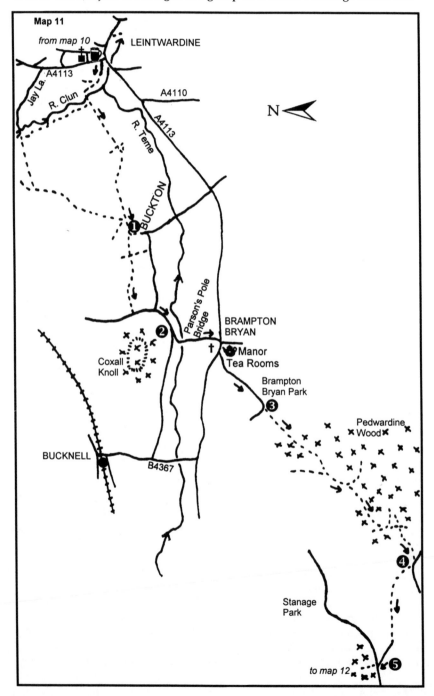

be seen ahead. Cross this stile to enter an orchard area and proceed in the same direction, the wooden buildings on the left, to cross a further stile which gives access to a track. Turn left along this and then immediately, (within 5 yards), right along another dirt track. In about 40 yards this reaches a T-junction with another track. Turn right to walk along this.

The hills to the left as these early fields are crossed are the Wigmore Rolls.

Just before entering the orchard area look behind for good views of Church Hill, behind Leintwardine, and Tatteridge Hill which were familiar on Stage 5 of the walk. On reaching the first track look ahead to see Coxall Knoll. The hills to the right of it are those behind Bucknell, such as Bucknell Hill and Hopton Titterhill. The hills to the left of Coxall Knoll are those above Brampton Bryan which will be climbed later on this stage. The Wigmore Rolls are now on the extreme left.

The track makes a sweeping bend to the left to head directly towards Coxall Knoll. Ignore a track going off right and a footpath going half right at the same junction, (SO386735), but go straight ahead on the wide track which now has a metalled surface. ❶

Where the track bends sharply left, (SO384735), take a footpath which goes straight ahead through a metal gate on the right-hand side of the track to enter a field. Follow the left-hand boundary of this to pass through another gate onto a track. Turn left and then immediately right to cross the track and pass through a metal gate into another field. Here again follow the left-hand boundary. Coxall Knoll remains directly ahead.

Coxall Knoll has an Iron Age hill fort at its summit. It has often been claimed to be the site of the last stand of the ancient British leader Caractacus against the Roman legions under Scapula in AD51 but this is now considered unlikely for no other reason than the fort here is not of any significant size.

On reaching a metal gate giving access to the bottom left-hand corner of a field pass through it and proceed half right up the field towards a gap in the boundary opposite. Pass through this and follow a boundary hedge which approaches, at a right-angle to, but does not meet the boundary just crossed. Keep this hedge on the immediate right as it is followed and where it turns away right continue half right across the field, towards a metal gate in the far right corner. Coxall Knoll is directly ahead while crossing the field. Pass through the metal gate onto a quiet road and turn left. Follow the road until a T-junction is reached and then turn right.

Walking this road, the River Teme will soon be seen down to the left. At a road junction go left. ❷

A right turn here and again at the next junction, onto the B4367, leads to Bucknell railway station on the Heart of Wales line – about a mile distant.

Shropshire Link bus services on the Ludlow-Leintwardine-Knighton routes also call at the station.

Remain on the road which bends sharply left to cross the Teme at Parson's Pole Bridge and eventually reaches the village of Brampton Bryan. Proceeding through the village the grounds of the Hall, which contain all that remains of the old castle, and then the small church of St. Barnabas, both on the right of the road, are passed. The A4113 is reached at a crossroads.

Brampton Bryan

There has been a settlement at Brampton Bryan since Saxon times. Domesday Book (1086) has the village as "Brantune" and records that it had previously been held by one Gunwar. By 1086 the manor was held by "Richard" for its owner Ralph (Ranulph) de Mortimer in return for guard services at Wigmore Castle, main seat of the Mortimers.

The grandson of 'Richard' was Brian Unspach who seems to have taken the village name as his surname at some point. His son became Brian de Brampton I. The connection with the Mortimers of Wigmore Castle continued with Brian de Brampton I laying the second foundation stone of Wigmore Abbey after Hugh de Mortimer, its founder, had laid the first, in 1179. It would appear that at some point the Bramptons either bought or were given the manor of Brampton Bryan by the Mortimers.

It was likely the Bramptons who built the first stone castle here, although there had probably been a wooden one on the site since about 1070.

In 1294 the male line of the Bramptons died out. A surviving daughter, Margaret, eventually married Sir Robert de Harley and so began the Harley ownership of the manor and village which continues to this day.

There have been many notable members of the family, some of whom have found their fame in London – Harley Street is named after the family. The most notable event in the village itself however happened during the Civil War when Lady Brilliana Harley held the castle, for the Parliamentarian cause, during a siege by the Royalists which lasted from 26th July to 9th September 1643. Sir Robert Harley,

Lady Brilliana's husband, was away fighting for the Parliamentarian cause elsewhere and her letters to him during this period survive and give a vivid insight to the conditions of the day. The Royalists destroyed the church, mill and twenty cottages during the siege – the entire village in fact. The siege was lifted when the Royalist force was called to march to Newbury in preparation for the coming battle there. Sadly Lady Brilliana died soon afterwards.

In 1644, with Lady Brilliana dead and Sir Robert still away, the Royalists again besieged the castle which surrendered on 17th April. Sixty-seven prisoners were taken, including the three youngest Harley children – all girls – who were imprisoned at Shrewsbury and only released when Parliamentarian forces took that town in 1645.

The castle was burned down – although there is some doubt as to whether it was the Royalists who did this after the second siege or the Parliamentarians later, when Sir Robert Harley fell out of favour with the leadership for opposing the execution of Charles I.

It was Sir Robert who oversaw the rebuilding of the church in 1656. This rebuilding cost £1200 and excluded the tower which was too ruined. The nave as rebuilt, and seen today, is of a great width. This was to enable the roof of the old castle banqueting hall, which had escaped fire damage, to be incorporated. The church was one of only six to be built in England during the Commonwealth.

The original church at Brampton was founded in 1240. What today's visitor sees is essentially the 1656 rebuilding with some 1888 restoration.

Perhaps the most interesting feature inside the church – St. Barnabas – is a surviving fourteenth century recess in the south wall which contains the effigy of a lady – possibly Lady Margaret de Brampton, who married Sir Robert Harley in 1309 after the male line of the de Bramptons died out. She is represented holding her heart in her hands.

The castle was rebuilt as a mansion in 1661, under Sir Edward Harley. The ruins of the old castle survive in its gardens.

Modern Brampton Bryan is little larger than the village destroyed in 1643.

There is a Post Office/Store and the Manor Tea Rooms in the village. A telephone box is situated on the A4113 on the left as the crossroads in the village is reached on the walk. There is a bus stop adjacent to it but the bus service is too limited to be of any use on this walk.

One feature of the village which immediately attracts the eye is the massive yew hedge around the grounds of the Hall – seen at its best near the church and opposite the Manor Tea Rooms. This is obviously of some considerable age and must present a mammoth task for those who have to trim it. It was being trimmed when we first walked this stage of the Elan Valley Way in September 1998.

On the pavement across the A4113 from the village green is another of the tap/pumps featuring a lion's head and similar to that seen on Stage 4 of the Elan Valley Way, at Knowbury. This particular example features a bell-shaped 'cup' attached to its handle but unfortunately was not in working order in May 1999.

The Elan Valley aqueduct is crossed as the route approaches Brampton Bryan Park but the crossing is not noticed. There is however one aqueduct related feature in the village that the walker will notice and, perhaps, regret – or rather the lack of a feature! Brampton Bryan has no pub! There was a pub here when the aqueduct was being built but two of the navvies employed on the undertaking chose to have a fight to the death there one day. The Harley family of the day closed the pub and vowed that there would never be another in the village.

Cross the A4113 and turn right along it. On reaching a small green with a chestnut tree at its centre, just past the Post Office/Store and the Manor Tea Rooms, bear left off the A4113 and along a metalled road which is marked as a Private Road/Bridleway.

Follow the road as it bends to the left and passes through a gate by a cattle grid. It proceeds up an avenue of trees to reach a farm settlement and passes through another gate, again with a cattle grid alongside, to enter Brampton Bryan Park. It next makes a sweeping right bend. ❸

At the start of a sharp right bend round to a wooden gate and cattle grid – the entrance to a private drive – (SO363718), leave the road to continue ahead, now climbing slightly. Aim to walk alongside and about 20 yards to the right of a row of large trees – an arrow painted in white on a small boulder at the top of the row will confirm the way. Passing this the path starts to climb steeply towards a coniferous plantation. On reaching the boundary fence to this follow the path around to the left to pass round the corner of it. A white arrow on a post points the way here.

*Stop and look behind here for glorious views over Brampton Bryan Park itself
and also of Coxall Knoll and the hills beyond it. On a very clear day the tower of
Leintwardine church may be seen to the right.*

Follow the path up and along the boundary of the coniferous plantation,
which is now on the right. The climb remains steep. The path continues
straight ahead, as the boundary to the plantation bends slightly away to the
right, entering open woodland and reaching a small gate. Pass through this
and continue climbing straight ahead. The path bends slightly to the right
to enter a more open area – dense bracken in season – the climb continuing
unabated as another boulder bearing a white painted arrow is passed.

*Views behind and to the right over to Mortimer Forest are now superb, on a good
day, while ahead and right the hills from Bucknell to Knighton are now visible –
Bucknell Hill, Stow Hill, etc. This area near the top of the climb is covered with
bilberries in season.*

The route attains a height of around 305 metres/1000 feet at the top of this climb.

Soon the path levels out and reaches a T-junction with a track,
(SO355713). Turn left along this. One of the white painted boulders marks
the junction.

Continue along the track for about 150 yards until reaching a junction –
with one track bending sharply around to the left and the other going
straight on. Take the latter – this time indicated by white arrows on a post.
The track initially runs between a field boundary, (wire fence), on the right
and woodland on the left.

*Turn here to look behind over the Teme valley. The outskirts of the village of
Bucknell are visible, slightly to the right, and the settlement of Heartsease, down to
the left. The large wooded hill is Bucknell Wood, the hill to the right of that with
fields part of the way up and woodland at the top is Bucknell Hill.*

*The route is now entering Pedwardine Wood. There now follows a superb
section of track with glorious views to the right and woodland to the left.*

Follow the track as it passes into thicker woods and meanders on. At a
T-junction of tracks turn left – a white arrow on a post pointed the way in
September 1998 but was missing by May 1999. Within 10 yards another
junction is met, with one track bending sharp left and the other initially
going right but then bending left and descending. Take the latter – as
indicated by a white arrow on a tree. The descent steepens, the track
narrowing and becoming more grassy. After about 200 yards on this track,
as it bends to the left, at a 'crossroads' of tracks turn right – more white
arrows here but this can still be a difficult junction to spot – onto another
track, (SO348704).

In just over 100 yards the track reaches a gate giving access from the
woods into a field. Go through this and follow a sunken path along the
left-hand field boundary, now descending. At the bottom of the field pass
through a metal gate and straight ahead down a slope. The path widens to
track width at the gate and, descending, passes a small quarry area, on the
right. On reaching the bottom it meets a farm drive. Turn left along this and
through a metal gate onto a quiet road. Turn right along the road. ❹

After about only 20 yards on the road turn right through a metal gate and
up a sunken track, (SO343701). It immediately climbs and bends left, and is

waymarked with red arrows. Where the track bears left to enter a field turn right through a metal gate to proceed up a very narrow and sunken path between two hedgerow boundaries – a route of some age. This path can be quite overgrown in late summer and muddy after wet weather. It climbs steadily and, bearing slightly left, passes through a metal gate.

Look behind here, where the boundaries of this very sunken path allow, for views back to Pedwardine Wood and the route recently walked.

Continue climbing the sunken path – in its upper stages it may be so overgrown as to make a diversion up to the neighbouring field on the right necessary. The buildings of Hill House Farm soon appear ahead. The path emerges onto a track which runs between two bungalows at the farm. Passing through a metal farm gate to reach a metalled section of track, by the entrance drives to the two bungalows, follow it between the large farm buildings, initially bearing slightly left. The old farm house is directly ahead and the metalled track/farm drive bends round to the right of it. Remain on it as it starts to climb.

About 100 yards after the farm house England (Herefordshire) is left behind and Wales (Powys) entered for the first time.

As the top of the climb is passed the farm drive drops slightly to a T-junction with a road. There are actually two separate arms of the farm drive as it meets the road – a triangular area of grass, a pine tree at its centre, between them. Aim directly between the two arms to cross the road and enter the woodland opposite through a gap in the trees. ❺

Drop down through the trees on an indistinct path which bears very slightly right. At the bottom of the wood bear right to where a metal gate gives access to a field. Head half left down the field to gates which can be seen in the bottom left-hand corner.

The prominent hill directly ahead as the field is descended is Stow Hill. The large building now coming into view below on the right is Stanage Park which was used for some scenes in the TV. serial Blott on the Landscape.

On reaching the gates pass through the one in the boundary ahead, (not the one on the left). Turn half right on entering the next field, heading towards the right-hand corner of an area of woodland, ahead left. There is a stile in the bottom boundary of the field, situated to the right of the corner of the trees. Cross this and bear half right to round the near left-hand corner of some substantial pheasant pens. Then drop left down into a rough meadow area to cross a couple of small streams. Maintaining the same direction, climb up the other side of this area to join a grassy track, turning right along it for some yards to pass through a wooden gate which has a black building, of corrugated iron and wood, beyond it, (SO331714).

Now on a stony track, pass to the left of the black building. The track bends round to the right to approach a substantial stone and brick bridge over a stream. Just before reaching this turn sharp left off it, through a wooden gate, and then bear very slightly right, rising along the left edge of a long grouping of deciduous trees.

Stanage Park house is across a small lake on the right here, the closest the route comes to it.

A traditional mole catcher had obviously been at work in the weeks preceding my walk along here in May 1999. Thirty-nine of the 'little gentlemen in velvet' were hanging from the fence alongside the track. The resulting aroma is best left to the imagination!

Keeping the main group of deciduous trees to the right continue straight ahead. A coniferous plantation soon appears on the right, beyond the deciduous trees. Aim to keep a constant distance from its boundary fence. Pass through a wooden gate, which may be open, a wooded hill visible ahead – The Knoll. The path bends very slightly left as it proceeds, the distance to the boundary of the coniferous plantation remaining constant however, until on passing its far corner it is left behind. As a very small

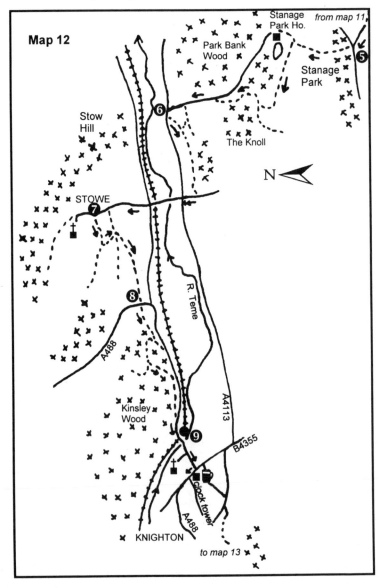

stream, in a slight dip, is crossed – this may be dry depending on the time of year and the weather – bear right to head for a track which can be seen rounding the corner of The Knoll. As a navigation guide, aim for the right-hand corner of the woodland on The Knoll and just to the left of a mast which can be seen above the trees in the wood opposite The Knoll, (Park Bank Wood on O.S. Explorer Map 201). The course of the 'seasonal' stream is alongside initially, while later on the boundary of the coniferous plantation in followed.

Stow Hill has loomed large to the right all the way along this section through Stanage Park. The route now turns to head straight for it.

On reaching the metalled track, just below the corner of The Knoll, turn right to walk along it. It makes a sweeping curve to the left and descends over a cattle grid to a T-junction with the main drive to Stanage Park. Turn left onto this, passing along an avenue of large trees to reach a gatehouse and the A4113 road. ❻

Turn left along the busy road. After about 50 yards on it turn left through a metal gate and into a field.

On passing through the gate look right to see one of the familiar valve chambers for the aqueduct.

Entering the field go straight across it to the boundary opposite and turn right to follow this. On reaching a gate by a pond, on the left, do not pass through it but continue to follow the boundary to the corner of the field. Here pass through a metal gate to enter another very large field. There are several poles in this, carrying overhead wires. Head directly towards the first of these seen as the field is entered, and gradually towards woodland at its left (top) boundary. On reaching that boundary follow it along.

Entering the very large field look half right to see the isolated little church of St. Michael and All Angels, Stowe, high on the slopes of Stow Hill. The climb up the road to it is the last climb of this stage of the walk.

Keeping the boundary with the woodland close on the left continue across the large field. At its far boundary pass through a wooden gate into another field. Bear half right to drop down to its far right-hand corner and on reaching this pass through a wooden gate – it may be necessary to unhitch an electric fence in front of this gate but plastic insulated grips are provided. Entering the next field head directly across it towards a wooden barn, the left of three barns ahead, and to the right of a house. Pass through a gate which is in the field boundary on the left of the barn – actually used for stabling – and turn left down a short track and onto a quiet road, (SO313724).

Turn right along the road. It immediately descends fairly steeply and soon reaches the A4113 near a telephone box.

Just before reaching the A4113 look left over a garden gate. Some people claim to have fairies at the bottom of their garden; the folk who live here have the Elan Valley aqueduct crossing a minor stream via a not so minor bridge. Do they pay water charges I wonder? On the other side of the minor road here, over one of the now familiar access stiles, lies a pipeline valve chamber.

Cross straight over the A4113 and proceed down the minor road opposite, signposted Stowe ½ Mile. The road soon crosses the River Teme and, shortly afterwards, the Heart of Wales Railway Line, heading directly towards Stow Hill.

Reaching the far side of the river the route leaves Wales (Powys) to re-enter England (Shropshire this time).

On reaching a crossroads go straight across, signposted Stowe, Stowe Church. The church can be seen ahead. A steady climb begins with a stream now running alongside the road on the right-hand side. The road begins to bear left as the settlement of Stowe is approached, passing Stowe Farm.

As the road bends sharply right and increases its rate of climb (by the entrance to the drive of the Old Vicarage), take a track going off to the left, (SO311736). ❼

Stowe

The village here was formerly of greater importance than its size today would suggest as it stood on the meeting place of one of the main Drovers' Roads from Wales into England and the old main road from Knighton to Bucknell. There is some evidence of deserted dwellings just below the church.

Stowe Church is a beautiful little stone building with a small wooden tower. It stands in a fold of the hills at a height of 225 metres/738 feet, below Stow Hill, and has magnificent views of the Teme Valley below. Powys Observatory, on its hilltop site, is directly opposite across the valley.

The church of St. Michael and All Angels is medieval in origin but the churchyard in which it stands is of an oval shape which suggests a sacred site of much earlier date. Limited restoration took place in Victorian times. Inside the timber roof is most impressive and indicative of the age of the building.

On the wall just inside the church door is a list of incumbents as far back as 1308.

In September 1998 some £35,000 was required for restoration work on the building – a tall order as only twenty-seven people live here.

To visit the church continue up the road which, as it bends right, increases its rate of climb significantly. Fortunately the climb is swiftly over, the church being less than 150 yards away.

The stony track immediately passes through a wooden gate, (which may be open), descending slightly as it does so, initially bending left but then bearing right. It crosses a small stream, in a culvert, and starts to climb gently, crossing a cattle grid and the stream once more. Remain on the track until some cottages, on the right, are reached and then turn very sharply left – through almost 180 degrees – to ford the stream and climb up to the top left-hand corner of the field where a fence is crossed, this giving access to a stony track at the top of the adjacent field.

(Note: At the time of writing there was no stile over the fence at the top corner of the field but the barbed wire could just about be stepped over. The blockage has been reported to Shropshire County Council for appropriate action. Until this is resolved an alternative route would be to proceed as above until the cattle grid is reached but then instead of crossing it turn left off the track and up through a metal farm gate to climb up the right-hand boundary of the field so entered. As the top of the field is reached the stony track is met and the route as above rejoined.)

Cross the stony track and pass through a metal gate opposite into a field, (SO309735).

Look behind here for a good view of Stowe Church and vicarage. Passing through the gate Knighton appears for the first time, ahead to the right. The large wooded hill to its right is Kinsley Wood.

On entering the field bear left to reach its left-hand boundary and follow this down it, heading directly towards Knighton. Pass through a metal gate to enter another field and again follow the left-hand boundary. Continue to do so through a further field, which is again entered via a gate. On passing through yet another metal gate to enter the next field follow the right-hand boundary. A road and the railway line appear below – about 150 yards away on the left – and the steady descent continues. Follow the right-hand boundary of the field down to the corner where a metal gate leads onto a road – the A488. ❽

Go slightly left across the road to cross a stile into a field. Bear half left to cross a sturdy footbridge over a small stream. Continue in roughly the same direction gradually approaching the left-hand boundary of the field and road beyond. Keep that boundary about 20 yards distant as the latter stages of the field are crossed. Cross a stile – situated about 20 yards in from the far left-hand corner of the field – and climb a short flight of wooden steps beyond to enter Kinsley Wood.

The steps emerge onto a broad forest track. Turn right and follow the stony track as it climbs and immediately swings sharp left. As a sharp right bend commences take a narrower track which goes down to the left off the main track. It initially descends but then levels out. Ignore a track going off sharp left but continue ahead, the track now running alongside a road which is about 40 feet below it on the left. After a while the track begins to lose height rapidly in preparation for meeting the road.

On reaching the road, (A488), turn right along it, the Heart of Wales Railway line, (and Knighton Station), alongside on the left. Turn left to cross a bridge over the railway. ❾

Crossing the railway Wales (Powys) is entered again and England (Shropshire) left behind, this time for good as far as this walk is concerned.

The road crosses the River Teme and bears right into Knighton. Follow the obvious main road through the town, ignoring any side streets – such as Church Road to the right, up which St. Edward's church can be seen. The 'main' road begins as Station Road and continues as Wylcwm Place, but remains the A488 throughout, eventually reaching a T-junction with Broad Street. Turn right here and walk up to the clock tower where this stage of the Elan Valley Way ends.

Knighton

The name literally means 'the town/settlement of the knights'. However its Welsh name, Tref-y-Clawdd, is more significant meaning 'The Town on the Dyke' which emphasises the importance of its position astride that fortification built under King Offa of Mercia around AD780. The crossing point on the River Teme here must have also contributed to the early growth of the settlement while in more recent times the arrival of the railway, in the 1860s, brought a degree of prosperity. Latterly the town has seen a growth in tourism due in no small part to its central position on the Offa's Dyke National Trail. The Offa's Dyke Centre is situated in the town.

The town was given the name of Tref-y-Clawdd in about AD840 by the Welsh king Rhodri Mawr, (Roderick the Great). It is in the Domesday Book (1086) that it is called Chenistetone – the town of the retainers or armed freemen, (later knights). After that it was variously referred to as Chnicheton, Kenithtun or Knyteton – by Saxon, Welshman or Norman.

The middle of the town – Broad Street – is marked by a fine clock tower of 1872, quite a common feature in Welsh towns. Off Broad Street by the clock tower is High Street, also known as the Narrows, which dates from Tudor times but today contains buildings mainly from the seventeenth century. One side of this street was called the 'Salutation Inn', the houses being dovetailed into each other suggesting they were once part of a single building.

Set back from the street where the Narrows joins Broad Street is the Old House. Its seventeenth century half-timbered front hides a medieval cruck built structure – formerly an open hall. Smoke-blackened roof timbers herein indicate the earlier existence of an open fire on a central hearth with no chimney but just a smoke hole in the roof above.

The other significant building in the town is the Church of St. Edward – situated in Church Road and seen to the right as the Elan Valley Way enters the town. There was previously an eleventh century church on this site, itself replacing an older building, but this was largely demolished in 1756 and all that now remains of it is the lower tower. The new church of 1756 has itself been replaced by the current Victorian building although the top of the tower is a survivor from it. The Victorian building was built in two stages – the nave in 1876 and the chancel 20 years later.

The dedication of the present church is to Edward the Confessor. If it seems unusual for a Welsh church to be dedicated to an English king/saint then it must be remembered that until the establishment of the Church of Wales, in the 1920s, Knighton was in the diocese of Hereford.

It is interesting to note that some medieval documents describe the church at Knighton as being merely a chapel of ease for the more important church at Stowe – visited earlier – more evidence of the former size and importance of the village of Stowe and the obvious reversal in fortunes of it and Knighton since.

When the eighteenth century church was taken down, in 1876, the oak from the box pews was reused as panelling in the lounge bar of the George & Dragon public house, in Broad Street, which itself dates from 1637. A good excuse to visit this pub!

Stage 7

Knighton to Bleddfa

> Distance: 12½ miles. No obvious part-way 'escape' point served by public transport.
> Maps: Landranger 148; Pathfinder 950, 971; Explorer 201.

Sharing the route of Offa's Dyke Path for the first mile and a half, the way climbs south out of Knighton. After parting company with the well waymarked national trail it heads, via high level tracks, towards and into the valley of the River Lugg. It drops down into Pilleth with its sad little church and early fifteenth century battle site. The Lugg is then crossed and followed eastwards for a short distance before a brief section of road walking leads to Litton and the start of the climb into Radnor Forest.

The climb into the forest is via the open Litton Hill and skirts the summit of the higher Llan-fawr. There are stunning views to be had across Radnor Forest, over the Lugg Valley and through the Presteigne Gap as height is gained. Thereafter the route follows the northern edge of the Radnor Forest, via woodland and more open tracks and paths, before a forest road takes it down into the small hamlet of Bleddfa.

The line of the Elan Valley aqueduct is crossed twice – as Knighton is left and as Bleddfa is entered – but on neither occasion is the crossing visible or obvious. The pipelines are in a tunnel to the north of the route for most of the stage.

STARTING at the clock tower walk down Broad Street and turn right through the arch of the Knighton Hotel and across the car park beyond. Continuing straight ahead climb up the steep road (Larkey Lane) to reach a T-junction.

Look behind here for good views across Knighton to Kinsley Wood beyond. The letters 'ER', formed by the planting of a different species of trees within a dark green coniferous stand in the wood may be seen. This commemorates the coronation of Queen Elizabeth II and these trees will not be felled until after her death.

Turn right and then immediately left off the road up Frydd Terrace, between the houses, as indicated by an Offa's Dyke sign. At the rear of the houses turn right, in front of a row of garages. Passing the end of these walk a few yards up the entrance drive to a house and then turn half left up a steep footpath which leads over a stile into woodland. On reaching a metalled track cross straight over it, a concrete Offa's Dyke Path marker a few yards up the path which continues the steep climb through the trees – Great Frydd Wood.

At the top of the wood cross its upper boundary fence, over a stile, and turn right to follow it along, Knighton Golf Course on the left. Initially still climbing, the path soon levels out, still following the boundary of the wood – to the right.

The climb out of Knighton is up Frydd Hill and the height here about 320 metres/1050 feet. As the trees to the right thin out there are good views of Garth Hill, topped by a mast, slightly to the rear.

Cross a stile, to the right of a metal gate, to enter a field and leave the Golf Course behind. Follow the right-hand boundary of the field, the woodland on the right now thinning out. Continue to follow the right-hand boundary through three further fields, each one entered over a stile.

Notice on the upright of all the stiles the little representation of an Offa coin, the symbol of the Offa's Dyke Association, although the waymarking throughout is with the National Trail 'acorn'. The Dyke itself has been on the right of the path

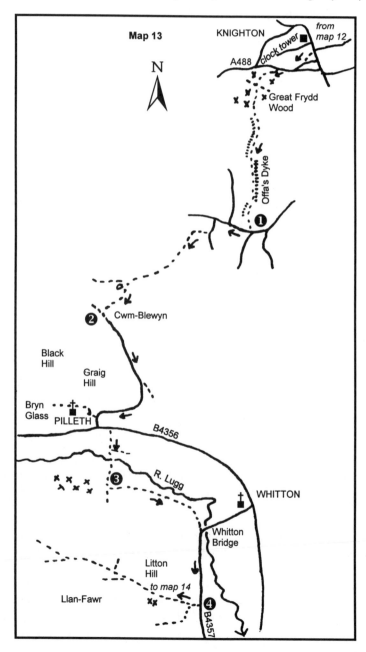

since it emerged from the woods but has been, until now, fairly insignificant in size. It is shortly to be crossed and thereafter becomes much more pronounced.

Offa's Dyke takes its name from Offa II of Mercia, the first Saxon leader to bear the title 'King of the English'. The dyke was constructed sometime after AD780 to mark and fortify the western boundary of his kingdom and was probably the result of an agreement between Offa and the Welsh, or Cymr. There appear to have been jointly administered laws governing trade and movement across the dyke and the recovery of stolen livestock. It was therefore almost as much a trade boundary as a defensive structure.

The prominent hill visible on the left along here, with the Powys Observatory building at its summit, does not appear to be specifically named on any of the Ordnance Survey maps of the area despite its height of 417 metres/1368 feet making it the highest peak for some considerable distance around. I have heard it called variously Reeves Hill, Stonewall Hill and Woodhouse Hill. The staff at the observatory however tell me its correct name is Llan-wen Hill – 'the hill of sunshine' – and they should know!

Follow the path along the right-hand boundary of the third field, with the bank of Offa's Dyke to the right. On reaching a gap through the earthwork, (at SO280708), cross it and continue to a stile over the right-hand boundary fence. Cross this and turn left to follow the boundary through the field so entered, the Dyke just beyond it and becoming more prominent.

Continue to follow the left-hand boundary fence through two more fields, both entered over stiles. On reaching the far boundary of the second of these cross a stile which is situated midway between the Dyke on the left and the field boundary on the right, where the field narrows. Go straight across the field so entered to a stile opposite. Cross this and again go straight across the next field to another stile opposite. Cross this and again initially go straight ahead, to eventually follow the right-hand field boundary to another stile. Cross this and continue to follow the right-hand boundary, the Dyke immediately on the right. On reaching a stile in the right-hand boundary cross it onto a road. ❶

On the field side of this stile is carved 'Chepstow 78 Miles' and on the road side 'Prestatyn 98 Miles'. On reaching the road we part company with Offa's Dyke Path.

Crossing the stile onto the road look straight ahead for the first view of the flattened conical shaped hill of Llan-fawr, (387 metres/1270 feet), at the north-eastern corner of Radnor Forest. The summit of this is skirted by the route of the Elan Valley Way as it climbs up into the forest later on this stage.

On reaching the road turn right. It immediately starts to descend and soon reaches a junction. Ignore a road going right but continue straight ahead, the road still descending. On reaching a second junction, (SO276699), turn left along a narrow road between two wire field fences. Just after this has made a bend to the left turn right along a track, indicated as a bridleway and with a nameplate for Radnor House at its entrance.

The initially metalled but then stony track makes a bold left turn in front of a house and passes between outbuildings, beginning to climb and bending slightly right. Go through a metal farm gate to enter a field and follow the track as it runs alongside the left-hand boundary. Passing through another metal gate follow the right-hand boundary of the next field, the track becoming more grassy. Remain on it as it continues to climb through another gate into the next field.

Good views of the hills to the left now open up. The highest point of these is Hawthorn Hill, (407 metres/1335 feet). Offa's Dyke Path runs along this ridge. The route here is climbing Rhos Hill.

The track bends to the right and is joined, on the left, by the field boundary fence. Following this it passes through another metal farm gate.

Turn and look behind here. To the half right the observatory on its high hill is visible while directly to the rear is Stow Hill, which so dominated the latter miles of Stage 6 of the Elan Valley Way. To its left is the mass of Panpunton Hill, which lies above and to the north of Knighton. The route is at a height of about 350 metres/1148 feet here.

Passing through yet another metal gate the track continues straight ahead, now enclosed on both sides by field fences. It begins to descend and passes through two further metal gates in quick succession, (the second being the middle of three gates ahead), the intervening area being used for the temporary impounding of livestock. On reaching a junction at a pond, just after the second gate, (SO264693), go left. The descent now becomes much steeper.

Passing through another gateway – gateless at the time of writing – the small settlement of Cwm-blewyn will be seen in the valley bottom below. Approaching it the track swings sharply right and crosses a stream which has been alongside on the right throughout the descent. Reaching the farmhouse it passes through another metal gate and crosses a stream in the valley bottom. Passing in front of the house it swings to the left to reach a T-junction of tracks. Turn left here onto a metalled track which runs parallel to the stream in the valley bottom – the latter being at the far side of the field on the left. ❷

Proceeding along the metalled track pass through two metal gates – both likely to be open. Soon the track starts to bear to the right and passes through another metal gate – again likely to be open.

Passing this third metal gate look to the left to see the village of Whitton below, its church to the right of the main settlement.

Descending the next section of track, bearing slightly right, ahead can be seen the hills of Radnor Forest with Llan-fawr prominent. As the descent becomes steeper look half left for wonderful views down the Lugg Valley, the river itself hugging the far side of it with its course recognisable from the trees along its banks.

Remain on the metalled track as it descends, still bearing slightly right. As the descent becomes steeper the track makes a sweeping bend to the right and, as this ends, passes a gate and cattle grid. The church and settlement of Pilleth appear ahead, four large trees high on the hillside above. The metalled track continues to descend, though not so steeply now, heading directly towards the settlement.

The two large hills to the right above Pilleth are Graig Hill and Black Hill, rising to 378 metres/1240 feet and 404 metres/1325 feet respectively. The hill behind Pilleth, with the four large trees on part way up, is Bryn Glas, now thought more likely to have been the site of the battle of Pilleth (1402) – see note below – than that as marked on OS. maps.

Another cattle grid with gates is passed and a small stream in a culvert crossed as the main farm settlement is entered, the track bearing left. Go straight on between the farm buildings to follow the route of the Elan Valley Way or take a bridleway to the right to visit the church. (The bridleway actually swings to the right around the church but by passing

Pilleth

Pilleth is mentioned in Domesday Book (1086) where it is referred to as 'Pelelei'. At this time it and the surrounding area, known as Maelienydd, were in the possession of the Mortimers of Wigmore, the powerful family of Marcher Earls.

The church of St. Mary, Our Lady of Pilleth, is stunningly sited on the remote hillside with beautiful views over the Lugg Valley, a typical Celtic site. The church is very simple inside and out. There is no electric lighting inside the building. Sadly its condition and state of repair is not all that could be hoped for. One of its walls leans alarmingly and is supported by a large wooden buttress outside while a 'temporary' roof, dating from the early years of the twentieth century, is not quite managing to keep the worst of the weather out. From the inside holes around the margins of the roof become obvious and water and green stains disfigure some of the internal walls.

The oldest parts of the existing building date from a thirteenth century structure which was lengthened and had a tower added in the fourteenth century. The church was burnt by Owain Glyn Dwr in the early years of the fifteenth century but was later restored, including a new tower. The remains of the base of the older, and larger, tower can be seen to the north of the existing structure.

In 1894 another fire, caused by an overheating chimney, again gutted the church – only the tower surviving on this occasion. The church remained a burnt out shell until 1905 when Walter Tapper, then Surveyor of York Minster, was asked to restore the building. This restoration was completed in 1911 and included the 'temporary' roof which is obviously much lower than the original and today looks better suited for a garage than a church. A suitable replacement is now a matter of some urgency.

The church contains an early thirteenth century octagonal font. The tower has its original medieval bell frame but two of the three bells are missing. The remaining bell dates from 1450 and was cast in Worcester.

Outside and by the tower is a Holy Well. Possibly an old pagan site it was well known in the Middle Ages, its waters being thought to cure eye diseases. At that time there was also a statue of the Virgin Mary, Our Lady of Pilleth, on the site.

Also in the churchyard is a plain unmarked curbstone marking the mass grave of some of the soldiers who died at the battle of Pilleth. Many bones dating from this time have been found in the churchyard – far more in fact than the size of the local population could account for – and these were buried on this particular spot by Sir Richard Green-Price in the mid nineteenth century. (The Prices were a very old established Radnorshire family who formerly lived at Pilleth Court, the large white building below the church.)

It was also Sir Richard Green-Price who buried more remains of the battle dead on the hill above the church – known as Bryn Glas and thought likely to be the actual site of the main battle. Six Wellingtonia trees were planted to mark the spot and four of these remain to dominate the whole site.

The battle of Pilleth took place on 22nd June 1402 between the Welsh under Owain Glyn Dwr and a larger English force under Sir Edmund Mortimer. Welsh victory was assured when the archers in Mortimer's army, mainly men of Welsh descent, went over to Glyn Dwr's side and turned their weapons against their erstwhile companions. It was a bloody battle with anything up to 1100 English dead and Sir Edmund Mortimer captured.

The savagery of the day did not end there, with the Welsh women camp followers then mutilating the corpses and demanding payment of ransom before burial would be allowed.

An interesting postscript to the battle is that the English King, Henry IV, delayed in sending the ransom demanded for the release of Mortimer – possibly because the Mortimers themselves had such a strong claim to the English throne – with the result that the latter himself made an alliance with Glyn Dwr, marrying one of his daughters. This was followed, in 1405, by the Tripartite Indenture, an agreement formalised at Bangor whereby Glyn Dwr, the Mortimers and the Earls of Northumberland were to unite against the king and split the country three ways – with Glyn Dwr taking Wales and the Borders, Northumberland the country north of the River Trent, and Mortimer the south. It seems unlikely that Mortimer was ever directly involved in this alliance, which came to nothing, and the main architect of it was probably the Earl of Northumberland. Owain Glyn Dwr, Sir Edmund Mortimer and Harry Hotspur are depicted as involved in this plotting in Shakespeare's *Henry IV, Part 1.*

The interior of the church of St Mary, Pilleth

through a small wooden gate and walking straight up the grassy hill ahead the churchyard can be entered at its bottom right-hand corner.)

Continue through the farm buildings and straight on down the metalled track to reach a road, (B4356). Cross it and turn left along it. After about 30 yards turn right to pass through a metal farm gate into a field, on a track signed as a bridleway. Follow the left-hand boundary of the field, crossing a small stream which then accompanies the track alongside the boundary hedge. On reaching a Y-junction and uneven ground – marking the remains of an old Motte and Bailey, (Castell foel-allt) – go slightly right, as the stream, field boundary and the other arm of the track bear away to the left, (SO258678). The track remains just recognisable but, as a rough navigation guide, keep a line of hawthorn trees immediately on the right as it swings slightly left around the site of the old fortification.

On reaching the River Lugg go through a metal farm gate onto a bridge over it. Cross the river and bear right along its bank to reach the right-hand boundary hedge of the field so entered. Follow this up the field to its top right-hand corner and pass through a metal farm gate there. ❸

The River Lugg rises in the hills of Powys, north-west of Llangunllo, and flows south-east to Presteigne and then east to pass through a gorge at Aymestrey after which it turns south and then again south-east to reach Leominster where it is joined by its main tributary, the River Arrow. It then heads south to join the River Wye to the east of Hereford. Its English name is derived from the Welsh 'Llugwy' meaning 'Clear Wye', the name 'Wye' itself coming from the Celtic 'Wy' signifying water.

On reaching the top of the first field after the river look behind for a good view of Pilleth and the hills behind.

Passing through the metal gate go straight ahead towards an isolated house but after 40 yards or so, (long before the house is reached), turn left along a track which immediately joins a more substantial track heading in the same direction – eastwards – along the Lugg valley. Bridleway arrows point the way.

The track soon becomes bounded by high hedges on both sides, the river out of sight and some distance to the left. Before too long there are gaps in the high hedgerows and views of the hills across the valley open up. Pass through a gateway with cattle grid. As an isolated cottage on the right, (Litton Cottage), is reached the river becomes visible on the left below and soon Whitton Church and churchyard can be seen across it, with the village itself beyond.

The hills across the Lugg Valley and behind Whitton are the same ridge seen earlier on this stage and include Hawthorn Hill – the highest point at 407 metres/1335 feet – and Cwm-Whitton Hill, Hengwm Hill, Gilfach Hill and, nearest the river, Furrow Hill. The Lugg makes a significant bend around the slopes of Furrow Hill while Offa's Dyke Path descends to the valley across it. The wood on its lower slopes is Gilfach Wood.

Turn and look behind here for good distant views of Pilleth and the hills behind. The site of the battle is now easy to imagine, the whole being dominated by the four Wellingtonia trees above the churchyard.

Just after passing a disused quarry, on the right, the track emerges through a metal gate onto a road, (B4357), with Whitton Bridge just to the left. Turn right to walk along the road. After about half a mile, just after passing the isolated building of Litton Court, on the left, the road dips slightly before making a significant bend to the left. Turn right here, (SO268663), along a metalled track signed as a bridleway. (*Navigation note: The bridleway/metalled track leaves the road mid way between Litton Court, on the left of the road, and a house set to the right of the road which has a barn by it. There are two arms off the road to the initial metalled track with a rough grass triangle between them.*) ❹

Where, after about 70 yards, the track loses its metalling and makes a sharp bend to the left leave it straight ahead through a metal farm gate, bearing yellow tape, to follow a track which runs between farm sheds and through another gate, to the right of a tall ash tree, into a field.

Follow the stony track as it begins to climb steeply and makes a sweeping bend left to reach a metal farm gate in the top boundary of the field. Passing through this, the climb becoming steeper, the track now bears slightly right past a small disused quarry, on the right, to another gate in the top boundary of the next field, a small conifer plantation immediately to the left. Passing through this metal gate the track climbs straight ahead, now in open country.

As this climb from the road proceeds look to the right to see the hills across the Lugg Valley, previously detailed. The course of Offa's Dyke Path across their ridge can easily be traced using O.S. Explorer map 201.

Also visible behind is the large bend forced on the Lugg by Furrow Hill – the course of the river recognisable by the trees along it; a road (B4356) lies beyond it and Gilfach Wood and the hill beyond that. The climb here is up Litton Hill.

Climbing this section we disturbed a buzzard from the small disused quarry.

The track climbs straight ahead, through bracken in season, and becomes grassy underfoot. When, after about 100 yards, it reaches a junction, with the option of some five tracks/paths of varying width ahead, left and right, take the middle track – the major one. On reaching another junction, this time with a grassy path going off to the right, again remain on the main track, which bears slightly left.

The summit of Llan-fawr, (387 metres/1270 feet) is half left ahead and should be kept well to the left throughout the climb.

The track bears slightly left towards the summit and becomes very broad. It runs just to the left of the corner of a field fence, (on the right), and about 100 yards right of another fence, (on the left) – at SO259666.

Look behind during this section of the climb, on a clear day, for superb views through the Presteigne Gap, (on the River Lugg), to Wapley Hill and Shobdon Hill, both of which lie along the Lugg Valley in Herefordshire. Both are wooded and their profiles resemble upturned boats from here. The Mortimer Trail – the 30 mile waymarked path from Ludlow to Kington – climbs both on its route. Shobdon Hill is the one to the left, and slightly more distant, and on a very good day the village of Byton may be visible on the lower slopes to its right.

While climbing this section in September we found an amazing variety of different and highly coloured fungi.

On reaching a junction where the track splits – the left arm heading towards the summit of Llan-fawr; the right still climbing but bearing well to the right of the summit – go right.

Look right along here to see Pilleth gradually coming into view. When we first walked this section there was a rainbow over the Lugg Valley with its one end directly on the church at Pilleth.

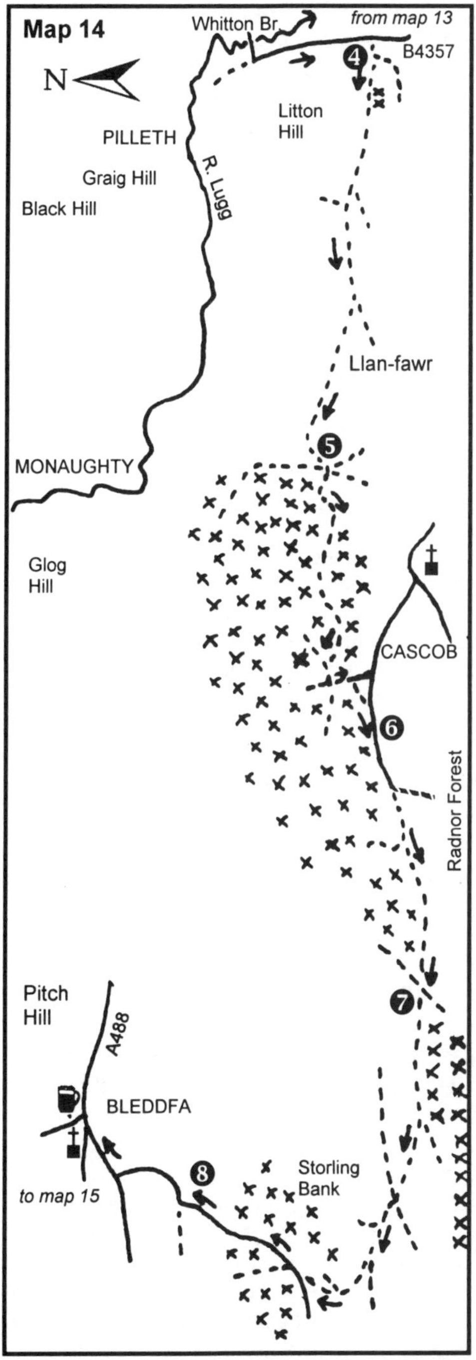

Map 14

N

from map 13

Whitton Br.

B4357

④

Litton Hill

PILLETH

Graig Hill

Black Hill

R. Lugg

Llan-fawr

⑤

MONAUGHTY

✝

Glog Hill

CASCOB

⑥

Radnor Forest

Pitch Hill

A488

⑦

BLEDDFA

✝

⑧

Storling Bank

to map 15

The views behind through the Presteigne Gap to Wapley and Shobdon hills remain superb while to the right, looking behind, the hills above Kington are now visible on a good day. Still looking behind and to the left, beyond the hills across the Lugg Valley, Stow Hill can be seen.

Follow the track as it skirts Llan-fawr, the summit well to the left. Ignore a number of smaller paths joining and leaving the main track along here. As another fairly substantial track joins, sharp left, the track begins to bear right, away from the summit. Pilleth is directly to the right at this point.

Looking right, over towards and beyond Pilleth, the course of most of this stage of the Elan Valley Way, (since the shared route with Offa's Dyke Path was left), can be made out. The views over in this direction are now superb. To the left a long high hill bearing a mast now comes into view. This is Black Mixen, not quite the highest point in the Radnor Forest at 650 metres/2133 feet.

As the track turns away from the summit a gradual descent begins. On reaching a metal gate, (SO251668), pass through it to enter a field. Proceed along the right-hand boundary of this, the descent soon becoming more marked.

The wooded hill half right is Black Hill and the village at the far end of it, at the foot of its slope, is Monaughty – directly ahead as the sweeping left bend (below) begins. The rounded hill beyond the village is Glog Hill.

Both grassy track and field boundary make a sweeping bend to the left, (through almost 90 degrees), as the bottom of the descent is neared. At the bottom, at a junction of tracks, go straight across a sunken track, bearing initially right and then climbing steeply around to the left, with the boundary of some woodland on the immediate right of the track. ❺

Follow the track as it climbs over an exposed section of bedrock and then bends to the right, (SO244671), before descending to enter the woodland through a gate.

Cascob – and a local legend

Look left just before entering the wood to see the small settlement of Cascob with its church – St. Michael's.

In the *New Testament, Book of Revelations* Michael is mentioned as a fighter against dragons. There is a local legend that the last Welsh dragon lies asleep somewhere deep in Radnor Forest and that four churches were built long ago to surround the forest and were dedicated to St. Michael to make sure that the dragon does not escape and ravage the countryside. The legend has it that if any of the four churches is destroyed then this will in fact happen.

The four churches are this one – St. Michael's, Cascob – and those at Cefnllys, Llanfihangel Nant Melan and Llanfihangel Rhydithon, the latter of which is visited on Stage 8 of the Elan Valley Way.

Michael's church at Cascob dates from the thirteenth century with a fourteenth century font and with its late fifteenth century roof restored in 1895. On the north wall of the sanctuary near the tower is an 'abracadabra charm' dating from the seventeenth century and supposedly used to exorcise a young woman. A collapsed west tower of the fourteenth century lies under a mound beside the current tower.

The church was one of those locally which was burnt by Owain Glyn Dwr in the early years of the fifteenth century.

As it enters the woods the track narrows to path width and, in a little over 100 yards, emerges into a small clearing from the far side of which a forest track departs straight ahead. Walk along this wide stony track which almost immediately begins a gentle climb which steepens as it bends left. Views are restricted along this section by a high bank along the right of the track and trees to the left.

The track makes a long bend to the right and begins to descend gently. At a T-junction of tracks go left, (SO234672), climbing slightly. After about another 100 yards, at a 'crossroads' of tracks, turn left, climbing to pass through a wooden farm gate – which may be open – onto a tarmac track which passes to the left of what is shown as Woodgate Farm on Explorer Map 201. (*Navigation Note: The buildings here include an active sawmill and when this is in operation it provides a good audible guide to the correct track to take through the woods. The noise should be coming from above and to the left as the left turn is made at the track 'crossroads'.)*

Proceed along the tarmac track for 30 yards – until after the sawmill/lumber yard has been passed – and then turn right, through a gate, into a green lane. Walk along this – the sawmill/lumber yard on the right. It climbs slightly at first and then – where there is a metal farm gate on either side of it – just as gently descends to emerge through a wooden gate onto a tarmac lane. Turn right along this, passing a lone house on the left, (Upper House), after which the lane becomes straighter and climbs noticeably. **6**

At a Y-junction, where the lane loses its metalled surface, bear right along an stony track, (SO228667). After about 90 yards, as the track commences a bend to the right, maintain direction by leaving it through a metal gate on its left, (which bears a bridleway sign), to enter a field. (The track just vacated bears right through its own metal gate to head into the woods.)

Head straight across the field following the right-hand boundary – woodland beyond. (There is no clear path or track across this field.) Pass through a metal gate and continue to follow the right-hand boundary of the next field, a rough grassy track now appearing underfoot. Passing through another metal gate the track continues to follow the boundary with the woodland. On reaching a metal farm gate in the far right-hand corner of the field pass through it to emerge onto a dirt track. Go straight across this onto another grassy track opposite, (SO220666). As the dirt track is crossed the woods which have been on the right-hand side end only to commence on the left. **7**

Look half right here to see the small village of Bleddfa in the valley below. The hill behind the village is Pitch Hill. Immediately to the right is the small settlement of Nant-y-corddi with Glog Hill behind it. The grassy track now walked is very good for bilberries in season.

Proceed along the grassy track which, after an initial level section, begins a gradual descent. On reaching a wooden gate ignore a track going up half left but pass through it into a field, following a boundary on the left which has woodland beyond it. After less than 100 yards pass through another gate into a large field. The short section between the two gates can be very muddy indeed in wet weather.

Go straight ahead across the field, its boundary with the woodland now some distance, (about 100 yards), away on the left. Head towards an obvious depression/valley some distance ahead. Following the now indistinct track across this field another more substantial track will be seen below to the right, the distance between the two tracks decreasing. As the depression/valley is neared the lower track makes a fairly sharp left bend across the line of the indistinct track which is being followed and is crossed just as the small valley is reached. Having crossed it walk above and to the right of the valley, (SO207667), the track underfoot now becoming clear again.

Since the large field was entered the views to the right, and Bleddfa, have been hidden by a low hill. This is Storling Bank. It rises to a height of 364 metres/1194 feet. The route is at a height of about 345 metres/1132 feet here.

Follow the grassy track as it bends round to the right, high above the small valley to its left. A small left bend precedes another fairly substantial bend to the right after which the track descends to pass through a gate – off its hinges at the time of writing – and continue to drop down to a stream in the valley. At a junction ignore a track going steeply up right but remain on the main track ahead. This section can be very muddy in wet weather.

Cross the stream, here in a culvert. The track begins to climb and soon regains its original height above the stream – which is now on the right. About 140 yards after the stream crossing, as the track turns away from the stream towards a metal farm gate, (about 75 yards ahead), take a footpath which leaves it on the right and continues to follow the edge of the small

Bleddfa

Bleddfa lies on the A488 road, at a height of 700 feet above sea level. The name is pronounced 'Bleth-va', with the emphasis on the first syllable, and is an anglicised version of the Welsh name 'Bleidd fach' meaning 'the place of wolves', although whether this means where wolves were driven down from the forest and killed – in a wolf-pit – or merely refers to the large numbers of these animals hereabouts is uncertain. Wolves roamed wild in the Radnor Forest until Tudor times.

The village has the Bleddfa Centre, (Gallery, Shop, Tea Room and Garden in old school buildings), the Hundred House Inn, a telephone kiosk, a small Post Office, and the church of St. Mary Magdalene – an unusual dedication hereabouts, probably Norman replacing an earlier Celtic one – possibly founded as early as the sixth century.

The present church dates back to the early part of the thirteenth century, the nave remaining from this structure. In the late thirteenth century the building was extended to double its size and the junction can be clearly seen both inside and outside. The tower dated from much the same period but collapsed in medieval times, also destroying much of the west end of the nave. Parts of the remains of this can be seen outside at the west end

of the building. Recent excavations of these ruins have revealed the cause of its demise to be burning which gives credence to the story that this is another of the churches locally which was burnt by Owain Glyn Dwr in the early years of the fifteenth century – just like those at Pilleth and Cascob passed earlier on this stage of the walk.

Inside the church, the octagonal font is medieval. The roof dates from the fifteenth/sixteenth centuries. Many of the internal roof timbers would have been painted and the rood beam still retains some floral decoration – red on a white background – with traces on others. The wooden bell turret at the west end of the stone roof was built in 1711. The church underwent renovation in 1818, 1907 and 1975-83. The porch and belfry were repaired in 1988.

There are the remains of a motte and bailey fortification to the east of the village. Dating from the twelfth century it was not rebuilt after Llywelyn ap Gruffyd destroyed it in 1262. Otherwise the only other building of any great age is the Hundred House Inn. Earliest reference to a building on this site dates from 1527. Courts of the Hundred were held at Bleddfa from 1524 onwards and continued to be held in the present building until 1867 when they were moved to Penybont.

valley along, above the stream. On reaching a rough, flat grassy area continue in the same direction along the right-hand edge of this, aiming for its far side and a point between a hazel tree on the left and a rowan tree on the right where a path which descends down wooden steps will be found. Follow the path and steps down to the stream below, a final bend to the right leading to a wooden footbridge across it, (SO200671).

Cross the footbridge over the stream, initially bearing left, as if to follow it upstream, but then after a few yards turning right to climb steeply up a path, the stream below to the right. The path climbs through open woodland and bracken in season. On reaching a large sycamore tree it splits, with one arm going each side of the tree. Take the left-hand path which continues to climb, passes to the left of a large oak tree and soon reaches a metal gate giving access onto a metalled forest track, (SO201672).

Turn right along the track which immediately climbs. After less than 50 yards ignore a forest dirt track which goes off steeply to the left but remain on the metalled track which meanders along and soon begins to descend. ❽

Pitch Hill is straight ahead as this section of track is walked, Bleddfa below in the foreground. Glog Hill is slightly to the right.

Passing a farm, (Neuadd), the track/lane makes a sharp, (almost 90 degree), bend to the right. Ignore a footpath going off to the left here. A sharp left bend follows and the now quite 'sunken' lane crosses a stream which is in a shallow culvert but which may be found to be flowing across the lane after wet weather. Continue along the lane which starts to climb and soon reaches the busy A488 road.

Turn right and walk down the road, crossing when a pavement begins opposite – just by the Bleddfa Centre. Bleddfa is reached in under 200 yards and this stage of the Elan Valley Way ends at the Hundred House Inn, just across the small triangular 'village' green.

Stage 8

Bleddfa to Crossgates

Distance: 11½ miles (Dolau 6¼ miles).
Maps: Landranger 148, 147; Pathfinder 971, 970; Explorer 201, 200.

The stage begins by following the last mile of Stage 7 in reverse. Forest tracks and paths lead directly west to more open country at Graig Hill, after which a clear track and later road take the route down into the valley of the River Aran and Dolau Station on the Heart of Wales Railway Line.

The single longest stretch of continuous road walking on the Elan Valley Way – almost 3½ miles in all, but of very quiet minor roads with good views, in the main – then climbs north of the valley before turning south-west to head directly towards Crossgates. The road is finally left behind to descend via tracks and paths to cross the River Ithon by a suspension footbridge. Thereafter the route arcs around to the north of Crossgates, using a mixture of paths, tracks and road. The stage ends, after a crossing of the substantial Clywedog Brook, just to the west of Crossgates.

For the first half of the stage the pipelines of the Elan Valley aqueduct are to the north of the route of the walk and deep in Dolau Tunnel – the longest tunnel section on the entire line of the aqueduct. Towards the end of the stage, as the descent to the crossing of the River Ithon is made, the aqueduct's own crossing of the river is seen below. It lies just downstream of the suspension footbridge which takes the walk across the river.

STARTING at the Hundred House Inn, walk across the small green and turn right up the road – A488 – which bends to the left and climbs. Take the first turning off the road on the left – just before the road bends to the right – and walk down a metalled lane which descends to cross a stream in a shallow culvert, (may flow across the lane in wet weather). Crossing this the lane begins to climb gently, bending sharp right and then left. Ignore a footpath going off to the right at the latter bend. Passing the buildings of Neuadd Farm, which is on the left, the lane begins to climb more steeply, a forested valley below on the left. On reaching the top of the climb it bears right, now with thick coniferous forest on the right and more open scrubby mixed forest to the left.

As the lane bends slightly left and begins to descend ignore a dirt track going off sharp right into the forest. A more pronounced right bend follows and on the left here is the metal gate through which the route of the walk emerged towards the end of Stage 7, at SO201672. Ignore it and the path beyond but remain on the lane/metalled track.

While climbing up the lane to this point look behind for views of Pitch Hill and Glog Hill, behind Bleddfa.

The metalled track continues to bend to the right and descend. A long straight section follows. Ignore a forest track going off to the right along this section. The track, still descending, bears left past a house, (on the left), and a bungalow, (on the right), losing its metalling and becoming stony. It continues to descend, a pond below to its left. Ignore a track going off to the right here – it is the long entrance drive to a house, soon passed. Instead remain on the main track which bears first left and then right to reach the valley bottom.

The track straightens and begins to climb, at first almost imperceptibly, a stream now to its immediate left. Shortly after passing through a wooden gate – which may be open – a house will be seen ahead, half-left and above the level of the track. Just before reaching a point level with this house, and about 120 yards after the wooden gate, turn right. (There is actually a three way choice here: on the left is a track to the aforementioned house, straight ahead there is a gate with a step stile alongside it leading into a field, and to the right is the track the route now takes – at SO192669). ❶

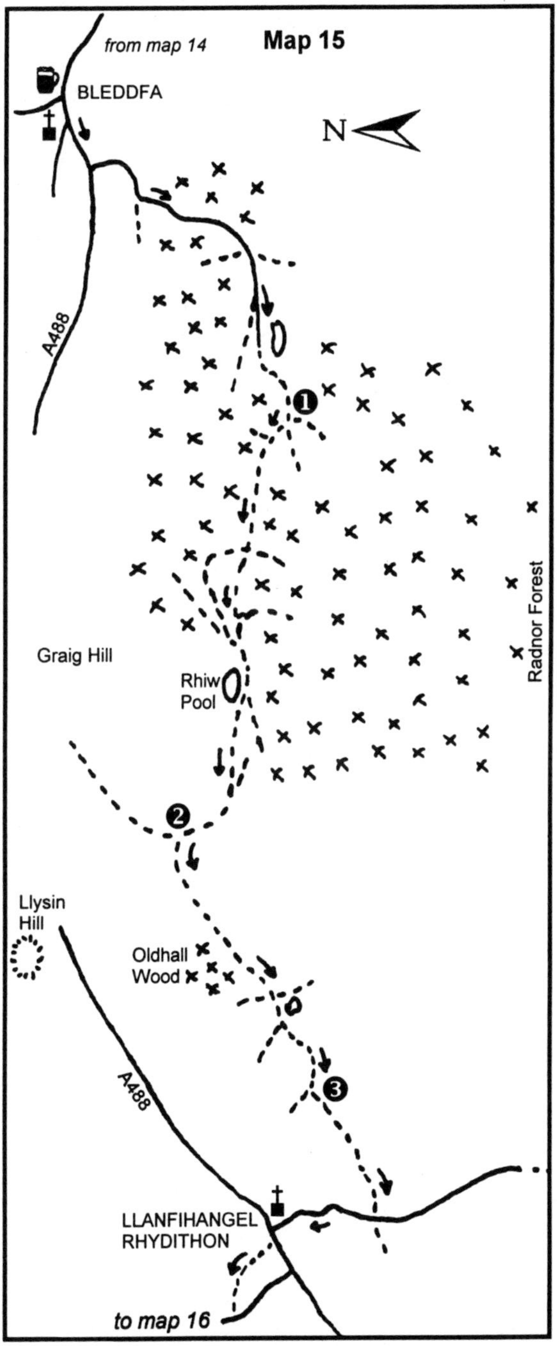

The stony track bears left initially and climbs, with a stream to its right-hand side. After a short distance it passes a house with a barn attached to its downside, on the left, becoming grassy underfoot. Ignore a track going off and down to the right to cross the stream via a small ford here but continue straight ahead to pass through a wooden gate and enter the forest. On passing through the gate into

Map 15

from map 14

BLEDDFA

N

A488

Graig Hill

Rhiw
Pool

Radnor Forest

❶

❷

Llysin
Hill

Oldhall
Wood

A488

❸

LLANFIHANGEL
RHYDITHON

to map 16

the forest the track narrows to path width, and can be quite muddy after wet weather. The climb steepens, the stream still to the right, in a deepening valley as the path gains height.

The steep climb continues, the path eventually reaching a forest track. Turn right along this and then, after about 25 yards, left off it to continue climbing up another grassy path which almost immediately widens to track width. There are bridleway marker signs at both turnings.

On reaching the forest track look behind for a good view of the route of the day so far.

The grassy track continues its steep climb, the stream still alongside to the right in its deep valley and the forest track beyond that and running parallel to both. Before long it makes a very sharp left turn, almost back on itself, to reach another forest track. Turn sharp right onto this broad track which climbs steadily and bends to the left. The stream and the first forest track are still running parallel, on the right, but soon the latter bends round to join the wide track now being walked from the right. Go slightly left at this junction. The climb ceases and a level section of walking ensues, a field ahead on the right with a large pond in it, Rhiw Pool. The route here is at a height of about 440 metres/1444 feet but any views have been restricted up to now by the dense mainly coniferous forest.

We climbed up this section to the pool with a strong smell of bog myrtle evident throughout. The plants themselves proved elusive however.

On reaching the pool leave the forest track, which here bends to the left, on its right to walk straight ahead along a grassy track which immediately passes through a wooden gate, bearing a bridleway sign. The track follows the forest boundary, to the left, as it crosses the field so entered.

From this first field views begin to open up ahead of the hills on the far side of the Aran Valley. Here the route is on Graig Hill.

The track becomes more distinct and bears slightly to the right, beginning a gradual descent. A metal farm gate will be seen ahead, this leading into the corner of a field to the right of the track. On reaching it do not pass through it but follow the track to the left of the boundary of the field, passing through two metal farm gates in quick succession as it proceeds – the field boundary to its right and the forest boundary to the left – bending right and still gradually losing height. Pass through another metal farm gate, (may be open), to meet another track at a T-junction. Turn right here – almost straight ahead, in fact. The track descends and makes a sweeping bend to the right past a disused quarry area, on the right. Here, as the track continues to bend to the right turn off it very sharp left to follow a grassy track along a field boundary, to the left as the quarry was passed but now on the right as it is followed, (SO173671). ❷

The track is designated as open to 'all traffic' and there are red arrow markers throughout the route from this point as far as the road above Llanfihangel Rhydithon.

The prominent hill directly ahead as the disused quarry is reached is Llysin Hill which rises to 427 metres/1400 feet and bears the remains of an ancient settlement at its summit.

The green track hugs the field boundary as both make an immediate sweeping bend to the right. It passes through a metal gate. Still alongside the boundary, pass through the lower of two adjacent metal farm gates, the track running below a coniferous forest plantation, on the left. When another track is joined keep straight ahead, following the right-hand boundary. As the track reaches a point level with the end of the coniferous plantation it begins to lose height and, after wet weather, may carry a small stream.

A fairly large deciduous wood, Oldhall Wood, is now one field distant on the right. The track continues its gentle descent, still with the accompanying field boundary immediately to the right, and eventually passes through a metal farm gate, bending to the right to hug the boundary wall of a house, Old Hall.

The track drops down to a 'crossroads' of tracks and a pond. Go straight ahead here, keeping the pond on the immediate left. Beyond the pond pass through a metal gate, cross a bridge over a stream, (Maes Brook), and, ignoring a footpath going off through a wooden gate on the right, follow the track as it bears left.

Passing through a wooden gate it begins to climb, a stream immediately to its left. The climb steepens and the track bears right and then left again, now lined by trees and more 'sunken'. As the climb eases the track bears right, soon reaching the top where, making a final bend to the right, it passes through a metal gate. Another metal gate alongside a cattle grid will be seen ahead. It bears a prominent 'Private Road' notice and on reaching it do not pass through it but turn left to climb up a track, (SO160665). ❸

Look behind here to see the recent descent to Old Hall.

The track passes through a metal farm gate, which may be open, and bends to the right, climbing quite steeply, a field boundary alongside to the right. It meanders up the field, still alongside the right-hand boundary, to a gateway at the top.

Climbing the field the high forest which the route crossed earlier on this stage can be seen behind – look left over the shoulder.

The gateway at the top of the field has no gate but instead is protected by a cattle grid. Cross this, the climb easing and the track making a sweeping bend to the right, a field boundary on its immediate left since the cattle grid.

Look behind here for views of the wooded hill of Oldhall Wood and Llysin Hill.

On reaching a metal farm gate, a farm building on its right-hand side and a surfaced livestock impoundment area beyond it, pass through it and two more in quick succession. The track begins to lose height quite rapidly and bends first right and then left to reach a junction of tracks. Ignore the one on the right – signposted as going to Penrochell – and go straight ahead to pass through a gate by a cattle grid. After a tiny initial rise the track once again descends and makes a sweeping right bend, with quite a drop on the right to a stream below, in a small side valley, which has crossed under the track at this point. Still bending right the track climbs, almost imperceptibly, and crosses more culverted streams. Remain on it as it straightens to approach and pass through a metal gate by a cattle grid which gives access onto a quiet road.

Turn right to walk down the road which immediately loses height rapidly.

Good views of Llysin Hill, very prominent to the right, as the descent of the road is made.

The road descends making a prolonged but gradual bend to the left. Soon the church of Llanfihangel Rhydithon will be seen below. Follow the road down to its junction with the A488 road. Turn left to continue with the route but right to visit the church.

The church is dedicated to St. Michael and is another of the four linked with the legend of the sleeping Welsh dragon in Radnor Forest (see the note on Cascob church at Stage 7 of the walk).

The church as seen today was built in 1838 on the site of a much older building. An ancient font which survives inside dates at least as far back as the fourteenth century but may be early Norman or even Saxon in origin. The graveyard contains the graves of three brothers who died during a blizzard in Radnor Forest. The first brother braved the blizzard to go out and search for a flock of sheep and when he failed to return the second brother set out to search for him. With both brothers overdue the third ventured out to look for them. After the storm was over a search party found the bodies of all three together in the snow.

Having turned left along the A488 cross it, as soon as it is safe to do so. After about 50 yards on the road turn right through a metal farm gate into a field – as indicated by a Public Footpath sign. Walk straight across the field to cross a stile in its far boundary and then straight across the next field to a point where it narrows. Here walk alongside the right boundary hedge to a stile in a corner. Cross the stile into a rough grassy area and proceed straight ahead across this and through a metal gate to emerge in a cul-de-sac of a small bungalow development. Follow this out to a T-junction with a road and turn right.

Look behind and slightly to the left while walking these fields and road for views of the church and the hills rising up behind it. Immediately behind the church from this angle is the bare Oldhall Bank, (422 metres/1384 feet), while behind that rises Fron-wen, (546 metres/1791 feet), and the high forest walked earlier on this stage.

Just before the name-sign for Dolau is reached a stream, Maes Brook again, comes alongside the road on the right and is crossed via a stone bridge. On reaching a road junction – with a road coming in from the right – continue ahead along the road. Ignore a narrow lane going off to the left, a nameplate for Dolau Farm at its entrance, but continue ahead past the warning signs for the railway crossing adjacent to Dolau station. On reaching the crossing go straight across it – or turn left onto the station platform if visiting the station (*see note on page 121*) or ending the walk here. ❹

 Dolau station, for trains on the Heart of Wales line.

Having crossed the Heart of Wales Line, by the level crossing at Dolau Station, proceed straight ahead along the road. Dolau Baptist Chapel, the chapel itself on the right of the road and graveyard on the left, is just beyond the crossing. A stream joins the road on its left-hand side, (a third

Dolau Station and the Heart of Wales Line

Dolau Station is worth a visit in its own right. In 1998 the station had just won the 'Wales in Bloom Best Station Award' for the fourth consecutive year. The Dolau Station Action Group members who care for the little unmanned halt and its masses of flowerbeds and hanging baskets do a wonderful job to the extent that a wait for a train here is always a pleasure. The walls of the small station shelter are covered with the awards it has won over the years, a selection of railway related poetry, and historic photographs of the line locally. There are also two fine examples of railway art, (paintings), on the platform.

Formerly also known as the Central Wales Line the through route between Craven Arms and Swansea was constructed piecemeal over 30 years and by six different railway companies, the last link in the chain being the Llanwrtyd Wells to Llandovery section which was completed in 1868 by the Central Wales Extension Railway and includes the Sugar Loaf Tunnel, a 283 yard long viaduct and a summit level of 820 feet. By the time the through route was opened all of the six original companies had passed under the control of either the London & North Western Railway or the Great Western Railway so the route operated very much as a joint concern. At the time of nationalisation in 1948 the line became part of the Western Region of British Railways.

The line was threatened with closure several times in the 1960s and that decade marked its downgrading from an important cross-country route to a light passenger-only route of more local importance. One of the reasons it has survived is that for many of the communities it

serves there is no viable public transport alternative. It has been estimated that to travel from Shrewsbury to Swansea using connecting bus services along the route of the line would take in excess of a week and that even then not all of the small settlements served by train would be visited!

Railway art at Dolau station

Whatever the full secret of its survival it remains a gem of a railway line with its unstaffed stations, request stops, ungated crossings, tunnels and viaducts – and above all miles and miles of glorious scenery. The 120 mile complete journey from Shrewsbury to Swansea takes around four hours.

The highest point on the line is Llangunllo, between Knighton and Dolau, at 980 feet.

The line is extensively used by walkers at weekends and there are programmes of organised walks running to/from several of the stations on the line, the brochures for which can be obtained at larger railway stations.

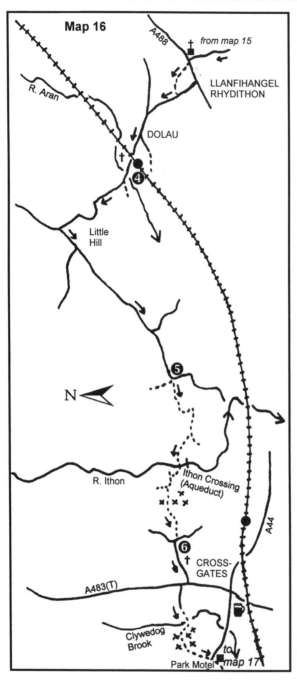

Map 16

from map 15

LLANFIHANGEL RHYDITHON

DOLAU

R. Aran

A488

Little Hill

N

R. Ithon

Ithon Crossing (Aqueduct)

A44

CROSS-GATES

A483(T)

Clywedog Brook

Park Motel

to map 17

appearance of Maes Brook on this stage), and accompanies it, finally joining the River Aran just to the left of where the road crosses the latter by a bridge, the confluence being clearly visible from the road.

Remain on the road, which soon begins to climb out of the Aran Valley.

The River Aran is the result of the coming together of several streams to the north-east of Dolau. It flows west to join the River Ithon, (Afon Ieithon), about three-quarters of a mile downstream of where this stage of the walk later crosses that river.

Passing a disused quarry, on the right, the rate of climb increases. A sharp bend to the left followed by three good bends to the right take the road round in a semi-circle before another sharp left bend restores it to its original heading. The climb finishes just before this last bend is reached and at the bend a slight descent commences.

On a clear day there are good views of the hills around a full 360 degrees here. Behind are the high hills of Radnor Forest and Llysin Hill. As the left-hand bend is rounded over to the left may be seen a flat-topped hill bearing a mast. This is Rhiw

Gwraidd, (436 metres/ 1430 feet), which will be seen again as this stage progresses and which dominates the first half of Stage 9 of the walk.

The road bends right, straightens and reaches a junction. Turn left – signposted Llanddewi 1½, Penybont 3½. After a little over 300 yards of straight road, at another junction, again go left – signposted Penybont 3¼. The road soon begins to climb, (the area hereabouts is named 'Little Hill' on Explorer Map 200), and eventually reaches a 'crossroads' with farm drives, that on the left signed as going to Penlan Farm. Remain on the road.

Rhiw Gwraidd is now half-right. As the top of the climb is reached there are good views of hills across the Aran Valley to the left. These include – left to right – Shepherds Tump, (460 metres/1509 feet), Coed-swydd, (412 metres/1352 feet), and Llandegley Rocks, (436 metres/1430 feet). The village of Llandegley lies in the gap between the latter two but cannot be seen. The high hills of Radnor Forest loom large behind this gap.

On reaching the top of the climb the road begins to meander. It undulates, but with an overall gradual descent, passes the entrance drive to Cwmwrach, on the left, and makes a sweeping bend to the left. As this finishes and it starts to bend right it passes the metalled lane to Rhydllyn, on the left, and the drive to Hill House, on the right. It continues to meander along past the drives to Nantleach and Blaen-y-cwm-mawr, both on the left. After a short gentle descent, gradually bearing left, it begins to climb again to a sharp left bend. ❺

As this bend begins, (SO112663), leave the road, turning right through a metal gate onto a metalled track, signed as a No Through Road and leading to Brynllefrith, (although the name sign on the gate seems to read 'Bryn Hyferth'), and then immediately left off it down a stony track.

The track initially follows a field boundary, which is on the left, bending slightly left and making a gradual descent. It then swings right to pass through a gate by a cattle grid and, still following the boundary on the left, heads towards an isolated farm and outbuildings ahead – Brynhoveth. The descent becomes more marked as the farmhouse is approached.

Descending this track the hill of Rhiw Gwraidd and its mast are directly ahead.

Follow the track as it crosses a second cattle grid and reaches the farm house. On passing the end of this building turn left, through a metal farm gate, to drop down through the farm yard and out through another metal gate at its far side. Bear right through a third metal farm gate and follow the field boundary, on the right of the track, the descent again becoming steeper and the track commencing a sweeping bend to the left.

Below, the Elan Valley aqueduct will be seen as it crosses the valley and the River Ithon.

Look out for the remains of a wooden stile in the boundary on the right of the track and turn right to cross this into the next field; (*Navigation Note: If a gate in the boundary is reached then the stile has been missed. The stile is about 100 yards after passing through the third gate, at the apex of the sweeping left bend.*)

Go across the field, generally following the contour of the land but losing just a little height as the far boundary is neared. Aim for a point immediately to the left of two large ash trees in the boundary. A stile across the wire boundary fence here was missing as of the time of writing but the

The Ithon Crossing under construction in 1898

(Viewed from a point below Brynhoveth Farm, near the route of the Elan Valley Way)

wire could easily be stepped over to enter the next field. Head slightly left down the field, roughly parallel to the aqueduct on the left, to a stile in its bottom boundary. Cross this and bear left, along the riverbank, to a suspension footbridge over the river. Cross this.

Take care! The suspension footbridge looked just a little worse for wear when I was here with one or two of the wooden planks underfoot in need of some attention, broken tension wires, and the whole structure crying out for a lick of paint. However take heart. It took myself and a fully loaded 55 litre rucksack – a fair old combined weight – with no trouble at all, and with the river below swollen by the worst flood waters in Wales for twenty years! Its condition has, however, been reported to Powys County Council for appropriate action.

The River Ithon, (Afon Ieithon), rises in the hills to the south of Newtown and flows southwards past Llanddewi Ystradenni and Penybont before looping north again to encircle Llandrindod Wells. It then resumes its southerly course to join the River Wye just south of Newbridge-on-Wye, to the north of Builth Wells. The Elan Valley aqueduct makes its own crossing of the Ithon less than 100 yards downstream of the suspension bridge, via a substantial bridge of its own.

Having crossed the suspension bridge bear half-right across the field now entered, towards some farm buildings beyond its far corner, (Tyn-dol). Exit the field here via a metal farm gate and then turn left to round the corner of the buildings. On reaching the end of the buildings, on the right – (just before reaching a metal gate leading into a green lane ahead) – take a footpath which goes off left over the boundary fence and up into a field, (SO102662). At the time of writing the stile here was missing but a 'temporary' replacement, in the form of some heavy duty plastic sacking wrapped around the barbed wire of the fence, had been provided.

Climb up the field heading gradually towards its right-hand boundary, where there is a stream in a deep side valley, and then following that up to the top of the field. Cross the remains of a stile in its top right-hand corner to enter a short wooded section. Proceed straight through this keeping the stream to the immediate right. On emerging from the trees into a field bear half-left across it, heading for a lone tree in the far boundary. The footpath should cross the boundary here but at the time of writing there was no stile so instead walk left along the boundary to pass through it via a metal farm gate and then walk back to reach and then follow the right-hand boundary of the field so entered.

Follow the right-hand boundary along to a point some 50 yards or so before the corner of the field is reached and then bear half-left across the field corner to drop down and pass through a gateway, (no gate at the time of writing), in the facing boundary and into the next field. Climb slightly to the right up this field to a metal gate in the top boundary which gives access onto a narrow road. (*Note: This exit point onto the road is some distance to the left of where it is shown on O.S. Explorer Map 200. The exit point for the course of the footpath as shown on that map is completely blocked. Should the original route of the path ever be reinstated – unlikely, but one never knows! – then on reaching the road a left turn followed by a right turn would be necessary to continue to follow the route of the walk, rather than as below.*) ❻

On reaching the road look behind for views of the hills of Radnor Forest. As Rock Road is entered Rhiw Gwraidd – the by now very familiar flat topped hill with the mast – is straight ahead. Rock Baptist Chapel, beyond and attached to the house of the same name, is worth a quick detour for the setting alone.

Turn right to walk along the road and then immediately left at a junction, into Rock Road. As it passes Rock House and Baptist Chapel, on the left, the road begins to descend. Remain on it until it reaches the A483 at a T-junction and then turn right, crossing the A-road as soon as it is safe to do so. Take the first turning on the left – just past an old milestone which reads 'Builth 11 Miles, Newtown 23' – into a metalled lane signed as a No Through Road.

After passing Old Mill Cottage and two more dwellings, on the left, the lane loses its metalled surface to become a wide track. It crosses Clywedog Brook, a tributary of the River Ithon, via a bridge – a footbridge to the right looking to be in poor repair and redundant. Having crossed the brook the track swings to the right, reaching some livestock pens. Beyond these it passes through a metal farm gate and heads towards coniferous woodland, a wire fence accompanying it on its right. Passing through another metal gate to enter the woodland the track bears right to climb up through the trees, a section which can be very muddy indeed in wet weather.

Remain on the track as it bears around to the left and continues climbing. On passing through another gate it leaves the wood and levels out, proceeding straight ahead to eventually pass through a gap at the right end of an old hedge boundary, a wire fence ahead, (SO082654).

On reaching the fence turn left to walk along a path – bounded by the wire fence on the right and the old field boundary trees on the left – which follows the narrow remnants of woodland.

As the path proceeds it becomes fenced in on both sides but the grassy corridor so formed is quite wide. On reaching a fence across this corridor cross a stile over it and continue along the grassy path which soon emerges alongside a garage belonging to a dwelling on the left. Go straight ahead onto a track. This leads to the A44 road just opposite the Park Motel.

Cross the A44. This stage of the Elan Valley Way ends here.

If staying at the Park Motel this is immediately ahead as the stage ends. The main settlement of Crossgates lies along the A44 to the left.

Proceeding along this road the Greenway Manor Hotel is on the left just before reaching a bridge over Clywedog Brook. The crossroads of the A44 and A483, which forms the centre point of the settlement is just over half a mile along the road from where the stage ends. Here will be found Guidfa House, a guest house, while right at the crossroads and about 75 yards along the A483 is The Builders Arms P.H. which also has accommodation.

Crossgates has two small shops, a large service station (with shop, restaurant and toilets) and one pub, The Builders Arms. There is a telephone kiosk to the left at the crossroads, along the A483.

Stage 9

Crossgates to Rhayader

Distance: 12 miles (Gwystre 2 miles, Nantmel 4¾ miles)
Maps: Landranger 147; Pathfinder 970, 969; Explorer 200.

For the first part of this stage the route flirts with the A44 road which is crossed twice. Little used footpaths and tracks take the route out of Crossgates and to the first crossing at Gwystre. Thereafter a track is followed to Carmel after which a quiet road is climbed to the isolated farm at Bwlch-mawr. Footpaths then take the route up and over into Nantmel and the second crossing of the A44.

A quiet road section follows, in the shadow of the prominent hill of Rhiw Gwraidd, before more tracks and footpaths, and finally a quiet road through the settlement of Nant-glas, take the route westwards and to the start of the final climb of the stage, up and over Gwastedyn Hill – with superb views of Rhayader and the hills behind the town as the top is reached. On descending from the hill the route enters Rhayader via a riverside walk along the Wye.

The Elan Valley aqueduct also follows the line of the A44 road for the early part of the stage. It is first seen as it crosses both a stream valley and the Carmel road at Carmel Bridge. Another two bridge sections are seen as the route enters Nantmel and two well houses are seen from a distance across the valley as the quiet road section after Nantmel is walked.

From the heights of Gwastedyn Hill another of these buildings is seen to the west of the River Wye and during the riverside approach to Rhayader the Wye Crossing of the aqueduct is passed – just one pipe, the fourth, going over the river here; the other three crossing underneath.

STARTING alongside the A44 road, facing the buildings of the Park Motel, take a track which skirts around the right-hand side of the motel grounds - signed 'Brookside, Private Drive'. On nearing this house leave the track, turning right to cross a stile with a small gate above it, situated just in front of a garage. Over the stile, turn left onto a narrow path confined between wire fences, which runs alongside and to the right of the property. Follow this path to reach Clywedog Brook, (it may be necessary to step over a single strand of barbed wire to reach the water's edge), and turn right along it.

On reaching a field boundary fence cross it via a metal fence/stile in the corner of the field, right at the water's edge. Follow the left-hand boundary of the field, an area of woodland separating it from the brook as the latter turns away left to its confluence with the River Ithon.

On reaching another field boundary ahead cross it through a gap in the hedgerow. Shortly after this turn left through a gap in the boundary alongside, descending through the edge of the trees and crossing a bridge spanning a small stream to reach another field. Follow the right-hand boundary of this, passing through a gap in a hedge boundary ahead. A group of farm buildings, (Abercamlo), will be seen ahead. Where the field boundary on the right bears right continue straight ahead to reach a metal farm gate just to the right of these. Pass through the gate onto a track and turn right, through another gate, to follow this out onto a quiet road. ❶

The footpath as indicated on the Explorer Map 200 and that actually present on the ground are at some variance from the turning left through the trees and over the

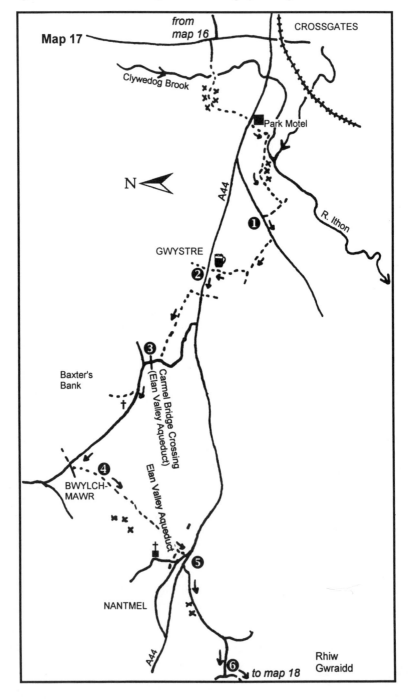

bridge up to the point where the right-hand field boundary bears away right approaching Abercamlo.

The O.S. map shows the initial turning towards the stream crossing to be some yards further on than it actually is, with the left-hand boundary of a field adjacent to that actually walked then being followed and the route passing through rough open woodland to cross a fence – this being at the point where the right-hand boundary fence of the field actually walked bears away right.

When this section was walked there was no sign on the ground of the route shown on the O.S. map while that actually followed was quite clear.

This variance of route may have something to do with a small nature reserve which has been established to the right of the route hereabouts. However, the O.S. map line of the footpath was confirmed as correct by reference to the definitive footpath map held by Powys County Council. The variation has been reported to that body so you may find that the original route is restored in the future – unless that is the 'diversion' is formally ratified.

The whole of this initial section from the A44 until the point on the quiet road where the Abercamlo farm track/drive reaches it, SO073650, looks rarely walked and the paths in danger of disappearing. Should the route be found to be completely impassable at any point then an alternative start to this stage is to proceed west along the A44 and take the first turning on the left, after about a quarter of a mile. Then proceed along the road for just under half a mile to reach the point referenced above.

Turn left along the road, almost immediately crossing a bridge over a stream, the latter then flowing alongside the road on the left for a short distance. Continue on the road past a commercial garage and house, on the right, but before reaching the next roadside house on the right turn right to walk along a metalled track, (SO069648). This rises gently, passes a bungalow, on the right, and bears left.

Climbing this track, views start to open up ahead. The hill of Rhiw Gwraidd, the distinctive mast on its flattened summit, is half left.

Where the metalled track swings left to form the drive of another bungalow, (Penburth), continue straight ahead on what is now a dirt track. After about 130 yards on this, on reaching a junction, SO066652, – one arm of the track going on ahead to bear slightly left; the other going right to pass through a metal gate – go right.

The track initially follows the right-hand boundary of the field entered via the gate. It remains an obvious track throughout and its only slight deviation in direction is where it bears left and then immediately right to pass a cattle feeder. The track is obviously heavily used by livestock and can be very muddy indeed in wet weather.

Follow the track to eventually emerge through a metal farm gate into a yard area with farm buildings, (Gwystre Farm). Pass to the right of the buildings, the track immediately descending to reach the A44. ❷

Limited bus service runs along the A44 here. The bus stops are just to the right as you reach the road with a telephone box and the Gwystre Inn also here.

Cross the A44 and turn left along it. After about 300 yards take a track off to the right, signed Cwmgwyddel. On reaching a metal gate which gives access to the farmyard, and may be open, go through it and bear round to the left, between the farmhouse and outbuildings, to pass through another gate into a field. Head straight ahead up the field, a stream about 30 yards away on the right.

Go through a gate in the far boundary, the track now climbing steadily ahead beneath trees and in a short 'cutting', with outcrops of rock to the left and the stream now immediately below on the right. This section opens out into another field, with higher ground to the left, and the track continues with the stream now once more about 30 yards distant. Pass through another gate and continue straight ahead following what now becomes a path just to the left of the trees which border the stream.

This is a pretty little valley walk. Ahead will be seen the crossing of the Elan Valley aqueduct – over valley, stream and road, and marked as Carmel Bridge on Explorer Map 200.

Nearing the far boundary of the field bear half-left, gradually making height, to reach its left corner, (SO057664). The footpath should gain access to a road at this point.

(Note: At the time of writing the way was blocked by a wire fence. This has been reported to Powys County Council but until any corrective action is taken by them then to gain access to the road turn left and walk back along the boundary hedge – on the right as it is walked. Just after passing a small ruined farm building a gate through the boundary gives access onto the road.)

Turn right to walk along the road which descends to pass under the aqueduct at Carmel Bridge. ❸

As the road descends the hill now straight ahead is Baxter's Bank, which rises to 361 metres/1184 feet.

Almost immediately after passing under the aqueduct there is a junction with a minor road going off to the right. Continue straight ahead, the road bending to the left to pass through a small settlement. Just after this ignore a footpath which leaves the road to the right, alongside a chapel building, beautifully sited by a stream, (SO054665).

Some wonderful home-made wooden road signs along here, warning of children at play!

The chapel and its graveyard by the stream is a haven of peace and tranquillity and well worth a few moments detour off the road.

Passing the drive to Hirfron, on the left, the road bends first right and then left and begins to climb more steeply, soon reaching the entrance drive to Brynsyfedd Farm, on the right. Remain on the road.

Passing the farm drive there are good views on the right of Baxter's Bank and its neighbouring hills. Also, if the day is good, look behind here for distant views of some of the hills which were familiar on Stage 8, with Llandegley Rocks directly behind and the high peaks of Radnor Forest rising up beyond.

The road continues to climb. Eventually the outbuildings of Bwlch-mawr will be seen ahead, on its left. On reaching the entrance drive to the farm turn left off the road as if to enter it but then go half-left, through metal gates, towards and then around the right-hand corner of the outbuildings, (SO045672), passing between them and a small group of conifer trees, through a metal gate and up a track in the field ahead. Almost immediately, go straight across a 'crossroads' of tracks, the track now bearing very slightly to the right, to climb up to and pass through a metal farm gate with a small tree beyond it. Passing through the gate the track disappears but continue to climb straight ahead, with the small tree to the right. The main farm buildings of Bwlch-mawr will be seen down below to the right. ❹

Continue climbing, heading towards the highest point of the hill ahead and very slightly away from the farm buildings, a small group of conifers ahead to the left. As height is gained and, on a good day, the views open up all around head directly towards the mast on the summit of Rhiw Gwraidd. A fence should by now be seen ahead. Head for a farm gate through this.

On a good day there are superb views all around from the top of this climb, at a height of about 365 metres/1197 feet. Rhiw Gwraidd, directly ahead, is about 2½ miles distant. As the gate is passed through and the path ahead walked look out for the first sighting of Nantmel Church half-right ahead and down in the valley.

On passing through the gate keep a field boundary fence immediately on the left as to the right a deep valley now begins to open up. The path begins to descend, following the fence. There is an area of woodland below to the right while across the valley the small farm settlement of Garth will be seen. On reaching a field boundary cross it, via a stile, into the top corner of the next field. Initially continue to follow the left-hand boundary of this but on reaching a metal farm gate in that boundary bear half-right down the field.

Descending this field on a clear day a glimpse of Llandrindod Wells may be had far over to the left. Half-right the long hill of Gwastedyn, climbed later on this stage of the walk, makes an early appearance.

Head down the field towards two metal farm gates, giving access to adjacent fields, at the bottom. Pass through the gate on the left and follow the right-hand boundary down the field so entered, an obvious track now underfoot. The church at Nantmel is almost directly to the right. Near the bottom of the field the track swings sharply left. Here leave it and continue to follow the right-hand boundary down to the corner of the field to join a track running across the bottom as it leaves the field to the right, through a metal farm gate.

Below to the right a section of the Elan Valley aqueduct will be seen as it crosses a stream in a deep side valley. Nantmel Church is up the grassy bank on the far side of this side valley.

Passing through the gate follow the boundary on the left around to the left and down to pass through another gate and onto a section of path with a very steep drop on its right to a stream in a side valley below – a section of the Elan Valley aqueduct striding across this. Head straight down this elevated section of path – the aqueduct immediately on the right, the path on the very edge of the drop to the stream. The buildings of Nantmel School, a road and a war memorial will be seen ahead. As the path makes its final descent towards these drop down into the 'gully' area to its left and head for a small metal gate. Pass through this and to the left of the school buildings out onto the road, which is a slip road off the A44. ❺

(Note: At the time of writing access onto the road was permanently blocked by the railings of the school playground. The definitive path was checked against maps held by Powys County Council and is as shown on the O.S. map - and as described above. Pending any official diversion of the path by the Council the road can be reached as follows. Having passed through the metal gate, follow the boundary on the left. After a few yards turn left to cross the boundary hedge via a small white wooden gate. This gives access to a small enclosure used by the school. Having passed through the gate turn right to follow the boundary down to the bottom corner of the enclosure and then turn left along the bottom boundary hedge until a wooden gate through it is reached. This gives access onto the road.)

To visit the church at Nantmel climb up the road which goes off the slip road just by the school. As this road is climbed notice a second smaller aqueduct crossing on the left. The churchyard is entered through a very old lychgate.

The church at Nantmel is dedicated to St. Cynllo, a fifth century Celtic king. The site is an ancient one but the oldest part of the existing church is the lower part of the tower, which dates from the thirteenth century. The church was rebuilt in 1792, a tablet at the base of the tower naming the architect as being David Thomas of Rhayader. The building was restored in 1870. In the churchyard near the church porch is a sundial dating from 1773.

There is a telephone box near the war memorial and school.

Limited bus service runs along the A44. Bus stops are outside the school.

Cross the slip road and walk past the war memorial and down to the A44. Cross the road and turn right to walk a short distance, (less than 100 yards), along it. Take the first road on the left. On leaving the A44 the road immediately narrows and bends to the right, crossing a bridge over a stream – a low bridge which looks to have been a hasty replacement for its collapsed predecessor alongside it to the left. The road makes another

Aqueduct construction crossing a side valley. (Date and location not known)

significant right turn and then bends to the left and starts to climb. Passing a small plantation of conifers, on the right, the climb becomes steeper. On reaching the steep drive up to Gilfach, on the left, the climb ceases and the road levels out, soon passing the drive to Llwyn-barried-fach, on the right. Remain on the road.

On reaching the entrance to the drive of Llwyn-barried-fach look to the right across the valley for a distant view of two well houses. The hill on the lower slopes of which the right of these is situated is Cefnnantmel.

Half left is the closest view yet of Rhiw Gwraidd with its mast, now about 1½ miles distant.

On reaching a minor road junction, (SO024654). bear right, turning slightly away from Rhiw Gwraidd – which has, until this point, been half-left and getting nearer but is now directly to the left. The quiet road continues on its new course, with grass and moss now growing along the centre of it in places, and before long the buildings of Cefnllyn will be seen ahead. The road swings right, the buildings well to the left, and soon reaches a junction with the drive to the settlement, (SO018655). **❻**

As the road reaches its junction with the drive to Cefnllyn look straight ahead for the first clear view of Gwastedyn Hill. The route climbs over this to reach Rhayader later on this stage.

Turn left along the drive to the farm and pass through a metal gate into its yard. Go straight across this, the farmhouse on the left, and follow the track through the gate opposite. The track bears left and then right and through another metal farm gate, a barn alongside to the right. Passing through this gate it bends to the left and follows a boundary fence on the right; the right of way however bears immediately left and follows the left-hand boundary hedge. Both meet at the far end of the field and pass through the right of two metal farm gates.

The right of way having rejoined the track, both follow the left-hand boundary of the field now entered.

Rhiw Gwraidd is a mile to the left as this field is crossed while to the right the long flat-topped mass of Gwastedyn Hill, (477 metres/1565 feet), is now prominent although over two miles distant.

Crossing the field the track becomes less distinct but continues to follow the left-hand boundary. Pass through a metal farm gate into another field – the gate may be open – and proceed straight ahead, the left boundary now some 20 yards distant. On initially entering this field there is a short tarmac section of track but within a few yards it becomes grassy again. Below and to the right the small lake of Llyn Gwyn will be seen and the grassy track, and the boundary to its left, now parallel the shoreline of this until, on rounding the end of the lake, both bear right, the track reaching a metal farm gate. Pass through this into another field and head straight across this to a metal gate on its far side which gives access onto a wide, stony track, (SO008646). While crossing the field keep Gwastedyn Hill half-right. **❼**

Turn right to walk along the track. It is initially level but soon, with a conifer plantation on the right hiding the waters of Llyn Gwyn beyond, there is a marked dip along its straight course. Eventually passing through a gate – which may be open – the track makes a 'crossroads' with a road, (SO006654). Turn left to walk along this.

After a while the road makes a sweeping left bend and passes the name-sign for Nant-glas. At a junction, on an equally pronounced bend to the right, ignore a road going off to the left. There is a telephone box here. On reaching the main settlement of Nant-glas the road crosses a stream, also called Nant Glas, and bends sharp left. As it straightens after this and climbs slightly towards the last bungalows of the hamlet look out for a

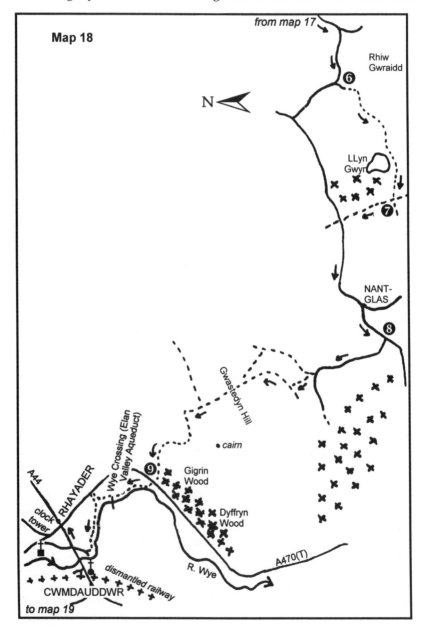

dwelling called The Grove, on the left of the road, and turn right just opposite this onto a metalled track, (SN994648). (*Note: Explorer Map 200 shows this track leaving the road immediately alongside a forested area but this has been cleared and the edge of the forest is now some distance to the left.*) ❽

This marks the start of the final climb of the stage, over Gwastedyn Hill. The hill of Rhiw Gwraidd is directly behind as it begins.

Walk up the metalled track. After a while it passes through a metal gate and into wilder, more open surroundings. The track meanders along, the climb becoming steeper. Eventually it makes a pronounced bend to the left to head towards Pen-y-ffynnon. As this bend begins there is a junction with a track going off to the right, (SN991658). Turn right onto this track but before reaching a metal farm gate, a few yards along it, go left through a small wooden gate to climb up a field, alongside its right-hand boundary. The climb up this field is possibly the steepest on the whole of the Elan Valley Way but the top is soon reached and a similar gate to that at the bottom of the field gives access to a path. Turn right to follow this. It has a boundary fence to its immediate right as it follows the contours of the hill, only gradually gaining height. There is initially a small stand of conifers just below the boundary to the right but as the path continues to contour its way gradually upwards these thin out.

The views are now superb. Directly behind are the hills of Y Gamriw, (604 metres/1982 feet), and Drum Ddu, (538 metres/1765 feet). Between these and Rhiw Gwraidd, (436 metres/1430 feet), which is almost directly to the right, is Trembyd, (475 metres/1558 feet). Below Rhiw Gwraidd the lake of Llyn Gwyn is visible and looking half-right Cefnnantmel, (402 metres/1319 feet), behind Nantmel is very prominent. Continuing around almost to a point straight ahead the large Camlo Hill, (509 metres/1670 feet), can be seen.

Climbing this section we witnessed a superb display of aerobatics by a red kite.

The path passes through a gate, steepens and gradually begins to bend left. The buildings of Bwlch-y-llys will be seen immediately below to the right and, as these are left behind, the path levels out somewhat. It is now wide and grassy and passes through bracken in season.

At a junction, just before another gate, ignore a path which descends sharp right, to Bwlch-y-llys.

Passing through the gate the path becomes less distinct. Continue on it straight ahead, across rougher terrain, towards a signpost beyond the next boundary fence.

Crossing this section look behind and half-left for a final view of where the A44 passes through the gap in the hills at Nantmel. On reaching the signpost look left to see a prominent cairn which is clearly visible from Rhayader on the early part of Stage 10. It stands at a height of about 470 metres/1542 feet. The route itself is at a height of about 440 metres/1444 feet here.

Pass through the gate at the boundary, adjacent to the signpost, (SN987667). Ignore a footpath indicated as going right here but continue straight ahead on a rough but wide grassy path which descends towards a rocky area, initially bearing slightly to the right but then, on passing through the rocks, swinging left. Approaching a wire boundary fence, to the left, the path bends right to head more steeply down hill, towards a gate in a boundary fence below. A sewage plant, adjacent to the River Wye, is almost directly ahead below as the descent is made.

As the path begins to drop down through the rocky area the views ahead are superb on a good day. Rhayader is spread out in the foreground below with encircling high hills beyond. Two distinct valleys can be seen between the hills straight ahead. In the one immediately ahead the course of the River Wye and the A470 road to the north-west of the town can easily be made out, with the hill mass of Moelfryn, (521 metres/1709 feet), beyond. The second valley, smaller and slightly to the left of the other, is the one used by the mountain road to Aberystwyth and by the Elan Valley Way early on Stage 10. The small lake of Gwynllyn and the rounded hill of Craig Ddu which overlooks it, (and is on its left), can be seen. To the left of this are the hills surrounding the Elan Valley.

To the right the large hill of Moel Hywel, (505 metres/1657 feet), is prominent. Looking more to the foreground and Rhayader the course of the River Wye can be made out. The crossing of the river by the Elan Valley aqueduct cannot be seen but to the left foreground below, and to the west of the river, one of the familiar well houses may be spotted.

Our descent here was accompanied by the cries of several buzzards which were launching themselves off the hill and engaging in aerial 'dogfights' with the local rooks.

Pass through the metal gate. A wide grassy path, slightly 'sunken' in places, bears half right and descends towards a field boundary on the right. On reaching the boundary bear left to follow it down the hill. As they descend both boundary and path, the latter now quite 'sunken', bear round to the left. The boundary fence eventually turns away to the right but another boundary, some 30 yards to the right, replaces it. The 'sunken' grassy track continues to bend to the left and descend.

Look out for a small gate leading through the boundary on the right – waymarked as a farm trail. When the 'sunken' path reaches a point opposite it ignore a path going straight ahead but remain on the 'sunken' path. This bends to the right to reach the boundary at the gate but then swings left again initially to follow the boundary more closely but then bearing left away from it and towards thick deciduous woodland, descending all the time. On almost reaching the woodland it makes a T-junction with a path descending alongside the trees. Turn right to continue the descent to the A470 road – now visible below – a stream

River Wye

The Wye is known as Afon Gwy in Welsh, the word 'Wy' being of Celtic origin and signifying water. The river rises on the slopes of Plynlimon, close to the source of the River Severn, and flows initially south by south-east, (passing through Rhayader, Newbridge-on-Wye and Builth Wells), before turning east, (through Hay-on-Wye and Hereford), and finally south, (through Ross-on-Wye, Monmouth and Chepstow) to enter the tidal River Severn. Its own main tributaries are the Ithon, Lugg and Monnow.

From Rhayader to Chepstow the river is now accompanied by the Wye Valley Walk, a long distance footpath of 112 miles. This is on the opposite side of the river to the Elan Valley Way as it approaches Rhayader.

alongside to the left, between the path and the woodland. **❾**

The woodlands to the left here are Gigrin Wood, immediately adjacent to the path, and Dyffryn Wood. Together they comprise Dyffryn Wood Nature Reserve and as the road is neared there is a notice board explaining what can be seen hereabouts. The reserve covers 65 acres and is mainly of oak woodland. On reaching the road the River Wye can be seen ahead, just one meadow beyond it.

The path reaches the A470 through a metal gate. Cross the busy road and turn right to walk along it for about 70 yards. Cross a stile on the left (SN980673) and follow the left-hand boundary fence of the field entered towards an enclosed area which is a sewage treatment plant. On reaching the near left-hand corner of this area cross a stile over its outer boundary fence and walk along a gravelled path between the outer and inner fences. Having walked along the left side of the sewage plant the River Wye is reached and the path swings right along the riverside boundary of the plant. On reaching the far end of this cross a stile and then a footbridge over a stream to enter a field. Continue along the riverbank through the field and at its far boundary cross another footbridge, over a stream, to enter the next field. Here again follow the riverbank.

Crossing this field, the line of the Elan Valley aqueduct will be seen to the right and soon the Wye Crossing appears ahead. Only one of the pipes, the fourth, actually crosses the river by the 'bridge' here; the others go underneath the river. The well house first noticed from Gwastedyn Hill is now seen perched on a low hill just across the river.

While photographing the Wye Crossing a red kite was seen overhead. Just a few decades ago these magnificent birds were faced with extinction as far as Britain was concerned, only a handful of breeding pairs remaining in their mid Wales stronghold. The recovery to today's situation, with an estimated 150 breeding pairs in Wales, is a triumph of conservation.

There is a Red Kite Feeding Station at Gigrin Farm, less than half a mile to the north-east of where this particular bird was seen. Here the birds can be watched from hides during the feeding season, from October to April. Feeding takes place at a set time each day – 2 p.m. at the time of writing.

Crossing this field the riverside path reaches the Elan Valley aqueduct's Wye Crossing. Continue past it along the riverbank and cross a stile out of the field, houses now on the right of the path, their garden boundary fences restricting its width and forcing it to the very water's edge. Eventually the narrow path bends to the right and a short flight of steps takes it between two of the dwellings and through a small wooden gate out onto the A470. Turn left along the pavement but after about 30 yards take a footpath going left, through a metal gate, down a few steps and back to the river. As the riverbank is regained the path crosses a sizeable side stream, the Rhyd-hir Brook. When the route was initially walked, in October 1998, the crossing was via a wooden footbridge but this had been washed away by floods by the time of our re-walk in June 1999, to be replaced by makeshift stepping stones. It is hoped that the bridge will soon be replaced.

(Alternative Route: Until the missing footbridge is replaced an alternative route to rejoin the river, if preferred, is to continue along the pavement of the A470, from the first 'return' option, for a further 120 yards and then turn sharp left down a track, the turning adjacent to a property called 'Waterdene'. On reaching the riverbank turn right.)

Stand on the footbridge (or at least near its site) facing the river and look half-left for a good view of Gwastedyn Hill and the cairn noted earlier.

Continue along the riverside path past an information board about the river. River and path are now some distance from the A470 and there are some picnic areas, with wooden tables and benches, en route. The church of St. Bride at Cwmdauddwr, on the opposite side of the river to Rhayader, will be seen ahead.

After rounding some playing fields, on the right, the path turns away from the river and emerges onto a track. Turn left to pass through a metal gate and onto a road. Almost immediately, at a T-junction, turn right to walk up a hill – Water Lane. At the top of this, at another T-junction, again go right into Bridge Street, which becomes West Street and leads to the Clock Tower/War Memorial at the crossroads in the centre of Rhayader, where this stage of the Elan Valley Way ends.

Rhayader

The town gets its name from the Welsh 'Rhaeadr Gwy' meaning the cataract/waterfall on the Wye – the cataracts were far more significant than they are today before the building of the stone bridge over the river in 1780.

There was also an important ford here, below the present bridge, from early times – used in turn by the Roman legions, drovers and the Cistercian monks as they travelled between their abbeys of Strata Florida and Abbeycwmhir.

The town has also been known locally as 'Bogey', after the Bwgy – a stream which flowed through it, and was used for drinking water, before it was culverted in 1877. (Its course was down North Street, West Street and finally Water Lane, at the bottom of which it entered the Wye.)

The town is the first settlement of any significance on the River Wye, being just 20 miles from the river's source. It stands at a height of 700 feet.

It is an ancient settlement, dating at least as far back as the fifth century. It is likely that its original nu-cleus was between the castle, overlooking the river, and the church. The present centre around the crossroads would seem to indicate a planned expansion in the thirteenth century.

The castle was built to guard the ford across the river. It had a short life and was probably never more than a largely wooden structure with stone foundations. It is unusual in that it was both built and destroyed by the Welsh. The first castle was built in 1178 by Prince Rhys ap Gruffyd but was destroyed during his wars against the Normans, in 1194. Within a year it had been rebuilt and garrisoned under Cadwallon but again fell to the Normans and came into the possession of Roger de Mortimer, Earl of Wigmore. The castle was finally destroyed by Llywelyn ap Iorwerth, (the Great), in 1231 although the land remained in Mortimer hands, eventually passing to the Crown under Edward IV in 1461.

In the reign of Henry VIII Rhayader became the county town of Radnorshire. The County Courts were held in the town and many of to-day's pubs can trace their origins to this period. This period of importance was brought to an abrupt end later in the sixteenth century when a judge was murdered near the town. County town status, and the courts, then passed to Presteigne.

There was more local lawlessness in the 1840s when farmers, drovers and landowners, suffering because of poor harvests and the general economic situation of the day, took their anger out on the local tollgates and tollhouses which were attacked and destroyed. The rioters wore women's clothing and blackened their faces, calling themselves 'the Daughters of Rebecca' – from a biblical reference in the *Book of Genesis*, ('And they blessed Rebecca, and said unto her let thy seed possess the gate of those which hate thee'). The riots were therefore known as the Rebecca Riots and lasted until local 'special constables' were reinforced by members of the Metropolitan Police, dragoons and infantry.

The railway reached the town in 1864 but the line was closed in 1962.

The town today still hosts an important livestock market and has a population of 2000.

Given the age of the settlement here there are few buildings of any great age or importance – the oldest surviving structure in the town being what was the Swan Inn, in West Street, which bears the date 1683.

The parish church of St. Clement, formerly dedicated to St. Cynllo, although being on an eighth century site only dates from the mid eighteenth century and was heavily restored after 1887, an earlier church on the site having fallen down in 1722. The font bowl is, however, early Norman.

The crossroads in the middle of the town is dominated by the Clock Tower/War Memorial which was erected on the site of the old Market Hall of 1762. The memorial was completed in 1924 and the designer/sculptor was a local man, Ben Lloyd.

There is a Leisure Centre, containing the Tourist Information Office, at the junction of North Street and Dark Lane and the bus stop for the service to Crossgates and Llandrindod Wells is near this.

Stage 10

Rhayader to Elan Valley Visitor Centre

Distance: 14 miles (Craig Goch dam 6½ miles, Pen-y-Garreg dam 8½ miles, Garreg Ddu viaduct 12½ miles).
Maps: Landranger 147; Pathfinder 969; Explorer 200.

The distance by road from Rhayader to the Elan Valley Visitor Centre is a little over 3½ miles but the final stage of the Elan Valley Way takes 14 miles, beginning a large semicircular detour by heading north-west from Rhayader and then westwards across high moorland to descend into the Elan Valley alongside the highest of its reservoirs – Craig Goch.

All of the dams and reservoirs in the Elan Valley itself are visited as the route then turns south. (The Claerwen Valley and its more recent and much larger dam and reservoir are not seen.)

The route finally crosses the Garreg Ddu viaduct, passing the Foel Tower – the actual starting point of the aqueduct to Birmingham – and Caban Coch dam before a visit to the Elan Valley Visitor Centre brings the 10 stage 128½ mile walk to its conclusion.

A mixture of quiet roads and tracks take the route out of Rhayader and up over into the Elan Valley. Thereafter the route uses tracks and footpaths to complete its journey.

The Elan Valley Visitor Centre is open between the beginning of April and the end of October. Outside of this period it is suggested that the route is retraced the short distance to Caban Coch dam if public transport is being relied upon for the journey back to Rhayader.

! **On the first section of the Stage there are two ford crossings of a stream, (Gwynllyn), which may be difficult or even impassable after very wet weather. An option to avoid these is included in the main text.**

STARTING at the Clock Tower/War Memorial, at the crossroads in the centre of Rhayader, walk along West Street and into Bridge Street to descend to and cross the bridge over the River Wye into Cwmdauddwr, where Station Road goes off to the right. Remain on the main road – B4518.

Crossing the river, look to the left for a view of Cwmdauddwr Church – St. Bride's – beyond the cataracts. Like St. Clement's in Rhayader the church was entirely rebuilt in the eighteenth century – 1778 – and again heavily restored, almost to the point of rebuilding, in 1866.

On the left of the road in Cwmdauddwr is a shop, 'Ty Craig', also known as the 'Rock House' or 'Rock Shop', where any donations for the upkeep of the chapel at Nant Gwyllt may be left. See the note on this chapel later on in this Stage.

Cwmdauddwr means 'Valley of the two rivers', that is the Wye and the Elan.

To the left Gwastedyn Hill, with its prominent cairn, looms large.

The road bears right and passes between old railway embankments, the bridge which formerly spanned it long gone. Just after this, as the road makes a sweeping bend to the left, turn right along a road signposted

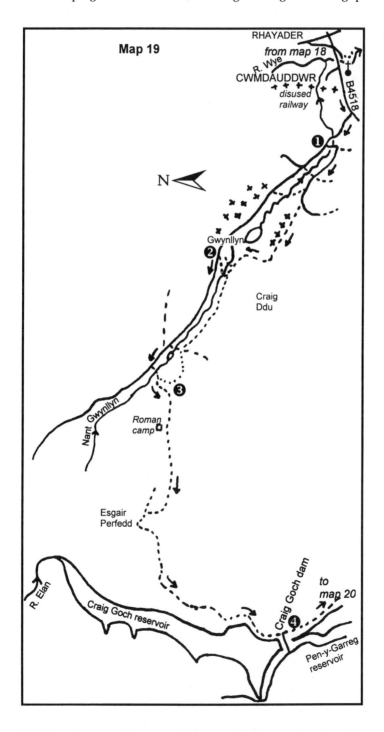

Rhayader's Railway

The railway reached Rhayader in 1864 and the station was in Cwmdauddwr up what is now Station Road. The line was that of the Mid-Wales Railway which ran between Moat Lane Junction, near Llanidloes, and Talyllyn Junction, near Brecon. It traversed 56 miles of wild country and reached heights of over 330 metres/1080 feet. The line was planned as part of a through route to link Lancashire with Milford Haven, carrying imported American cotton from the Welsh port to the mills and a return cargo of finished goods for export, but hoped for profits never materialised.

The line worked as an independent concern until 1888 when it entered into a working agreement with the Cambrian Railway and it was finally absorbed into that same company's network in 1904. In the 1920's the Cambrian Railway's lines passed under the control of the Great Western Railway.

The line was important, in the days before the motor car, in opening up the mid-Wales area and its small communities to passengers and goods. It gained in importance when the Elan Valley dams and reservoirs were under construction, between 1892 and 1904, with the laying of the Elan Valley Railway lines from a junction with it, to the south of Rhayader.

The line was closed, as part of the 'Beeching' cuts, in 1962.

In the garden of the last property on the right before the railway embankment is reached are some old railway distance posts.

'Aberystwyth Mountain Road'. It initially has a pavement but on reaching three sets of semi-detached houses, on the right, this ends.

The rounded hill of Craig Ddu, (464 metres/1522 feet), makes its first appearance of the stage ahead here. Gwastedyn Hill is directly behind.

The road meanders along, fairly level, and soon crosses a bridge over a stream, (Nant Gwynllyn), which then runs alongside it on the left. About 80 yards after the bridge, opposite a milestone reading 'Aberystwyth 29 miles, Rhayader ½', turn left onto a minor road, (SN962681). (There is a sign for Tynpistyll Farm at the junction and also signs saying 'No Through Road' and 'Weak Bridge'.) ❶

Crossing a bridge over Nant Gwynllyn the road bends first left and then sharp right, around a house, (Upper Mill). Ignore a track going off the road to the left at the sharp right bend but continue around the bend on the road – having now rounded three sides of Upper Mill.

The road climbs gently for a while. Ahead the valley begins to close in, between the rounded mass of Craig Ddu and the slopes opposite, (Wennallt).

Ceasing its gentle climb the road meanders along on the level. Remain on it, ignoring a footpath going off right and a bridleway left. Ahead, above the road on the left, an isolated farmhouse, (Parc Farm), will be seen and the bottom of its drive – with an old railway wagon here being used as a shed – soon passed. With Craig Ddu directly ahead the road makes a short descent before beginning to climb again and bending slightly left. Ignore a bridleway departing right, through a metal gate. The mountain road vacated earlier can now be seen opposite, on the right, as it begins to climb up the valley and the small lake of Gwynllyn appears ahead down in the valley bottom.

The road continues to bend slightly left soon reaching a line of oak trees, along its right-hand side, and with a small deciduous wood ahead and also on the right.

On reaching the edge of the woodland, the road bends sharply to the left and climbs. At the bend leave the road, turning right to walk along a substantial farm track (SN950685). A blue bridleway sign points the way along this unmetalled track and there is also a farm nameplate – Treheslog Farm.

The track initially follows a boundary with the small deciduous (oak) wood – on the right. Passing the end of this it crosses a stream, (Nant Pant-y-llyn), via a very low bridge/culvert, the rounded hill mass of Craig Ddu directly ahead with the buildings of Treheslog Farm at its foot.

As the track reaches the farm turn right to pass in front of the buildings and through a metal gate at the far end of them. The track now heads directly towards the small lake of Gwynllyn and has the slopes of Craig Ddu on its immediate left. It bears round to the left, following the lower slopes of the hill mass, and begins to climb. It is bounded along its right-hand side by a rough stone wall, with a wire fence behind, while the steep lower slopes of Craig Ddu form a natural boundary to the left. The stream of Nant Gwynllyn is visible in the valley below while the road on the opposite side of the valley is now much nearer to, and somewhat higher than, the track.

With the noise of waterfalls ahead, the climb up the track becomes steeper. Ignore a footpath which leaves the track on the right to descend into the valley. When the waterfalls come into view ahead the track bears to the right, at a Y-junction, towards them. On reaching the stream ford it at a shallow point (SN941695) and turn half right to follow a path which climbs steeply up and across a scree slope to the road above. On reaching the road turn left up it. ❷

There are superb views to be had from the path up the scree slope. On a clear day the entire valley is seen with the lake of Gwynllyn reflecting the sky in the foreground, the dominant mass of Craig Ddu alongside, and the long mass of Gwastedyn Hill, with its prominent cairn, in the background. Most of the route of the stage to date can be made out.

Note: After very wet weather the ford at these waterfalls may become impassable as will a second ford to be crossed further up the stream. If this happens there is a possible alternative path which remains to the west of the stream, (Nant Gwynllyn), and so avoids both fords. See ★ on page 144 for details of this.

The road meanders along and climbs steadily, the stream down to its left. After a little over half a mile a track departs left off the road to cross the stream by a ford just above some sluice gear set on a low wall. Remain on the road but look ahead here to see some prominent sheepfolds on its left. As the road approaches these, still climbing, a track joins it from the right, a bridleway signpost at the junction, while ahead a similar signpost will be seen indicating a track going off to the left. Turn left off the road along this track, (SN929699), which immediately bears right towards the sheepfolds and reaches the stream.

Ford the stream and continue on the same course to reach the sheepfolds. *If the fords were passable now continue reading from* ✪ below.

★ Note: *As with the first fording of Nant Gwynllyn this crossing can become impassable after very wet weather. If so, then to avoid both fords remain on the west bank of the stream for the following alternative route.*

Where the track from Treheslog Farm originally fords the stream, (SN941695), do not cross but instead continue up and along the stream, high above it on a narrow path which remains fairly distinct all the way to the small sluice and ford, referred to in the main text, above – *in fact this path might be considered as an alternative to the initial half mile on the road, even in drier weather.*

After the sluice has been passed the path becomes less distinct and can get very boggy, (with a number of side streams, the crossing of which can divert a direct route somewhat), but is quite safe to walk as long as one takes care where to tread. As far as can be managed head directly towards the area of sheepfolds which will be seen to the left of the stream ahead. On reaching these the main route is rejoined. (*A reasonably less boggy route through the area of side streams deviates from the direct route to the sheepfolds to pass a small ruined building which is marked on Explorer Map 200 at SN929697.*)

(*Tip: If very boggy ground is encountered tread on the clumps of tussock grass or rushes rather than on moss. This may appear a rougher walk but will certainly be drier and safer underfoot. If bog is encountered while attempting to cross side streams then head upstream where a rocky, drier crossing place can usually be found.*)

✪ On reaching the sheepfolds/pens bear half-left on a rutted grassy track which curves up and around to the right – the most distinct of several tracks which head off in the same direction here. ❸

Climbing along the track from the sheepfolds there are good views behind back through the valley just walked. Explorer Map 200 shows the site of a Roman Marching Camp at SN923698 but there is no real trace of it on the ground. It lies alongside where the track makes a first fairly substantial bend to the right, a slightly raised area of ground to the right of the track. One can only imagine the thoughts of any soldiers billeted here in this bleak place so many miles from home.

The grassy track climbs and meanders along, the sole survivor of several tracks which left the sheepfolds in the same general direction only to peter out. Soon after a substantial bend to the right – the site of a Roman Marching Camp – the initial climb eases. Numerous small paths leave the track along this section but remain on the clear grassy main track throughout.

This is a wonderful section of grassy track walking with the hills around the Elan Valley now beginning to come into view ahead and to the left. Looking behind, on a good day, there are views of hills back as far as Radnor Forest, with the mast on the top of Black Mixen, familiar on the latter miles of Stage 7, just visible. Over to the left - roughly South South-West - the prominent peak with an apparent large cairn on top is Drygarn Fawr, at 645 metres/2116 feet the highest point in mid Wales. It is about eight miles distant.

As the track bends to the right the wooded slopes of Gwaelod-y-rhos, above the southern end of Pen-y-garreg reservoir, may be seen over to the far left on a clear day. The climbing ceases as the summit of the flat-topped moorland, (Esgair Perfedd), is neared; the route being at a height of about 485 metres/1591 feet here - the highest point of the Elan Valley Way. The surrounding area and the track itself may be boggy after wet weather.

The track again bends right and then eases left. As it does so it becomes less distinct. A wind farm may be seen across to the far right on a clear day.

On meeting another track at a T-junction turn left. There is a bridleway marker post just before the junction. Ahead will be seen two further bridleway marker posts. The still indistinct track bears half-left at the first of these and left about 20 yards before the second. It then heads past a further marker post, (SN911698), soon becoming more distinct. The distant wind farm is directly behind at this point.

Follow the track which begins to descend slightly and bends right. Craig Goch reservoir finally comes into view ahead and the descent becomes steeper, the track heading directly towards a small 'V' shaped line of conifers on its far side. It then bends left to descend parallel to the reservoir.

Follow the steep grassy track down to where it becomes stony at the bottom and then walk along it above the reservoir, fording a side stream *en route*.

Eventually the track passes through a small wooden gate, alongside a larger gate marked 'Elan Estate', beside Craig Goch dam. There is a small toilet block to the left of the track just beyond the dam. ❹

Craig Goch is the highest of the Elan Valley Reservoirs and has a surface area of 217 acres and a capacity of 2028 million gallons. The dam is the only one in the Elan Valley built to a curved design. It is 120 feet in height and 513 feet long. There is a narrow road across it.

The dam marked the terminus of the Elan Valley Railway No.4 Line, which ran from a point adjacent to the next dam down the valley – Pen-y-garreg – along that reservoir to this point. The old trackbed has recently been resurfaced to provide an all-access footpath/cycleway along the left-hand side of Pen-y-garreg reservoir. This is known as the Elan Valley Trail and the Elan Valley Way now follows it.

Bus stop for the Royal Mail post bus service is across the dam.

Passing the toilet block go through a wooden gate sited similarly to the one above the dam and walk along the wide track ahead – an old railway trackbed with a fine compacted surface. Pen-y-garreg reservoir, with its small round wooded island, will be seen down to the right ahead.

The well surfaced track makes for easy walking and all side streams along it have been so there is no fording to be done. The track initially passes below rocks and then later below deciduous forest – mainly oak – as it follows the reservoir. Further along it enters that same woodland. Where the reservoir bends to the left the track does likewise, passing through a deep rocky cutting which reveals its railway track origins.

The deep cutting was known as 'Devil's Gulch' by the navvies working on the construction of the Elan Valley Railway and problems with hard rock strata here led to the curve being far sharper than had been planned and the works being delayed by three months.

Devil's Gulch under construction in 1895

As the track emerges from the cutting Pen-y-garreg dam, and the steep slopes of Graig Dolfaenog beyond, can be seen ahead. The wooded slopes at the southern end of the reservoir are Gwaelod-y-rhos – seen earlier on the stage when crossing the uplands.

After a while the track passes through a gate and crosses a significant side stream, (Nant Hesgog), via a sturdy bridge – again of railway origin – to reach Pen-y-garreg dam. ❺

Pen-y-garreg is the middle of the three Elan Valley dams. It is 123 feet high and 528 feet long. The reservoir above it, and of the same name, has a surface area of 124 acres and a capacity of 1332 million gallons.

The small rounded building housing the gearing of the dam is surmounted by a small domed roof bearing a weathervane in the shape of a fish. As I passed this when first walking the route, on a wet October day, a heron flew immediately overhead – but was not fooled!

Just past the dam are two gates, a small one to the right giving access to a path going down below the dam and a larger one to the left used by the track. Pass through the latter and continue along the track. After a while it crosses another large side stream, (Nant y Blymbren), via a bridge – a black wooden hut alongside the track on the left. Just beyond this there is a parting of ways – a bridleway climbing left while the Elan Valley Trail descends to the right through a gap in a wooden fence (SN916675). Go right.

The well-surfaced track descends through coniferous forest. After about 200 yards on it look out for a path coming in on the left, steeply down from

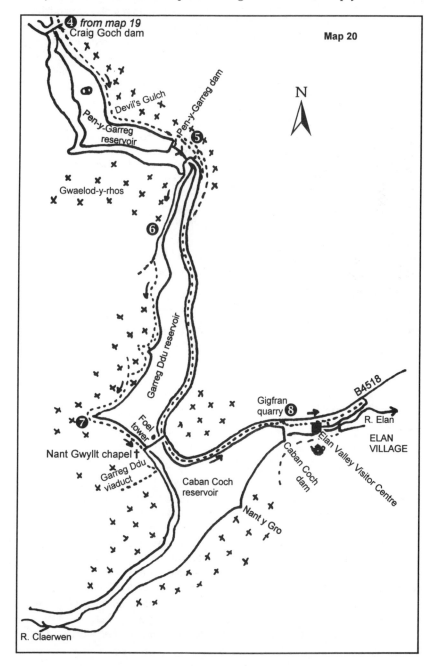

Shelley and the Elan Valley

Hidden below the waters of Garreg Ddu reservoir are the ruins of Cwm Elan House. The poet Percy Bysshe Shelley stayed here for short periods in both 1811 and 1812, the house at that time being owned by his uncle, Thomas Grove. In 1812 Shelley, with new bride Harriet Westbrook, attempted to purchase the neighbouring Nantgwyllt House but were prevented from doing so by lack of funds. That house was also submerged as the reservoir filled and lies further around the valley, beyond Garreg Ddu viaduct.

Shelley was enchanted by the area and one wonders what he would have felt about the dams and reservoirs which have effectively drowned these wild valleys. Of the area around Cwm Elan he wrote that 'rocks piled onto each other to tremendous heights, rivers formed into cataracts by their projections

and valley clothed with woods present an enchantment'.

Shelley is the best known literary figure connected with the area but he was not the first to fall under its charms. In 1798 William Lisle Bowles, a friend of Thomas Grove, wrote a poem entitled 'Coombe-Ellen', (Cwm Elan), which includes the following lines:

'No sound is here.
Save of the stream that shrills,
and now and then
A cry as of a faint wailing, when
the kite
Comes sailing o'er the crags, or
straggling lamb
Bleats for its mother.'

Perhaps not that much has changed here although the 'shrill' of the streams was more a 'roar' when I was here after the storms of October 1998.

the bridleway above, and crossing the track to continue down through the forest on the right. Turn right down this descending steeply through the trees to reach a road.

Turn right to walk along the road. Almost immediately it bends left to cross a stone bridge over the river. Pen-y-garreg dam can be seen to the right as the bridge is crossed (SN915673).

Bus stop for the Royal Mail post bus service just after the bridge is crossed.
There is a telephone box just before the bridge.

Remain on the road as it climbs after crossing the bridge. It makes a sweeping bend left, as the bridge is crossed, and then a hairpin bend to the right. At the apex of this bend take a track going off to the left - marked as a footpath and initially metalled. It is waymarked as the Elan Woodland Trail; waymarking which continues all the way to Garreg Ddu viaduct. It leaves the road through a wooden gate, which may be open, and runs along well above the level of Garreg Ddu reservoir, to the left, and below the coniferous forested slopes of Gwaelod-y-rhos. As the end of the forest is reached the track – still metalled – passes through a wooden gate. ❻

The course of the trackbed of the old Elan Valley Railway No.3 Line – now well-surfaced and used for the Elan Valley Trail – can be clearly seen on the opposite side of Garreg Ddu reservoir, with the road and the sheer slopes of Graig Dolfaenog beyond.

The track continues high above the water. Before long it passes through a wooden gate to enter the 'yard' of the remote farmstead of Tynllidiart, on the left, losing its metalled surface. Continue straight ahead through another wooden farm gate to enter a field and follow its right-hand boundary. On reaching the far side of the field ford a stream, (Nant yr Henwrach), and pass through a metal farm gate, the track now reaching more open surroundings. Continue to follow the boundary on the right. As a metal gate in this is reached the track becomes indistinct and narrows to path width. Footpath markers point the way as the path continues to follow the right-hand boundary.

Cross a boundary fence ahead via a step stile and a stream beyond it by a footbridge. 'Duck boards' take the path slightly uphill through a boggy area. At the end of these the path turns left, down towards the reservoir, the route still well marked by footpath waymark posts.

The path descends to a wooden gate, with a metal farm gate and stile alongside to the left of it. Go through this and continue towards the water's edge, passing a 'Broadleaved Woodland' information board. The path, now almost at the water's edge, bears right, into the trees. A section of very narrow path, about 25 foot above the water, follows.

Across the reservoir the sheer slopes and rocky outcrops of Creigiau Dolfolau dwarf the road below them.

When the path meets a track, at a T-junction, turn right to follow the latter which meanders and undulates along through the mainly oak woodland and soon begins to bear right, narrowing to path width.

Cwm Elan House and the advancing waters of the reservoir

Nant Gwyllt Chapel

Nant Gwyllt is a chapel of ease for the parish of Cwmdauddwr. It is reached by walking along the road past the viaduct and turning up a drive to it, just before reaching a stream. The drive turns back towards the viaduct and climbs up to reach the chapel. The building replaces one which was submerged when the reservoirs filled.

Inside the chapel is a beautiful window representing the theme of the 23rd Psalm with Jesus as a shepherd, a sheep and lamb at his feet. This faces the reservoir and the light coming through it is very effective in the dark building. The chapel is unusual in that visitors are asked to leave the inner door open to air the building but to close the two outer gates against sheep.

Sad to report but visitors are also asked not to leave any donations at the chapel. Twice in recent times the donation box has been robbed and on the most recent occasion the box was actually chipped out of the wall. Any donations can be left at 'Ty Craig', (the Rock Shop/House), in Cwmdauddwr – see note under Cwmdauddwr at the start of this stage.

As the path bears right look left across the reservoir for a first view of the Foel Tower.

On reaching a junction of paths, by another 'Broadleaved Woodland' information board, go left along a path which immediately descends towards the water and bends right to reach a wooden gate into a field, a stile to its left, (SN910648).

As the path bends to the right, before reaching the gate into the field, look left for good views of Garreg Ddu viaduct, built on top of the submerged dam, and the Foel Tower alongside. Nant Gwyllt Chapel is also in view. There are further good views to be had while crossing the field.

Enter the field and bear half-left to drop down to its bottom, (left-hand), boundary. Follow this along, initially beneath trees and rocky outcrops, to cross a stile over it to the left and approach a stream, Nant Methan.

Foel Tower and the Carreg Ddu viaduct

Garreg Ddu

Garreg Ddu viaduct is built on a sub-merged dam, the purpose of which is to enable the statutory amounts of compensatory water for the River Elan, (Afon Elan), and River Wye to be released, notwithstanding low water levels in the reservoir, without disrupting the supply to Birmingham. The road over the viaduct gives access to the Claerwen Valley, its dam and reservoir.

The Foel Tower, adjacent to the viaduct on the far side here, houses the gear controlling the water flow to the filter beds and aqueduct and so marks the starting point of the water's 73½ mile journey to Frankley, Birmingham.

The reservoir to the north of Garreg Ddu viaduct and submerged dam is known as Garreg Ddu reservoir while that to the south is Caban Coch reservoir. The waters are retained behind the Caban Coch dam, visited later, and the surface area of the two expanses of water is 500 acres; the total capacity 7815 million gallons.

Cross the stream via a footbridge and bear half-left to climb up the bank ahead. Another footbridge takes the path over a small side stream and the climb then ends, the path meandering through the trees towards the edge of the reservoir. Fording more minor side steams it soon reaches the water's edge - a matter of only some 5 to 10 feet away - and continues alongside this.

Very good views of the Foel Tower and Garreg Ddu viaduct across the water through the trees to the left here.

Crossing a boundary fence, via a step stile, follow the path as it bears right to climb up initially a slight rise which becomes steeper as it progresses, a stream on its left. At the top, at a T-junction with a wide stony track, turn left, (SN906643).

The track immediately crosses the stream (culverted), descends slightly and bears first left and then right to cross a cattle grid. Passing a small disused quarry area, on the right, it bears right to follow an arm of the reservoir and on reaching the head of this bends sharp left to cross a stream, Llwydnant, via a bridge and then proceed along the opposite side. ❼

Walking through the woods along the side arm of the reservoir, persistent rasping calls led us to a woodpecker's nest in a hole, high in a tree.

As the stream is crossed the open deciduous woodland the track has been running through gives way, on the right, to coniferous forest beyond a boundary fence – Llanerchi Wood. Passing another 'Broadleaved Woodland' information board the main body of water is reached again, the Foel Tower straight ahead.

Remain on the track as it continues along the edge of the reservoir. Passing through a gate, with a cattle grid alongside, it reaches the road at Garreg Ddu viaduct, Nant Gwyllt Chapel in the trees up to the right.

Just before reaching the road, and opposite the Foel Tower, look down to the edge of the reservoir to see the point where the water from the Claerwen reservoir enters. It has travelled to this point through the Dol y Mynach Tunnel.

Before crossing the viaduct take a few moments to look at the information board concerning the Elan Valley Water Scheme which stands to the left at its approaches.

Bus stop for the Royal Mail post bus service just after the viaduct is crossed.

The Elan Valley Railway

The four lines and sidings of this railway were laid before construction work on the dams could begin. The No.1 Line ran from a junction with the Mid-Wales Railway, (Cambrian Railway), south of Rhayader to Elan Village, the No.2 Line from Elan Village to Caban Coch dam, the No.3 Line from Caban Coch to Pen-y-garreg dam, and the No.4 line from Pen-y-garreg to Craig Goch dam. At their peak there were thirty-three miles of track in operation. The railway was virtually redundant within a few years of the construction of the Waterworks being completed and the track was lifted some time afterwards. When the Claerwen dam came to be built, between 1946 and 1952, the materials and workforce were taken to the site by road, via Garreg Ddu viaduct.

One of the Elan Valley locomotives

Walk across Garreg Ddu viaduct - there are narrow pavements - and turn right onto a section of old railway trackbed on which a compacted stony surface has been laid. This is reached either through a wooden 'Elan Valley Trail' gate or over a step stile across a wall where metal railings have been lowered. Follow the track along the edge of the reservoir, eventually crossing a culverted stream and, after about one mile of walking, reaching Caban Coch dam.

Leave the section of trackbed - again either through a gate or over a step stile - and walk across the viewing enclosure at the edge of the dam. ❽

This trackbed was part of the Elan Valley Railway's No.3 Line.

As a sweeping left bend, on both track and water's edge, is rounded look across the reservoir to see a small inlet opposite where the stream of Nant y Gro enters. There was formerly a small coffer dam at this point but it was destroyed during the Second World War when it was used by Barnes Wallis to calculate the size of bomb needed for the famous 1943 'Dambusters' air raid.

Submerged under Caban Coch reservoir are two large rocks known as the 'Devil's Clogs'. Legend has it that the Devil bet that he could jump across the valley with two large stones in the heels of his shoes. He jumped but as he was halfway across the valley a cock crowed heralding the dawn. As the Devil was supposed to lose his power with the coming of daylight the two boulders fell from the sky and landed in the middle of the River Elan.

On reaching Caban Coch dam look right to see the large disused quarry area, Gigfran Quarry, now used as a car park. Stone from this quarry, and from one on the opposite side of the reservoir, was used to construct and face the dam. Caban Coch is the lowest of the Elan Valley dams. It is 122 feet high and 610 feet long.

Bus stop for the Royal Mail post bus service at the car park adjacent to Caban Coch dam.

At the far side of the viewing enclosure again either pass through the wooden 'Elan Valley Trail' gate or over a step stile to follow another compacted stony track which runs along high above the Afon Elan, (River Elan), right. Follow the track, above gorse bushes, to reach a wooden gate through a fence. Passing through this leave the track, dropping down slightly to the right to walk along the edge of a wide grassy terrace well above the river.

The stony track and grassy 'terrace' area are the remains of the trackbed of the Elan Valley Railway No.2 Line.

As the wide 'terrace' ends rejoin the compacted stony track. The Elan Valley Visitor Centre will be seen on the immediate right, down by the river.

Continue along the track to a point just past the Visitor Centre car park, below, and then turn half-right down a grassy path towards the access road to the Visitor Centre. (Stone steps and a steep path descend directly to the Visitor Centre at the same point but do not use these.)

At a junction of paths, part of the way down, go right to reach the access road. Cross the road and walk to the edge of a flat grassy picnic area, above

---

The Elan River

The Afon Elan rises in the hills to the north-west of the reservoirs. It flows east and then south-east before entering Craig Goch reservoir. Below Caban Coch dam it flows north-east and then south-east to join the River Wye just under two miles to the south of Rhayader.

There are two bridges across the Elan just below the Visitor Centre which can be seen from the high track. They lead to Elan Village. One is a suspension bridge, the third on this site and now deemed unsafe for traffic, and the other is its replacement, a Bailey bridge.

By the river at the Visitor Centre is Christopher Kelly's 1986 bronze statue of Shelley, inspired by his poem *Prometheus Unbound*.

Nearby is a hydro-electric turbine, one of two which were originally installed either side of the river below Caban Coch dam to generate electricity. In operation between 1952 and 1995 it generated 200 horsepower/150 kilowatts and over 13 million gallons of water passed through it daily. A new turbine has now been installed in the turbine house to the south of the river. This generates 800 kilowatts, enough to power 800 dwellings.

the river. Here turn right to walk to the Visitor Centre, passing the Shelley statue and defunct turbine, (see notes), en route.

The Elan Valley Visitor Centre marks the end of the Elan Valley Way.

The Elan Valley Visitor Centre, situated in old workshop buildings, is open daily between the beginning of April and the end of October. It contains an exhibition area, audio-visual theatre, café, book and gift shop, and an information desk. Telephone 01597 810898 for the Information Office, 810899 for the café and 810880 for the Rangers.

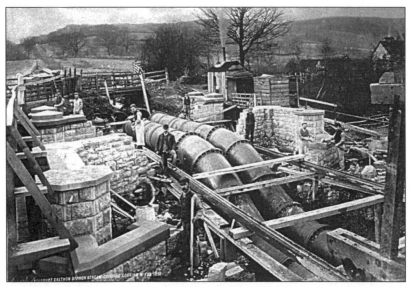

Stream crossing under construction at Caethon (not on the route of the Elan Valley Way) in 1897.

Acknowledgments

This walk could not have been designed nor the book written without the help and kindness of many people and my thanks go out to all of them. To anyone I may have forgotten below, my apologies. The memory is not all it used to be.

In particular my thanks to:

Mark Chapman (Rights of Way Officer with Powys County Council) – for advice as regards rights of way in the Crossgates, Carmel Bridge and Nantmel areas.

The Revd. Norman Davis (Blakedown) – for information regarding Broome and its church.

David Edwards (Heart of Wales Line Travellers Association) – for information on the history of the Heart of Wales Railway.

Peter Groves (Meridian Books) – for advice, help and encouragement, and for agreeing to publish this book; and for his company during the re-walking of stages 1 to 4.

The Revd. Robert Horsefield (Cleobury Mortimer) – for the information on Hopton Wafers Church and village.

Alan Jones – for the help and company on several stages of the walk, and tolerance of the worst of my bad walking habits over 20 years.

Stroma Lennox – for information on, and pulling everything together at, Cleobury Mortimer.

Shona Lewis (Rights of Way Officer with Shropshire County Council) – for advice as regards the rights of way in Stowe Parish.

'Red' and Tom Morrow – for the test walking. Sorry about the problems on Stage 4!

Gillian Mortimer (Senior Librarian, Ludlow Library) – for research and information into the origins of The Sheet and Downton Castle.

Rita Morton – for making available her collection of slides showing the dams and aqueduct under construction, and allowing us to reproduce some in this book.

Sarah Parish and Louise Ellis (Severn-Trent Water, Birmingham) – for information/maps as regards the route of the Elan Valley aqueduct and other help on the project.

Alwyn Pound and Dave Bate (Severn-Trent Water, Ludlow) – for technical information regarding the Elan Valley aqueduct and its pipelines.

Patricia Reynolds – for permission to use the photograph of her painting on Dolau Station.

The Revd. Geoffrey Shilvock (Wolverley) – for information regarding Wolverley church.

The Society of Authors, as the literary representatives of the estate of A.E.Housman, for permission to use the lines from A Shropshire Lad quoted in Stage 3.

Lucy Torode and members of the Wolverley and Cookley Historical Society – for information on Cookley and Wolverley and a most enjoyable history walk around the latter.

Dave Walker – for the initial germ of an idea for the walk and advice regarding the book.

'Zog' (North Herefordshire Footpath Warden) – for sharing his knowledge of the footpaths of the area and advising as to the routing of Stage 6.

Also the staff at/of Kidderminster, Bewdley, Ludlow, Llandrindod Wells and Rhayader Tourist Information Centres, Offa's Dyke Association, Elan Valley Visitor Centre and Rangers, and the Wyre Forest Visitor Centre.

Recommended Further Reading

K. Beddoes & W.H. Smith. *The Tenbury and Bewdley Railway* (Wild Swan Publications, 1995)

T. Clift. *The Central Wales Line* (Ian Allan, 1982)

D. Davenport. *The Shelleys at Nantgwillt 1812* (Diana Davenport)

B. Geens. *The Severn Valley Railway at Arley* (Wild Swan Publications, 1995)

G. Hodges. *Owain Glyn Dwr & the War of Independence in the Welsh Borders* (Logaston Press, 1995)

J. Jeremiah. *The River Severn, A Pictorial History* (Phillimore, 1998)

C. W. Judge. *The Elan Valley Railway* (Oakwood Press, 1987)

J. I. Langford. *Staffordshire and Worcestershire Canal* (Goose & Son, 1974)

J. Marshall. *The Severn Valley Railway* (David St. John Thomas, 1989)

E. A. McBride. *Elan* (Dwr Cymru Welsh Water, 1987)

R. Morriss & K. Hoverd. *The Buildings of Ludlow* (Alan Sutton, 1993)

R. Morton. *The Building of the Elan Valley Dams* (Rita Morton, 1996)

M.R.C. Price. *The Cleobury Mortimer & Ditton Priors Light Railway* (Oakwood Press, 1995)

M. Salter. *The Old Parish Churches of Herefordshire* (Folly Publications, 1998)

M. Salter. *The Castles and Moated Mansions of Shropshire* (Folly Publications, 1988)

M. Salter. *The Old Parish Churches of Shropshire* (Folly Publications, 1988)

M. Salter. *The Castles of Mid Wales* (Folly Publications, 1991)

M. Salter. *The Old Parish Churches of Mid Wales* (Folly Publications, 1991)

M. Salter. *The Old Parish Churches of Worcestershire* (Folly Publications, 1995)

M. Salter. *The Castles of Herefordshire and Worcestershire* (Folly Publications, 1989)

A. Sidebotham. *Brampton Bryan, Church & Castle* (Audrey Sidebotham, 1990)

S. C. Stanford. *The Archaeology of The Welsh Marches* (S.C. Stanford, The Old Farm House, 1991)

M. A. Vanns. *Severn Valley Railway, A View from the Past* (Ian Allan, 1998)

The Foel valve tower under construction in 1903

Aqueduct related features passed en route

Stage 1

Bartley Reservoir.
Frankley Reservoir.
Valve chamber near A451.

Stage 2

Site of former crossing of Staffordshire & Worcestershire Canal.
Valve chamber in field alongside road leading to Eymore Wood.
Section of Aqueduct, including valve chambers, in Seckley Wood, (above Severn crossing).
Severn Crossing.

Stage 3

Valve chambers along a section of Aqueduct near Buttonoak, Wyre Forest.

Stage 4

River Rea Crossing, near Cleobury Mortimer.
Well house, Earls Ditton.
Two sections of pipeline at the foot of Titterstone Clee Hill.
Valve chambers in fields near Caynham.
Ledwyche Brook Crossing.
Steventon Bridge, (River Teme Crossing).

Stage 5

Two bridges crossing side valleys, two well houses, and several valve chambers along a section of Aqueduct in Deepwood, Mortimer Forest.
Valve chambers on Tatteridge Hill and from road to Downton.
Downton Bridge, (River Teme Crossing).

Stage 6

Valve chamber in field near A4113 at Stanage Park.
Valve chamber near A4113, near Stowe.
Crossing of small stream in garden near A4113, near Stowe.

Stage 7

(None)

Stage 8

River Ithon Crossing.

Stage 9

Carmel Bridge Crossing.
Two bridges crossing side valleys at Nantmel.
Two well houses alongside A44, near Nantmel.
Well house near River Wye, Rhayader.
Wye Crossing, Rhayader.

Stage 10

Craig Goch Reservoir and Dam.
Pen-y-garreg Reservoir and Dam.
Garreg Ddu Viaduct and Submerged Dam.
Foel Tower.
Garreg Ddu and Caban Coch Reservoirs and Caban Coch Dam.
Elan Valley Visitor Centre.

Index

Also from Meridian…

THE MONARCH'S WAY

by Trevor Antill

A long distance walk, waymarked and shown on O.S. maps, that closely follows the route taken by Charles II after his defeat by Cromwell's forces at Worcester in 1651. Starting from Worcester it goes first north, then south through the Cotswolds and the Mendips to the coast, then along the South Downs to Shoreham where Charles escaped to France. Visiting many historic places, perhaps previously known to readers only through the history books, it also goes through some of the finest scenery in western and southern England.

Book 1: Worcester to Stratford-upon-Avon. 175 miles.

ISBN 1 869922 27 1. £5.95. 112 pages. 19 photos, 8 drawings, 19 maps.

Book 2: Stratford-upon-Avon to Charmouth. 210 miles.

ISBN 1 869922 28 X. £6.95. 136 pages. 21 photos. 23 maps.

Book 3: Charmouth to Shoreham. 225 miles.

ISBN 1 869922 29 8. £6.95. 136 pages. 21 photos. 25 maps.

WALKS TO WET YOUR WHISTLE

by Roger Seedhouse

Eighteen walks covering some of the most beautiful countryside in Shropshire and along its Staffordshire borders, each providing an opportunity to visit a pub in which the walker will feel welcome and comfortable. The main walks range in distance between 7 and 11½ miles but each has a shorter alternative of between 2¾ and 5¼ miles.

ISBN 1 869922 34 4. £5.95. 112 pages. 17 photos. 18 maps.

MORE WALKS TO WET YOUR WHISTLE

by Roger Seedhouse

Following the author's highly successful first book he now presents a second collection of walks with a pub in Shropshire and along its Staffordshire borders.

ISBN 1 869922 36 0. £5.95. 112 pages. 24 photos. 18 maps.

AND THE ROAD BELOW

by John Westley

The entrancing account of the first complete walk around the coastline of the British Isles, a distance of 9,469 miles, that earned for the author a place in the *Guinness Book of Records*. Undertaken in aid of multiple sclerosis this book shows how a relatively inexperienced walker could, with courage and an over-riding determination to succeed, overcome what seemed at times to be near-insurmountable problems. *The author has donated half his royalties from the sale of this book to the Multiple Sclerosis Society and this sum will be matched by an equal contribution from the publishers.*

ISBN 1 869922 25 5. £8.95. 208 pages. 11 photos.

Prices applicable January 2000 and may be subject to change.

Available from booksellers or direct from Meridian Books. Please send remittance, adding for postage & packing, £1.00 for one book, £2.00 for two or more books, to:

Meridian Books, 40 Hadzor Road, Oldbury, West Midlands B68 9LA

Please send for our complete catalogue.